The CASE STUDY ANTHOLOGY

To Andrew—may the pen still be mightier than the mouse,
when you grow up

The CASE STUDY ANTHOLOGY

Editor
Robert K. Yin
COSMOS Corporation

SAGE Publications
International Educational and Professional Publisher
Thousand Oaks ■ London ■ New Delhi

For information:

Sage Publications, Inc.
2455 Teller Road
Thousand Oaks, California 91320
E-mail: order@sagepub.com

Sage Publications Ltd.
1 Oliver's Yard
55 City Road
London EC1Y 1SP
United Kingdom

Sage Publications India Pvt. Ltd.
B-42, Panchsheel Enclave
Post Box 4109
New Delhi 110 017 India

Printed in the United States of America

Library of Congress Cataloging-in-Publication Data

Yin, Robert K.
The case study anthology/Robert K. Yin.
    p. cm.
Includes bibliographical references and index.
ISBN 0-7619-2925-8 (Cloth)
ISBN 0-7619-2926-6 (Paper)
  1. Social sciences—Methodology. 2. Case method. 3. Social sciences—Research—Methodology—Case studies. I. Title.
H61.Y564 2004
001.4′32—dc22

                      2003026095

This book is printed on acid-free paper.

04   05   06   07   10   9 8 7 6 5 4 3 2 1

Acquisitions Editor:	Lisa Cuevas Shaw
Editorial Assistant:	Margo Crouppen
Production Editor:	Denise Santoyo
Copy Editor:	Annette Pagliaro
Typesetter:	C&M Digitals (P) Ltd.
Indexer:	Kathy Paparchontis
Cover Designer:	Michelle Lee Kenny

Contents

Preface

A "case study anthology" has always seemed to be an oxymoron. By their nature, case studies are lengthy manuscripts. The good ones are usually book-length already. Paring down such works risks losing the essence of good case studies—which may very well be the depth of their inquiry combined with the grandness of their scope. So, over the years I had not given much thought to a case study anthology, though many years ago I had seen the value of editing two readers, one in urban affairs and the other on race, national origin, and culture.

Not surprisingly, I was initially hesitant when Deborah Laughton, who had been my main editor at Sage on two earlier books on the case study method, indicated the potential need for an anthology. I asked her to give me some time to collect my thoughts and round up some possible readings, before agreeing to proceed. There had always been some favorite case studies of mine. The main question was whether excerpts from them could serve as fair representations. Another question was whether a rich enough array of excerpts could be assembled, because I had noted that the most useful anthologies usually have many selections, not just a few.

The double whammy for the proposed anthology, moreover, was that it was to focus on methodology—not on a specific subject area, such as education, community development, or management studies. My quick additional checking suggested that methodological anthologies are frequently adopted by libraries and reference collections, but not necessarily used in academic courses or research. So, on top of the problem of fairly excerpting lengthy case studies, a methodological anthology risked poor distribution and hence wasteful scholarship.

Well, the rest is history. I did eventually agree to proceed, and the product is before your eyes. In my opinion, the collection in this case study anthology does cover a meaningful waterfront, from the perspective of case study methods. The selected works also cover a broad variety of (again, in my opinion) attractive topics. In addition, I found myself pleased to include some older case studies (from two or more generations ago), combating my intuition that contemporary social science students and academicians tend to find the past increasingly irrelevant.

Methodology aside, the selected works are well worth reading—even if they are outside your field of specialization. Whether the anthology draws sufficient interest among scholars, and whether it helps to advance your use of or appreciation for the case study method, only time will tell.

Acknowledgments

This anthology has only been made possible by the authors of its 19 selections. Most of the selections are excerpts from much longer works—usually books. To keep the anthology within a reasonable length, substantial omissions had to be made. You, the readers, have complete control over the obvious remedy: Let this anthology be your *introduction* to the selected works, not their last word. I hope you will obtain and read the original works in their entirety. In this way, we all will honor the original authors.

The anthology also represents a new plateau in what has become my lifelong quest to strengthen case study research. During the earlier stages of this journey, support and encouragement came from Larry Susskind (then the head of the Department of Urban Studies and Planning at M.I.T.), Nanette Levinson (then a professor in the School of International Service at American University), Professor Erik Maaloe and his colleagues at the Aarhus School of Business in Denmark, and Professors Leonard Bickman and Debra Rog of Vanderbilt University—who also have served as series editors for my two earlier books on case study research. Over the past decade, and certainly within the context of research at COSMOS Corporation, several others have helped to keep the journey going. They include John Redman (then of the National Institute of Standards and Technology), who willingly supported the training of experienced researchers to show the relevance and importance of the craft to manufacturing and technological topics; Shakeh Kaftarian (then of the U.S. Department of Health and Human Services' Center for Substance Abuse Prevention), who pressed to combine case studies with other quantitative research; Bernice Anderson (the National Science Foundation), who has valued case studies for their ability to cover complex topics such as education reform in mathematics and science education; and the many members of COSMOS Corporation's excellent research staff, who continue to practice case study as well as other forms of social science research.

Most recently, I have had the pleasure of continuing a still incomplete, 10-year dialogue about the case study method with Bob Stake (professor at the University of Illinois at Urbana-Champaign), reflecting ongoing work in the field of education. However, the most immediate instigator for this anthology, C. Deborah Laughton of Sage Publications at the time, deserves the greatest thanks and recognition.

Sage also arranged for a review of the initial outline of the anthology by a special panel of professors who represent different fields but teach courses related to case studies. The panel provided individual comments (anonymously) that were extremely helpful in the anthology's final design, and hopefully improved the anthology's relevance and usefulness to potential readers. I offer my sincere thanks to the members of the panel, all but one of whom subsequently agreed to be identified in this acknowledgment:

Paul Beamish, Associate Dean of Research,
Ivey Business School, University of Western Ontario

Rosann Webb Collins, Associate Professor,
College of Business Administration, University of South Florida

Larissa A. Grunig, Professor, Communication,
University of Maryland

Sharon D. Kruse, Associate Professor,
Educational Foundations and Leadership, University of Akron

Katherine C. Naff, Associate Professor,
Public Administration, San Francisco State University

Randy Stoecker, Professor,
Department of Sociology and Anthropology, University of Toledo

Sandra P. Thomas, Professor and Director of the Ph.D. Program in Nursing,
University of Tennessee, Knoxville

Despite all of this attention, support, encouragement, and feedback, only I as the editor bear the final responsibility for this anthology.

Introduction

WHAT TO EXPECT FROM THIS ANTHOLOGY

This anthology takes you on two tours. The first tour is substantive: to experience the panorama of topics covered by some of the best case studies that may ever have been done, including a case study that is now 75 years old and still in print! The second tour is methodological: to see how case study research[1] has been practiced—by some of the best social scientists, past and present, in the country.[2]

Together, both tours take you through an exciting terrain. The substantive tour investigates such topics as:

- A mass vaccination of the American public in the 1970s—of the sort now envisaged to combat bioterrorism;

- Nuclear confrontation between the United States and the former Soviet Union, threatening life on the entire planet;

- The emergence of social class in American society in a New England city;

- The operation of the country's major computer chip firm—a Fortune 100 firm, in Silicon Valley;

- Civil disorder in Los Angeles in the 1990s (not 1960s);

- The reform of major urban school systems in Houston, Texas, and Chicago, Illinois;

- The reduction of serious crime in New York City under Mayor Rudolph Giuliani;

- Competition in the global marketplace by South Korea's major manufacturing firm;

- The workings of the country's major preschool program, *Head Start*;

- A methadone maintenance (drug treatment) clinic in Syracuse, New York; plus

- Eight additional topics.

The methodological tour shows how case studies investigate real-life events in their natural settings.[3] The goal is to practice sound research while capturing both a phenomenon (the real-life event) and its context (the natural setting). One strength of the case study method is its usefulness when phenomenon and context are not readily separable, a condition that occurs in real-life but cannot easily be duplicated by laboratory research. Another strength is that the method enables you, as a social scientist, to address "how" and "why" questions about the real-life events, using a broad variety of empirical tools (e.g., direct field observations, extended interviews, and reviews of documents and archival and quantitative records).

Completing the two tours successfully will increase your ability to bring a powerful social science method to bear on significant social events. Could you ask for more?

Audiences for the Anthology. Regardless of your field of interest, you are likely to have been exposed to case studies of one form or another. Whether your field is an academic discipline (e.g., sociology, political science, or psychology) or a practice field (e.g., education, urban planning, community psychology, public administration, business management, health sciences, communications, or international affairs), your encounters should have included case studies done for research purposes (i.e., collecting and analyzing empirical evidence to address some research question).

Disappointingly, not all of these encounters may have been happy ones. Some researchers, based on their encounters, may have subsequently vowed to refrain from doing case studies and relying on case study evidence. These researchers may have been frustrated by the apparent lack of rigor in case study research. Other researchers remain willing to be swayed but cannot readily find or cite better case studies for their own or others' review. Yet other researchers already are satisfied with their use of the case study method but would like more examples.

The present anthology tries to meet the needs of all three audiences and also recognizes that the same individual may have suffered through all three variants at some point within the same career.

The Anthology's Selections. The anthology has 19 selections. They span a broad variety of topics and different social science disciplines, striving to demonstrate the applicability of the case study method to the bulk of social science research. Besides the breadth of the selections, they also were chosen as good examples of social science writing. Some of the selections represent excerpts from classic case studies. A good number of selections cover conditions in specific locales across the country (see Box 1).

Before going further, let's stop for a moment. Go to one of the 19 selections and read (or browse) it. If you want a contemporary topic, try the selections in Chapters 1, 12, or 19. If you want a sample of what

Box 1   Locales Covered by Anthology's Selections

Atlanta, GA (Chapter 8)*

Cambridge, MA (Chapter 9)

Chicago, IL (Chapter 11)

Clinton Township, MI (outside of Detroit) (Chapter 8)

Houston, TX (Chapter 19)

Los Angeles, CA (Chapter 13)

Louisville, KY (Chapter 8)

Merced, CA (Chapter 18)

Muncie, IL (Chapter 3)

New Bedford, MA (Chapter 8)

New York, NY (Chapter 17)

Oakland, CA (Chapter 5)

San Antonio, TX (Chapter 8)

San Francisco, CA (Chapter 8)

Silicon Valley, CA (Chapters 12 & 14)

Syracuse, NY (Chapter 16)

Washington, DC (Chapter 8)

---

*Note that Chapter 8 covers seven locales, but none in great depth. Missing from the list is the suburb just north of Boston, MA, which was the scene for the *Yankee City* study (Chapter 4).

might be a classic case study, try Chapters 2, 3, or 4. If you want to see how case study research has been reported in academic journals, as opposed to books, Chapters 7 or 18 are good examples. After reading or perusing any of this anthology's selections, you can return to this Introduction.

As with most anthologies, no one should expect to read the book from cover to cover. You hopefully have either looked through or read at least one of the selections. It should have piqued your interest. However, try not to limit your subsequent choices for reading additional selections to only your substantive topics of interest. The anthology does not concentrate on any particular subject matter (e.g., Box 2 shows how the selections might be categorized according to one scheme[4].) Rather, the anthology deliberately covers diverse topics, and its organizing principles are methodological.

Box 2   Distribution of Anthology's Selections, by Academic Subjects

Subject	Chapter Numbers	
	Primary Designation	Secondary Designation
Community development	3, 4, 18	5, 8, 13
Criminal justice	13, 17	
Education	9, 11, 15, 19	
Health	1, 16	
International affairs	2, 6	
Businesses and organizations	10, 12, 14	6, 19
Public policy	5, 7, 8	1, 2, 15

USING THIS ANTHOLOGY

Methodologically, the selections fall into five sections. Covering all five will not only help you to appreciate the existing case study literature but also may help you to design and conduct your own case study. To assist in this process, each selection has an individual introduction that highlights both the methodological issues and the substantive significance of the selection. The introductions should give you an idea of what you can learn by reading each of the selections. The broader themes underlying all of the selections and the anthology's five sections are as follows.

Section I: Theoretical Perspectives and Case Selection. This first section deals with the challenge of starting your case study. You must establish its rationale. The process includes both defining the ideas to be examined ("theoretical perspectives"[5]) and selecting the specific "case" to be the subject of your case study ("case selection"). You must satisfy both parts of the process as you start.

Note the distinction between the "case" and the "case study." The "case" is the real-life set of events from which data will be drawn. The case can be a concrete affair (e.g., a national crisis, as in Chapters 1 and 2 of the anthology, or the social life in a community, as in Chapters 3 and 4). The case also can be an abstract process (e.g., the implementation process, as illustrated in Chapter 5). In contrast, the "case study" is the substance of your research inquiry, consisting of your research questions, theoretical perspectives, empirical findings, interpretations, and conclusions.

Some investigators have benefited by having access to important cases (e.g., Chapters 1 and 2). The investigators have then developed significant case studies about these cases. One way of making your own case study significant is to embed it in a larger research literature (i.e., by examining hypotheses and covering theoretical issues identified as important to your field). In this manner, any lessons learned from your case study can then contribute to the building of new knowledge in your field.

Other investigators have benefited by defining an important topic for their case study. They have then selected a relevant case to be investigated (e.g., Chapters 3, 4, and 5).[6] Of course, the investigators still had to have access to the case, in order to collect the needed data. However the case itself was not necessarily a momentous or extraordinary set of real-life events. In fact, the case might have reflected an "average" circumstance.

You can succeed by having a good "case" or by designing your "case study" to address important theoretical considerations that will yield important new ideas. The more that you have both an important case and a well-designed case study—and follow data collection and analysis procedures carefully—the more likely your research will make an important contribution to a field and also attain a high level of professional recognition.

Section II: The Strength of Multiple Cases. The five chapters in Section I all have single cases as the subjects of their case studies. Relying on single cases, however, is not the only way of doing case study research. You also might have two or more cases as the subject of your single case study—what would then be called a "multiple-case study." Thus, in defining your case study, another early consideration is whether you will limit it to a single "case," or whether your case study will consist of two or more cases. The three selections in Section II all represent multiple-case studies. One apparently single case (Chapter 6), in fact, comes from a book that covered eight other cases. The other selections cover two cases (Chapter 7) and seven cases (Chapter 8) respectively. The selections show different ways of treating the multiple cases.

Collecting and analyzing data from two (or more) cases requires much more work than working on a single case. At the same time, the rewards can be greater, especially if you have the opportunity to choose your multiple cases to satisfy an important consideration from the standpoint of research design (e.g., by choosing extremely contrasting cases; potentially replicating cases [Chapter 7]; or some other desired variation among the cases [Chapters 6 and 8]. With such designs, the data from the multiple cases can strengthen your case study findings and make your interpretations more robust.[7] Having multiple cases also provides a side benefit. If your case study depends on a single case and your data collection encounters some unexpected difficulty, you may not be able to complete a case study of any sort. When such difficulties arise with a case that is only one of your multiple cases, you would still have the other case(s) to fall back upon.

Section III: Quantitative Evidence and "Embedded" Units of Analysis. Case studies can rely on both quantitative and qualitative evidence. The quantitative evidence can come from coded behaviors (Chapter 9), surveys

(Chapter 10), or archival information about an array of organizations, such as a large number of schools (Chapter 11). The analysis of the quantitative evidence also can range from simple tallies (Chapter 9) to state-of-the-art statistical techniques (Chapter 11).

Interestingly, case studies that involve more quantitative data also may more frequently involve "embedded units of analysis." Such units reside within (and are smaller than) the main unit of analysis—the whole "case." For instance, in a case study about a single school, the behavior of teachers within individual classrooms would be the embedded units (Chapter 9). Alternatively, in a case study about a single organization, the members of the organization would be the embedded units. These members also might have been the subjects of a formal survey (Chapter 10). Similarly, a case study may be about the reform of a whole system of schools. Then the individual schools within the system would be the embedded units whose characteristics could be tallied and statistically manipulated (Chapter 11).

Especially challenging under these circumstances is to avoid losing sight of the original case. For instance, if the results of a member survey only are used to investigate member behavior and characteristics, the original inquiry regarding the organization as a whole may not be well addressed. One of the selections in this section (Chapter 10) devotes considerable attention to this problem of balancing the whole case and its subunits, although, as the authors point out, there are no easy solutions.

Section IV: More Illustrations of Case Study Evidence. Section IV contains yet additional examples of different types of case study evidence: observations of physical facilities (Chapter 12); intensive use of documents such as newspapers (Chapter 13); reliance on data from open-ended interviews (Chapter 14); and a mixture of traditional evidence, such as quoted materials from interviews and documents, citation to findings from related research, and direct participation in the case (Chapter 15).

Many textbooks already tell you how to deal with these types of evidence. The selections in Section IV, however, go beyond the textbooks and show how evidence is put together around a particular case study. The data are still presented so that they can be reviewed and interpreted by the reader, apart from the author's own interpretations. A constant challenge is knowing how, nevertheless, to integrate the discussion of the evidence to make it an integral part of your case study.

Section V: Analyses and Conclusions. Analyzing case study data can assume many forms. In addition, rather than following the traditional linear sequence of doing laboratory research (e.g., defining hypotheses, collecting and presenting data, analyzing data, and then offering interpretations and conclusions) case study analysis can occur while you are still in the middle of collecting data. For example, when doing fieldwork, you may make a decision to search for additional field evidence on a particular topic, based on a preliminary analysis of your field data. In fact, an emerging realization is that analysis may occur at a variety of junctures when doing case studies. Such a pattern, rather than the neatly packaged step implied by the traditional linear sequence, might be one reason why analyzing case study data—especially qualitative data—has been an elusive craft.

The selections in Section V highlight the varieties of analyses used in case studies, ranging from the use of chronologies and analysis of behavior in clinical settings (Chapter 16), to the linking of crime-control initiatives with subsequent crime trends (Chapter 17), to an extensive analysis of economic development outcomes associated with the closing of a military base (Chapter 18). However, many of the chapters in the first four sections of the anthology, although intended to illustrate other procedures in the case study method, also already contained considerable amounts of analysis. You may especially want to revisit Chapters 7, 8, 11, 13, and 15, to see if you can isolate additional examples of relevant analytic techniques.

Providing a summative analysis and citing the major accomplishments from a case can be one way of bringing your case study to conclusion. The anthology's final selection (Chapter 19) shows, in exemplary fashion, how this part of the case study method can be practiced.

ADDITIONAL NOTES ABOUT THIS ANTHOLOGY

Methodological anthologies are a challenge to assemble. One challenge, already observed, is to mediate between the breadth of covering multiple substantive topics—versus the thinness in covering any single topic. A parallel challenge is to mediate between methodological breadth and depth.

Regarding the methodological challenge, this anthology deliberately favors depth rather than breadth. The depth—and thus the anthology's methodological niche—reflects the case study method described in an earlier text, first published in 1984 and now in its 3rd edition (*Yin,* 2003b). The method applies the norms of doing empirical research to the conduct of case study research. Moreover, the desired research can rely on quantitative or qualitative data.[8] The sacrifice in breadth arises because the anthology does not cover related methods, such as other forms of qualitative research or the conduct of field-based inquiries more generally.[9] The anthology also is not a "how-to" book, providing concrete guidance to carry out specific research procedures, such as gaining the approval for a case study investigation from an institutional review board (IRB), or arranging the logistics to conduct case study fieldwork.

Yet another challenge arose in the editing process. Whether appearing in books or as journal articles, most of the selected works needed to be pared down, to allow the anthology to cover a variety of selections without becoming cumbersome in length. The older selections also were edited for language (related to gender, race, and technology) that American society no longer favors.

SUMMARY

So, in various ways this anthology compromises breadth, depth, length, and language—in all, a possibly steep price—just to go on two tours. My bet is that you will still feel good about taking them.

Notes

1. The entire anthology emphasizes the use of case studies as a *research* tool, whether to study individuals (e.g., see Bromley, 1986) or groups and organizations (e.g., Yin, 2003b). Case studies also enjoy extensive use as a *teaching* tool (e.g., Bock & Campbell, 1962; and Christensen & Hansen, 1981), as a way of improving *practice* (e.g., Pigors & Pigors, 1961), and as a form of clinical or *archival record*, but none of these latter uses is the subject of the anthology.

2. Interestingly, the array of authors includes eminent social scientists who have not necessarily specialized in using the case study method. In fact, at least two of the authors have gained widespread recognition in doing state-of-the-art statistical research.

3. All the methodological definitions and terms used in this anthology can be found and are elucidated in a textbook on case study research that has been widely used since its first edition in 1984 (see Yin, 2003b). A companion text (Yin, 2003a), now in its second edition, contains case applications of the methodology.

4. Of course, many selections are cross-cutting, and using other categories would result in different schemes. For instance, another scheme might distinguish between the selections dealing with the delivery of *local* public services (e.g., Chapters 5, 8, 9, 11, 13, 15, 16, 17, and 19) and the selections dealing with the policies and programs of the *federal* government (e.g., Chapters 1, 2, 5, 7, 8, 15, and 18).

5. This term is not intended to suggest that you need any formally articulated theory. For instance, if you start with a "discovery" motive, that is your theoretical perspective. However, you should not settle for an oversimplified theoretical perspective, either.

6. The real-life research process is not so cut and dry (i.e., either selecting a case first or defining a case study first). Case selection and case study design may be interactive processes, whereby you iteratively arrive at the final choices. The entire situation has its parallel in laboratory research, where an investigator also has a dual need—to select and design a specific experiment but also to establish the broader (theoretical) significance of the experiment that is to be done.

7. An important assumption here is that you are interested in generalizing the findings from your case study, to go beyond the specific circumstances of the cases that you studied. The recommended generalization process relies on *analytic*, not *statistical* generalization and is discussed in Mitchell (1983), Gomm, Hammersley, &

Foster (2000), and Yin (2003b), although these authors use different labels for the same concepts. The logic underlying the desired generalization process is discussed in an incisive but little known article by Donald Campbell (1975).

8. However, the case study method does not fall cleanly within the province of either quantitative or qualitative methods. In fact, how the case study method is to be categorized among other social science methods has been the subject of extensive writing. For instance, while no method of social science research, by definition, can replicate the scientific method in the natural sciences, the present anthology has been organized from the perspective that *emulating* the principles of scientific research (e.g., starting with explicit research questions, using a research design to address these questions, collecting and fairly presenting evidence to support interpretations, and referencing related research to aid in defining questions and drawing conclusions) will produce strong case study research. At the same time, an international handbook on education research divides the various social science methods into scientific and humanistic research, and places the case study method under the latter (Keeves, 1998, p. 7). The humanistic tradition offers such strengths as an emphasis on prolonged engagement in the field, "thick" description, and the celebration of the particular rather than the general (e.g., Stake, 1994; and Simons, 1996).

Despite the terms "scientific" and "humanistic," which are too stereotypic, the two orientations to doing case study research are not necessarily conflicting. They may be seen as differences in emphasis (e.g., Stenhouse, 1988; and Yin, 1994). However, in designing a new case study, you should be sensitive to these differences in orientations and whether key members of your audience have particular preferences.

9. For example, the anthology does not have any selections on the use of participant-observation, in which a research investigator adopts a "real-life" role while also investigating the topic at hand. See Platt (1992) for an extended discussion of the relationship between participant-observation (and sociological fieldwork) and the definition of the case study method as it has been used in this anthology.

References

Bock, E. A., & Campbell, A. K. (Eds.). (1962). *Case studies in American government: The Inter-university case program.* Englewood Cliffs, NJ: Prentice-Hall.

Bromley, D. B. (1986). *The case-study method in psychology and related disciplines.* Chichester, Great Britain: John Wiley.

Campbell, D. T. (1975). 'Degrees of freedom' and the case study. *Comparative Political Studies, 8,* 178–193.

Christensen, C. R., & Hansen, A. J. (1981). *Teaching and the case method: Text, cases, and reading.* Boston, MA: Harvard Business School.

Gomm, R., Hammersley, M., & Foster, P. (2000). Case study and generalization. In R. Gomm, M. Hammersley, & P. Foster (Eds.), *Case study method: Key issues, key texts* (pp. 98–115). Thousand Oaks, CA: Sage.

Keeves, J. P. (Ed.). (1988). *Educational research, methodology, and measurement: An international handbook.* Oxford, England: Pergamon Press.

Mitchell, J. C. (1983). Case and situation analysis. *Sociological Review, 31,* 187–211; reprinted in R. Gomm, M. Hammersley, & P. Foster (Eds.). (2000). *Case study method: Key issues, key texts* (pp. 165–186). Thousand Oaks, CA: Sage.

Pigors, P., & Pigors, F. (1961). *Case method in social relations: The incident process.* New York: McGraw-Hill.

Platt, J. (1992). 'Case study' in American methodological thought. *Current Sociology, 40* (1), 17–48.

Simons, H. (1996). The paradox of case study. *Cambridge Journal of Education, 26,* 225–240.

Stake, R. E. (1994). Case studies. In N. K. Denzin & Y. S. Lincoln (Eds.), *Handbook of qualitative research* (pp. 236–247). Thousand Oaks, CA: Sage.

Stenhouse, L. (1988). Case study methods. In J. P. Keeves (Ed.), *Educational research, methodology, and measurement: An international handbook* (pp. 49–53). Oxford, England: Pergamon Press.

Yin, R. K. (1994). Evaluation: A singular craft. In C. Reichardt & S. Rallis (Eds.), *New Directions in Program Evaluation, 61,* 71–84).

Yin, R. K. (2003a). *Applications of case study research* (2nd ed.). Thousand Oaks, CA: Sage.

Yin, R. K. (2003b). *Case study research: Design and methods* (3rd ed.). Thousand Oaks, CA: Sage.

Section I

Theoretical Perspectives and Case Selection

The Epidemic That Never Was

Policy-Making and the Swine Flu Scare*

Richard E. Neustadt and Harvey V. Fineberg

---

editor's introduction:

Methodological Significance

If you are going to do a case study, you are likely to devote a significant portion of your time to that case study. To be avoided is committing much of your time and resources and then finding that the case study will not work out. Therefore, in using the case study method, your goal should be to select your case study carefully. Try to spot unrealistic or uninformative case studies as early as possible.

More ambitiously, try to select a significant or "special" case or cases for your case study. The more significant your case—combined with the use of other methodological features emphasized throughout the rest of this anthology—the more likely your case study will contribute to the research literature or to improvements in practice (or to the completion of a doctoral dissertation). Conversely, devoting your efforts to a fairly "mundane" case study may not even produce an acceptable

---

study (or dissertation). If you do not have access to a special case, the recommended approach is to consider any candidate for your case study with great care and forethought, even if the process takes more time than you would have anticipated.

Set your goals high. You may only have a once-in-a-lifetime opportunity to contribute to case study research. Also consult actively with your peers and colleagues about your selection. Choose the most significant case possible. Your success might result in an exemplary study (or dissertation). Your study might present new theoretical or practical themes. It also might capture, as with the present selection, a case of lasting relevance—if not value—decades later.

Substantive Note**

In the swine flu scare, the United States government tried to immunize its whole population against a threat of world epidemic from a potentially deathly and new influenza strain, known as "swine flu." The scale of the immunization effort was unprecedented, with more than 40 million citizens immunized in 10 weeks during the fall of 1976. The venture also was marked, not surprisingly, by controversy, delay, administrative troubles, legal complications, the threat of unforeseen medical side effects, and a progressive loss of credibility for public health authorities.

The entire experience echoes to the present time, about 30 years (a generation) later. The governments of the world are preoccupied with the threat of maverick countries using weapons of mass (biological) destruction. The biochemical defenses may have changed and even improved, but the political and community forces—at national, state, and local levels—may still be those at work in the "swine flu scare" years earlier. At that time, Neustadt and Fineberg already concluded their case study with such topics as "thinking twice about medical knowledge." In retrospect, wouldn't this earlier case study have been an excellent case study to have had on your resume?

**Some passages in this substantive note come from the authors' Introduction, p. xix.

The New Flu

The proximate beginning of this story is abrupt. On the East Coast of the United States, January 1976 was very cold. At Fort Dix, New Jersey, the training center for Army recruits, new men fresh from civilian life got their first taste of barracks and basics. A draft of several thousand came in after New Year's Day to be instructed by a cadre back from Christmas leave. The fort had been almost emptied; now in the cold it was full again. By mid-January many men began reporting respiratory ailments. A relative handful was hospitalized. One, refusing hospitalization, went on an overnight hike and died.

After a county medical meeting on another subject, the state's chief epidemiologist bet the senior Army doctor that Fort Dix was in the midst of an influenza virus epidemic. To win, the latter sent a sample set of cultures for analysis in the state laboratory. He lost. The lab turned up several cases of flu traceable to the Victoria virus, which had been the dominant cause of human influenza since 1968. But the lab also found other cases of flu caused by a virus it could not identify. With foreboding, Dr. Martin Goldfield, the civilian epidemiologist, sent those cultures to Atlanta, to the Federal government's Centers for Disease Control (CDC). A similar virus, also unidentified, was isolated from the dead man, and a culture was sent to CDC. In the evening of February 12, the Center's Laboratory Chief, Dr. Walter Dowdle, reported the result to his superiors—in four cases, including the fatality, the unknown virus was swine flu. This caused more concern than surprise at CDC.

Four things combined to create the concern. First, these four recruits could have been infected through human-to-human transmission. Not since the late 1920s had this form of influenza been reported in as many persons out of touch with pigs. There might have been a number of occasions unreported; no one knew. Second, for a decade after World War I a virus of this sort was believed to have been the chief cause of flu in human beings. Since then it had confined itself to pigs. Were it returning now to humans, none younger than 50 would have built up specific antibodies from previous infection. Third, the Fort Dix virus differed in both its surface proteins, termed "antigens," from the influenza virus then circulating in the human population. This difference, in expert terms an "antigenic shift," would negate any resistance carried over from exposure to the other current viruses. In 1976, leading experts assumed that pandemics follow antigenic shifts as night follows day.

And finally, in 1918, a pandemic of the swine flu virus, the most virulent influenza known to modern medicine, had, in a so-called "killer wave," been associated with some 20 million deaths worldwide, 500,000 here in the United States. Many were taken by bacterial pneumonia, a complication of influenza now treatable with antibiotics, but an unknown number succumbed to the flu itself. Among the hardest hit then had been able-bodied persons in their twenties and early thirties. Parents of small children died in droves. So did young men in uniform. Virulence cannot as yet be tested in the lab. Could the Fort Dix swine flu be a comparable killer? No one at CDC had any reason to suppose it was—contrasting the 1920s to the circumstances of the one death now—but still. . . .

The absence of surprise reflected expert views at that time about epidemic cycles and about the reappearance of particular types of viruses in people. It was widely thought—on rather scanty evidence—that antigenic shifts were likely about once a decade (interspersed with slighter changes, "drifts," each second or third year). There had been shifts in 1957 and in 1968, both followed by pandemics—Asian flu and Hong Kong flu respectively—and public health officials were expecting another by, say, 1978 or 1979. 1976 was close. The very day the Fort Dix cases were identified at CDC, *The New York Times* carried an Op Ed piece by Dr. Edwin D. Kilbourne, one of the country's most respected influenza specialists, extolling cycles and affirming that pandemics occur every 11 years— another one of which, he warned, was surely coming soon:

> Worldwide epidemics, or pandemics, of influenza have marked the end of every decade since the 1940s—at intervals of exactly eleven years—1946, 1957, 1968. A perhaps simplistic reading of this immediate past tells us that 11 plus 1968 is 1979, and urgently suggests that those concerned with public health had best plan without further delay for an imminent natural disaster.[1]

In addition, an influenza virus recycling theory was just then receiving attention, and this suggested swine-type as a likely next strain to appear. The idea was that the flu virus had a restricted antigenic repertoire and a limited number of possible forms, requiring repetition after a time period sufficient for a large new crop of vulnerable people to accumulate. The Asian flu of 1957 was thought to have resembled flu in the pandemic year of 1889. The Hong Kong flu of 1968 was thought to be like that of 1898. Swine flu, absent for 50 years, fit well enough, no surprise. The theory had been originally proposed by two doctors who wrote in 1973:

> A logical sequel to the data presented and supported here would be the emergence in man of a swine-like virus about 1985–1991. . . . Regardless of one's view as to the origin of recycling of human strains of influenza, the matter of being prepared to produce swine virus vaccine rapidly should receive consideration by epidemiologists. Man has never been ably to intervene effectively to prevent morbidity and mortality accompanying the emergence of a major influenza variant, but the opportunity may come soon.[2]

Although some experts were skeptical about the regularity with which previous strains might be expected to reappear, no one doubted that a swine flu virus might well re-emerge in the human population.

On February 12, alerted by preliminary lab reports, Dr. David Sencer, CDC's director, asked a number of officials from outside his agency to join him there for a full lab report on February 14. The Army responded, as did Goldfield from New Jersey. And from two other parts of CDC's parent entity in HEW [now the U.S. Department of Health and Human Services, HHS], the Public Health Service (PHS), Dr. Harry Meyer and Dr. John Seal came as a matter of course. Meyer was director of the Bureau of Biologics (BoB) in the Food and Drug Administration; Seal was the deputy director of the National Institute for Allergy and Infectious Diseases (NIAID) in the National Institutes of Health. (NIAID's director left these relations to Seal.) The BoB was responsible for licensing and test-ing flu vaccines, the NIAID for federally sponsored flu research. The duties of Meyer and Seal overlapped, but they were accustomed collaborators. Both were accustomed also to work closely with CDC, its labs and its state services.

Among their recent objects of collaboration had been workshops held at intervals since 1971 on how to better the quite dismal record of 1957 and of 1968 in getting vaccine to Americans ahead of a pandemic. This matter was much on Seal's mind and especially on Meyer's. His bureau had been the subject of a Senate inquiry three years before and needed nothing less than the black-marketing and discrimination characteristic of vaccine distribution in 1957.

To this group, enlarged by CDC staff, Dowdle reported his laboratory findings. The question at once became whether four human cases were the first appearance of incipient pandemic or a fluke of some kind, a limited transfer to a few humans of what remained an animal disease that would not thrive in people. All agreed that based on the present evidence there was no means of knowing. Surveillance was the task at hand. Since their uncertainty was real, they also agreed that there should be no publicity until there were more data: Why raise public concern about what might turn out an isolated incident? Some days later CDC scrapped this agree-ment on the plea that uninformed press leaks were imminent, and Sencer called a press conference for February 19. He must have hated the thought that an announcement might come from some place other than CDC. However that may be, the press conference got national attention:

In *The New York Times,* Harold Schmeck reported, February 20:

> The possibility was raised today that the virus that caused the greatest world epidemic of influenza in modern history—the pandemic of 1918–19—may have returned.

This story (on Page 1) was headed: *U.S. Calls Flu Alert on Possible Return of Epidemic Virus.*

The 1918 reference was included in brief notices that night, on CBS and ABC news telecasts. NBC went them one better and showed 1918 still pictures of persons wearing masks. Lacking further information, the media did not follow up on the story for a month. But 1918 left a trace in certain minds—some of them TV producers and reporters. From within CDC, we have encountered a good deal of retrospective criticism at press tendencies to "harp" on 1918 prematurely, with no evidence whatsoever about prospective virulence or even spread through 1976. These NBC pictures are cited along with *The New York Times* headline. But the reference was included in the CDC press briefing, and indeed without it, what was known about Fort Dix so far was scarcely news at all. Publicity had no effect on the effort to establish what the Fort Dix outbreak meant. In Fort Dix itself, where the Army conducted its own investigation shielded from civilians, the Victoria strain proved dominant, at least for the time being. There were plenty of new influenza cases; none was caused by the swine virus. On the other hand, that virus was isolated from a fifth soldier who had been sick in early February, and blood tests confirmed eight more old cases of swine flu, none of them fatal. Moreover, a sampling of antibody levels among recruits suggested that as many as 500 had been infected by swine flu. This implied human transmission on a scale that could not reasonably be viewed lightly. Around Fort Dix, however, in the civilian population—which was Goldfield's territory for investigation—analysis of every case of flu reported, by a medical community on the alert, showed only the Victoria strain. Elsewhere in New Jersey, Goldfield's inquiries turned up no swine flu. The Army's inquiries turned up none at camps other than Fort Dix. The NIAID network of university researchers and the state epidemiologists in touch with CDC reported none untraceable to pigs. The World Health Organization, pressed by CDC, could learn of none abroad. One death, 13 sick men, and up to 500 recruits who evidently had caught and resisted the disease—all in one Army camp— were the only established instances of human-to-human swine flu found around the world as February turned into March, the last month of flu season in the Northern Hemisphere.

On March 10 the group that had met February 14 reassembled at CDC and under Sencer's chairmanship reviewed its findings with the Advisory Committee on Immunization Practices (ACIP). That committee consisted of a set of outside experts appointed by the U.S. Surgeon General, independently advising CDC; in fact, it was almost a part of CDC— nominated, chaired, and staffed at Sencer's discretion. BoB deadlines now forced his pace. One ACIP function was to make vaccine recommendations for the next flu season available to manufacturers. The annual questions were: vaccine against what viruses, aimed at which population groups? For 1976 these questions had already been reviewed in a January ACIP meeting. The committee had recommended Victoria vaccine for the "high-risk groups" as then defined, some 40 million people over 65 in age or with certain chronic diseases. By March 10, the four active manufacturers had produced in bulk form about 20 million doses of Victoria vaccine for the civilian market. If Fort Dix meant a change or addition, now was the time to decide. Indeed, for a regulatory body like the BoB, responsible for setting standards and for quality control, March was already late. Vaccine is grown in eggs; a vaccine against swine flu would require new supplies replacing those just used for the Victoria vaccine. Then immunization trials would be needed if there was a new vaccine; also extensive testing would be necessary. And what about the vaccine now in bulk? Whatever surveillance had turned up by now would have to suffice for some sort of decision. . . .

[On March 24, President Gerald Ford announced:]

I have been advised that there is a very real possibility that unless we take effective counteractions, there could be an epidemic of this dangerous disease next fall and winter here in the United States. Let me state clearly at this time: No one knows exactly how serious this threat could be. Nevertheless, we cannot afford to take a chance with the health of our nation. Accordingly, I am today announcing the following actions.

. . . I am asking the Congress to appropriate $135 million, prior to their April recess, for the production of sufficient vaccine to inoculate every man, woman, and child in the United States. . . .

Field Trials

On March 25, the day after the President's announcement, a meeting chaired by Meyer at the BoB—with CDC and NIAID and the producing laboratories represented—drew several key conclusions. These had been in the air March 10 or even earlier; this meeting tacked them down.

First, manufacturers should produce enough swine vaccine for everyone—roughly 200 million doses—and start deliveries in June for use from July on. Neither now nor later were dates for the mass immunization made precise. The aim was to start before August—as early in July as deliveries allowed—and to finish before winter. (In their April testimony, Sencer and Cooper said November; whereas Meyer, closer to production, said late December.)

Second, since this would fully occupy available facilities of active manufacturers, no more Victoria vaccine should be produced. What was at hand would be made bivalent by adding swine vaccine in bulk. This would produce some 30 million bivalent doses, to be used for high-risk groups, mainly the elderly.

Third, the rest of the swine flu vaccine would be turned into monovalent doses and used on a one-person, one-dose basis, thus ensuring wide availability. This assumed that one dose would give adequate protection without bothersome effects on adults and children alike. The assumption was colored by recent improvements in vaccine purification. But it rested fundamentally on logistical concerns: How could one hope to get vaccine and kids together twice?

Fourth, the needs of the armed forces, also those of the Veterans Administration, although separately determined and contracted for (as usual), had to fit inside these targets, with deliveries coordinated in a fashion to which military doctors were distinctly unaccustomed. Production orders from still other sources, including other countries if they came, had to wait for American deliveries. Diversions of American supplies would be a matter for the White House. (So, indeed, was the compliance of DoD: Cavanaugh later got stuck with both.)

Another assumption was hidden, or more precisely muffled, in these calculations, namely that the manufacturers would grow the monovalent vaccine fast enough to guard against an early fall pandemic. In 1918, the virulent phase had begun in August. The manufacturers now argued, in Hilleman's words at the meeting:

> . . . you couldn't possibly have 200 million doses by fall . . . If you are talking about one dose per egg, which is more what it looks like [instead of the hoped-for two doses] you are talking about a different situation.[3]

The day before, the President had pledged vaccine to everyone. A week later, Cooper, on the Hill, would state his goal as "95 percent of all Americans." Hilleman's discrepancy seems to have left Meyer untroubled.

On April 2, Sencer in Atlanta hosted a monster meeting to acquaint state health officials and representatives of private medicine with these targets (Congress willing) and with CDC's conception of administrative follow-through based on state immunization plans. Prompt filing of these plans was sought by CDC. Funding and technical assistance were to follow. Vaccine distribution would begin as soon as field trials, tests, and bottling allowed, and states should start at once to put it into people. Taking maximum advantage of the time at hand, the states now had a chance to immunize the country, or most of it, before the next flu season.

Here was a challenge for the Public Health officialdom from coast to coast, an opportunity to do in 1976 precisely what had not been done in 1968 or 1957—and at Federal expense with the President responsible. Energy and time and personnel might have to be withdrawn from other uses, to be sure, but not much money begged from any legislature except Congress; his trouble, not theirs. Besides, there was the vision of the Kilbournes and the Coopers: Preventive medicine raised high in public consciousness. Who could be against that? . . .

Between October 1 and December 16, more than 40 million Americans received swine flu shots through Sencer's program. (Defense and VA programs accounted for some millions more.) This is twice the number ever immunized before for any influenza virus in a single season. Considering the obstacles, it is an impressive number. It also is a number oddly distributed. Some states, albeit small ones, inoculated 80 percent of their adults in that time period. Others immunized not more than 10 percent. Delaware was at the top of that range, New York City near the bottom. Variations in between are striking: Houston, Texas, inoculated only 10 percent of its adults, whereas San Antonio, Texas, immunized nearly one-third. Despite coincident deaths, Pittsburgh, Pennsylvania, vaccinated nearly 43 percent whereas Philadephia, home of Legionnaire's Disease, managed but 23 percent. And so forth.[4] These variations cry out for explanation. So far as we know, CDC has not pursued them and may lack the resources to do so. . . .

One state that was conscientious in its conduct of the national program was Minnesota, where nearly two-thirds of the eligible adults were immunized. In the third week of November, a physician there reported to his local health authorities a patient who had contracted an ascending paralysis, called Guillain-Barré syndrome, following immunization. The physician said he had just learned of this possible side effect from a cassette-tape discussion of flu vaccination prepared for the continuing education of family practitioners by a California specialist. The Minnesota immunization program officer, Denton R. Peterson, dutifully called CDC and spoke to one of the surveillance physicians there. The latter expressed no interest in this single case, but Peterson was sufficiently bothered to conduct a literature search and did indeed discover previous case reports. "We felt we were sitting on a bomb," he told us. Within a week three more cases, one fatal, were reported to Peterson. Two came from a single neurologist who remarked that he had observed this complication of flu vaccine during his residency training. More anxious than ever, Peterson again called CDC, where the surveillance center was just being told by phone of three more cases in Alabama. The next day they learned of an additional case in New Jersey. By then CDC was taking the problem seriously. Center staff surveyed neurologists in 11 states to ascertain the relative risk of this rare disease (estimated at five thousand cases annually) among the vaccinated and unvaccinated. When the preliminary results suggested an increased risk among the vaccinated, Sencer sought advice from usual sources: NIAID, BoB, ACIP, and his own people. The statistical association did not convince them all.

But what struck everybody, sensitized by their long summer, was the thought: Until the risk (if any) is established, it cannot be put into a consent form! The statistical relationship would have to be reviewed and immunization halted in the interim. After everything that had already happened, everybody took that to mean virtual termination. Even the least imaginative could conjure up the television shots of victims in their beds, wheel chairs, and respirators.

With some trepidation about White House willingness to stop, Sencer called Cooper on December 16, and fortuitously reached him in the White

House Staff Mess, lunching with Cavanaugh. Mathews by chance was at another table. The three huddled quickly; Cooper then excused himself and made a call to Salk. The switchboard reached Salk in Paris. Without enthusiasm he concurred with Sencer's view. Cooper and the others then walked down the hall to [President] Ford. He heard them out, sighed, and agreed. For most intents and purposes the swine flu program was over. With no disease in sight nine months after Ford's announcement, even a rare side effect could turn him around.

That afternoon Cooper announced suspension of the swine flu program, saying that he was acting "in the interest of safety of the public, in the interest of credibility, and in the interest of the practice of good medicine."[5] . . .

Legacies

The swine flu program ended, but in terms of Federal policy it left at least three legacies. With these the Secretary [of HEW] still is dealing or has yet to deal. One is a national commission on immunization policy. Another is liability policy. The third is an expanded Federal role in influenza immunization. The three interlock. They still evolve. They carry far beyond March 1977, the month we made our stopping-point for detailed reconstruction. But during 1977, while we worked on 1976, we tried to keep an eye on these three legacies. . . .

Notes

1. *The New York Times*, February 13, 1976, p. 33.

2. N. Masurel and W. M. Marine (1973). Recycling of Asian and Hong Kong Influenza A Virus Hemagglutinins in Man. *American Journal of Epidemiology, 97*, 48–49.

3. Bureau of Biologics Workshop, March 25, 1976, transcript, p. 128.

4. Figures are taken from unpublished data compiled by the CDC. Percentages are based on populations 18 years of age and older, as of the 1970 census. This means that for 1976, [the] percentages are overstated in areas of recent, rapid growth.

5. For the full text, see HEW press release, December 16, 1976.

Essence of Decision

Explaining the Cuban Missile Crisis*

Graham Allison and Philip Zelikow

editor's introduction:

Methodological Significance

Chapter 1 of this anthology emphasized the desirability of choosing a significant or special case. However, you may only have access to such a case under rare circumstances. Another way of boosting the potential contribution of your case study is to place it within a compelling theoretical framework. The framework should guide your data collection and also may lead to important ways of generalizing from the case study's findings.

The present selection illustrates the use of such a framework. Part of the framework is based on a few sharply focused questions. The authors used these questions to organize the data to be collected for a single but highly complicated case study. The authors also introduced three theories, all well based in the prevailing research literature, to explain the findings from the case study. Such an approach contributed to the authors'

***Editor's Note:** This is the introductory chapter from *Essence of Decision: Explaining the Cuban Missile Crisis, Second Edition* by Graham Allison and Philip Zelikow. Copyright © 1999. Reprinted with permission from Addison-Wesley, New York, NY. The book was first published in 1971, with Graham Allison as the sole author. The second edition contains extensive new material, including reinterpretations of the original work, based on huge amounts of new evidence that emerged after the original publication. With the exception of one deletion, and minor edits, the introduction is presented as written by the authors.

ability to generalize the study's findings to a much broader array of political and international situations—even though the original findings only came from a single case.

The selection is from the introduction to an entire book—which is the complete case study. However, the introduction differs from most. Rather than merely serving as a prelude to the ensuing case study, the introduction also previews the implications and lessons to be learned from the case study. Such creativity, as well as the ingenuity underlying the selection of the three sharply focused questions (a fourth question deals with the "lessons learned" and is not really a substantive question), should not be taken for granted. The more you can strive for similar results, while also thoroughly examining a huge amount of evidence ("tens of thousands of pages") as did Allison and Zelikow, the more your case study also could become a classic.

Substantive Note

The book from which this introduction has been extracted has been a bestseller in the field of political science for over 30 years. As a case study, the book focuses on one of the most serious crises in modern history—when the United States and the former Soviet Union stood "eyeball to eyeball" for 13 days in October 1962. The confrontation could have resulted in nuclear holocaust, threatening the survival of human life on this planet. As a contribution to the field of political science, the book compares three different theories of government action in foreign affairs: a rational (single) actor model, an organizational behavior model, and a government politics model. These theories had not been so cogently articulated or applied to a set of real-life events until the book's original publication in 1971. The introduction also neatly represents these theories in more common terms by alluding to three alternative ways of playing a hypothetical game of chess.

Not indicated by the introduction is another distinctive aspect of the case study. The original case study was based on an extremely broad array of evidence, including government documents and interviews with a large number of officials.

The subsequent collapse of the Soviet Union, after the book's first edition had been published, led to a unique opportunity to examine additional critical documents that had not been previously available to the researchers. Thus, the present introduction comes from a revised version of the original case study, appearing in the book's second edition. All of these characteristics—the significance of the case, sharpness of the research questions, contribution to theory, and exhaustive review of evidence—combine to make the book an example of a classic case study.

The Cuban missile crisis stands as a seminal event. History offers no parallel to those 13 days of October 1962, when the United States and the Soviet Union paused at the nuclear precipice. Never before had there been such a high probability that so many lives would end suddenly. Had war come, it could have meant the death of 100 million Americans and more than 100 million Russians, and millions of Europeans as well. Other natural calamities and inhumanities of history would have faded into insignificance. Given the odds of disaster—which President [John F.] Kennedy estimated as "between one out of three and even"—our escape seems awesome.[1] This event symbolizes a central, if only partially "thinkable," fact about our existence in the nuclear age.

The missile crisis is among the most studied episodes in modern history. Nonetheless, even the central questions have eluded satisfactory answers:

Why did the Soviet Union place strategic offensive missiles in Cuba? For what purpose did the Russians undertake such a drastic, risky departure from their traditional policy? Given the repeated American warnings that such an act would not be tolerated, how could Khrushchev have made such a major—potentially fatal—miscalculation?

Why did the United States respond with a naval quarantine of Soviet shipments to Cuba? Was it necessary for the United States to force a public nuclear confrontation? What alternatives were really available? What danger did the Soviet missiles in Cuba pose for the United States? Did this threat justify the president's choice of a course of action that he believed entailed a realistic chance of disaster? Did that threat require more immediate action to disable the Soviet missiles in Cuba before they became operational?

Why were the missiles withdrawn? What would have happened if, instead of withdrawing the missiles, Khrushchev had announced that the operational Soviet missiles would fire if fired upon? Did the "blockade" work, or was there an "ultimatum" or perhaps some "deal"? Why did the

Soviets remove the missiles rather than retaliate at other equally sensitive points—Berlin, for example?

What are the "lessons" of the missile crisis? What does this event teach us about nuclear confrontations and the risks of nuclear war? In the aftermath of the Cold War, what does it imply about crisis management and government coordination? Is this a model of how to deal with adversaries?

The tens of thousands of pages of relevant evidence now finally accessible to students of this crisis pose a serious challenge in themselves. Simply reading carefully all the evidence is an assignment requiring many months. We two have made a best effort to take full advantage of the storehouse of declassified documents, memoirs, oral histories, interviews, and even the formerly secret tapes of most of the White House deliberations in offering an analysis of the missile crisis. Here, the missile crisis also serves as grist in a more general investigation. But the central premise of this study is that satisfactory answers to questions about the missile crisis will require more than additional information and analysis. Real improvement in our answers to questions of this sort depends on greater awareness of what we (both laymen and professional analysts) bring to the analysis. When answering questions such as "Why did the Soviet Union place missiles in Cuba?" what we see and judge to be important and accept as adequate depends not only on the evidence available but also on the "conceptual lenses" through which we look at the evidence. A primary purpose of this study, therefore, is to explore the fundamental yet often unnoticed choices among the categories and assumptions that channel our thinking about problems like the Cuban missile crisis.

The General Argument

When we are puzzled by a happening in foreign affairs, the source of our puzzlement is typically a particular government action or set of actions: Soviet emplacement of missiles in Cuba, American troops being sent to the Persian Gulf, Germany ceding sovereign control over its currency by adopting the Euro, and the failure to defend the undeclared "safe havens" in Bosnia. These occurrences raise obvious questions: *Why* did the Soviet Union place missiles in Cuba? *Why* were five hundred thousand American soldiers in the Persian Gulf? *Why* did Germany give up the Deutsche-Mark? *Why* did the United Nations do so little to defend Srebrenica in July 1995? In pursuing the answers to these questions, the serious analyst seeks to discover why one specific state of the world came about—rather than some other.

In searching for an explanation, one typically puts himself or herself[2] in the place of the nation or national government confronting a problem of foreign affairs, and tries to figure out why one might have chosen the action in question. Thus, analysts have explained the Soviet missiles in Cuba as a way of defending Cuba against American attack. U.S. troops went to Saudi Arabia to undo and deter aggression. Germany joined its European Union partners in a common currency to advance the cause of European integration. The United Nations failed to act in Bosnia because member nations involved lacked the will to resist Serb aggression.

In offering (or accepting) these explanations, one is assuming that governmental behavior can be most satisfactorily understood by analogy with the purposive acts of individuals. In many cases this is a fruitful assumption. Treating national governments as if *they* were centrally coordinated, purposive individuals provides a useful shorthand for understanding policy choices and actions. But this simplification—like all simplifications—obscures as well as reveals. In particular, it obscures the persistently neglected fact of government: The "decisionmaker" of national policy is obviously not one calculating individual but is rather a conglomerate of large organizations and political actors. What this fact implies for analysts of events such as the Cuban missile crisis is no simple matter. Its implications challenge the basic categories and assumptions with which we approach events.

More rigorously, the *argument* developed in the body of this study can be summarized in three propositions:

1. Professional analysts of foreign affairs and policymakers (as well as ordinary citizens) think about problems of foreign and military policy in terms of largely implicit conceptual models that have significant consequences for the content of their thought.[3]

In thinking about problems of foreign affairs, professional analysts as well as ordinary citizens proceed in a straightforward, informal, and nontheoretical fashion. Careful examination of explanations of events such as the Soviet installation of missiles in Cuba, however, reveals a more complex theoretical substructure. Explanations by particular analysts show regular and predictable characteristics that reflect unrecognized assumptions about the character of puzzles, the categories in which problems should be considered, the types of evidence that are relevant, and the determinants of occurrences. Our first proposition is that bundles of such related assumptions constitute basic frames of reference or conceptual models in terms of which analysts and ordinary laymen ask and answer the questions: What happened? Why did it happen? What will happen? Assumptions like these are central to the activities of explanation and prediction. In attempting to explain a particular event, the analyst cannot simply describe the full state of the world leading up to that event. The logic of explanation requires singling out the relevant, critical determinants of the occurrence, the junctures at which particular factors produced one state of the world rather than another.[4] Moreover, as the logic of prediction underscores, the analyst must summarize the various factors as they bear on the occurrence. Conceptual models not only fix the mesh of the nets that the analyst drags through the material to explain a particular action; models also direct the analyst to cast nets in select ponds, at certain depths, in order to catch the fish he is after.

2. Most analysts explain (and predict) behavior of national governments in terms of one basic conceptual model, here titled Rational Actor Model (RAM or Model I).

In spite of significant differences in interest and focus, most analysts and ordinary citizens attempt to understand happenings in foreign affairs as the more or less purposive acts of unified national governments. Laymen personify actors and speak of their aims and choices. Theorists of international relations focus on problems between nations in accounting for the choices of unitary rational actors. Strategic analysts concentrate on the logic of action without reference to any particular actor. For each of these groups, the point of an explanation is to show how the nation or government could have chosen to act as it did, given the strategic problems it faced. For example, in confronting the problem posed by the Soviet installation of strategic missiles in Cuba, the Model I analyst frames the puzzle: Why did the Soviet Union decide to install missiles in Cuba? He focuses attention on certain concepts: goals and objectives of the nation or government. Finally, the analyst invokes certain patterns of inference: If the nation performed an action of this sort, it must have had a goal of this type. The analyst has "explained" this event when he can show how placing missiles in Cuba was a reasonable action, given Soviet strategic objectives. Predictions about what a nation will do or would have done are generated by calculating the rational thing to do in a certain situation, given specified objectives.

3. Two alternative conceptual models, here labeled an Organizational Behavior Model (Model II) and a Governmental Politics Model (Model III), provide a base for improved explanations and predictions.

Although the Rational Actor Model has proved useful for many purposes, there is powerful evidence that it must be supplemented by frames of reference that focus on the governmental machine—the organizations and political actors involved in the policy process. Model I's implication that important events have important causes (i.e., that monoliths perform large actions for large reasons) must be balanced by the appreciation that (1) monoliths are black boxes covering various gears and levers in a highly differentiated decision-making structure and (2) large acts result from innumerable and often conflicting smaller actions by individuals at various levels of organizations in the service of a variety of only partially compatible conceptions of national goals, organizational goals, and political objectives. Model I's grasp of national purposes and the pressures created by problems in international relations must confront the intranational mechanisms from which governmental actions emerge.

Organization theory provides the foundation for the second model, which emphasizes the distinctive logic, capacities, culture, and procedures of the large organizations that constitute a government. According to this Organizational Behavior Model, what Model I analysts characterize as "acts" and "choices" are thought of instead as *outputs* of large organizations functioning according to regular patterns of behavior. Faced with the fact of Soviet missiles in Cuba, a Model II analyst frames the puzzle: From what organizational context, pressures, and procedures did this decision emerge? He focuses attention on certain concepts: existing organizational components, their functions, and their standard operating procedures for acquiring information (e.g., about American strategic forces or intentions); the definition of feasible options (e.g., sending proven but medium-range ballistic missiles to Cuba vs. building new intercontinental-range missiles); and implementation (e.g., actually installing missiles in Cuba without being discovered). The analyst invokes certain patterns of inference: If organizations produced an output of a certain kind at a certain time, that behavior resulted from existing organizational structures, procedures, and repertoires. A Model II analyst has "explained" the event when he or she has identified the relevant Soviet organizations and displayed the patterns of organizational behavior from which the action emerged. Predictions identify trends that reflect existing organizations and their fixed procedures and programs.

The third model focuses on the politics of a government. According to this model, events in foreign affairs are characterized neither as unitary choice nor as organizational outputs. Rather, what happens is understood as a *resultant* of bargaining games among players in the national government. In confronting the problem posed by Soviet missiles in Cuba, a Model III analyst frames the puzzle: Which results of what kinds of bargaining among which players yielded the critical decisions and actions? He focuses attention on certain concepts: the players whose interests and actions impact the issue in question, the factors that shape players' perceptions and *stands*, the established procedure or "*action channel*" for aggregating competing preferences, and the *performance* of the players. The analyst invokes certain patterns of inference: If a government performed an action, that action was the resultant of bargaining among players in this game. A Model III analyst has "explained" this event when he or she has discovered who did what to whom that yielded the action in question. Predictions are generated by identifying the game in which an issue will arise, the relevant players, and their relative power and bargaining skill.

A central metaphor illuminates the differences among these models. Foreign policy has often been compared to moves and sequences of moves in the game of chess. Imagine a chess game in which the observer could see only a screen upon which moves in the game were projected, with no information about how the pieces came to be moved. Initially, most observers would assume—as Model I does—that an individual chess player was moving the pieces with reference to plans and tactics toward the goal of winning the game. But a pattern of moves can be imagined that would lead some observers, after watching several games, to consider a Model II assumption: the chess player might not be a single individual but, rather, a loose alliance of semi-independent organizations, each of which moves its pieces according to standard operating procedures. For example, movement of separate sets of pieces might proceed in turn, each according to a routine, the king's rook, bishop, and their pawns repeatedly attacking the opponent according to a fixed plan. It is conceivable, further-more, that the pattern of play might suggest to an observer a Model III assumption: A number of distinct players, with distinct objectives but shared power over the pieces, could be determining the moves as the resul-tant of collegial bargaining. For example, the black rook's move might contribute to the loss of a black knight with no comparable gains for the black team, but with the black rook becoming the principal guardian of the palace on that side of the board.

A single case can do no more than suggest the kinds of differences among explanations produced by the three models. But the Cuban missile crisis is especially appropriate for the purposes of this study. In the context of ultimate danger to the nation, a small group of men weighed the options and decided. Such central, high-level crisis decisions would seem to be ideal grist for Model I analysis. Model II and Model III are forced to compete on Model I's home ground. Dimensions and factors uncovered by Model II and Model III in this case should, therefore, be particularly instructive.

Broader Implications

At the suggestion of colleagues who have used this book in professional school courses as well as in undergraduate instruction, we state here at the outset five further "big ideas" that emerge by implication and illustration in the chapters that follow.

First, our central argument can be applied broadly in arenas beyond foreign affairs. Understanding that ordinary explanations, predictions, and evalua-tions are inescapably theory-based is fundamental to self-consciousness about knowledge. This insight is especially important in professional training where individuals learn to apply a theory or approach, for example, in law, economics, or business. Similarly, the Rational Actor, Organizational Behavior, and Governmental Politics models can be applied beyond foreign policy to the domestic policy of national governments;

state and local governments; nongovernmental organizations such as the United Nations or Red Cross; schools, universities, and hospitals; business enterprises; and other aggregate actors whom one encounters in normal, everyday life.

The proposition that what you see does not necessarily equal what you get can be confusing, even disturbing. Nonetheless, if we are successful, the chapters that follow will persuade the reader that the categories and assumptions he has been using comfortably, unselfconsciously matter more than he suspected. As economists consider why an Indonesian economy that grew at a rate of more than 10 percent per annum for two decades crashed in 1998, declining at a rate of more than 15 percent; or lawyers consider whether an individual is likely to be convicted of perjury; or business leaders assess investment opportunities using present value calculations, each inevitably proceeds within the terms of one set of categories and assumptions, rather than others. The more powerful or comfortable the frameworks being applied, the more painful the recognition that it is not the whole truth. (For theorists, the proposition is that these categories and presumptions cannot be tested within the theory.)

Concepts like "state actor," "perjury," or "GNP" clarify some dimensions of the buzzing confusion one faces, on the one hand, as they inescapably distort or limit one's grasp of other dimensions of the phenomena, on the other. Consider the table on which the book you are now reading is resting. Through normal lenses with 20–20 vision, it appears to be a solid object. This means that if placed on the table, the book will rest there stably. But imagine examining the same table under an electron microscope. What would one see? Mostly empty, unoccupied space—space through which neutrons can pass with minimum effect.

Second, because simplifications are necessary, competing simplifications are essential. When explaining, predicting, evaluating, or planning, one should in principle consider all significant causal factors at all critical points in the process that leads to the occurrence in question. But because most explanations or predictions are offered in real time, where both analysis of the question and attention to the answer are limited, simplification and shorthand are necessary. Concepts and theories, especially ones that do real work, become accepted, conventional, and efficient for communicating answers. Particularly in explaining and predicting actions of governments, when one family of simplifications becomes convenient and compelling, it is even more essential to have at hand one or more simple but competitive conceptual frameworks to help remind the questioner and the answerer what is omitted. They open minds a little wider and keep them open a little longer. Alternative conceptual frameworks are important not only for further insights into neglected dimensions of the underlying phenomenon. They are essential as a reminder of the distortions and limitations of whatever conceptual framework one employs. Like the first point, this is a general methodological truth applicable in all areas of life, especially relevant where professionals have learned a theory or language that allows them to sort, analyze, and communicate findings readily.

Third, while this book focuses principally on explanation, inferences that come from explanations and prediction (or betting), the central arguments have important implications for an array of related assignments, including: *(1) evaluation* or appraisal of actions by individuals, institutions, or aggregates; *(2) prescription* of what is to be done; and *(3) management* of a sequence of actions, by oneself or by a group, to achieve a chosen objective. The basic logic of explanation requires one to identify both specific circumstances in the case in question and generalizations from prior experience about instances of this kind. This allows one to understand why the event was (or is) to be expected, given this combination of circumstances and regularities. Predictions or bets about future events are, in effect, the logical flipside of explanations. Further assignments including evaluation and prescription require more than explanation. But each rests on a foundation of judgments about the causal process involved—judgments that differ significantly depending on which of the conceptual models informs the assessment.

Fourth, the conceptual and historical analysis developed in this book has important implications for the current foreign policy agenda. These begin with the fundamental question of risks of nuclear war. In the aftermath of the Cold War, should Americans continue to be concerned about the risk of nuclear weapons exploding on American territory? On what grounds can individuals like former Senator Sam Nunn and Senator Richard Lugar conclude that the risks of one or a dozen nuclear weapons exploding on American soil is now higher than during the Cold War? Why do countries acquire nuclear weapons, for example, India and Pakistan in 1998, but not South Korea or Sweden? What are the prospects of nuclear war between new nuclear countries, for example, India and Pakistan, or Israel and a potential nuclear weapons neighbor like Iran, Iraq, or a terrorist group? From actions the president of the United States and the chairman of the Soviet Union actually took in 1962, the crisis lets us examine a dozen plausible sequences of events and actions that end with nuclear weapons exploding on American and Soviet cities.

Beyond nuclear issues, sensitivity to causal factors illuminated by each of the models should inform a fundamental rethinking of national security strategy, foreign policy, and the role of the United States (and other nations) in the post–Cold War environment. An era that continues to be called by what it comes after—the post–Cold War era—rather than what it *is*, may best be considered an "era of confusion."[5] The reasons for confusion are not difficult to identify. For most of the second half of the twentieth century, containment of expansionist Soviet or Chinese Communism provided the fixed point for the compass of American engagement in the world. In 1990, the Cold War ended in a stunning, almost unimaginable victory that erased this fixed point from the globe, an erasure sealed by the disintegration of the Soviet Union in 1991. Most of the coordinates by which Americans got their bearings in the world have now been consigned to history's dustbin: the Berlin Wall, a divided Germany, the Iron Curtain, captive nations of the Warsaw Pact, Communism on the march, and finally the Soviet Union itself. In the aftermath of this avalanche of events, American foreign policy, as well as the foreign policy of most of the other great powers, mostly drifts. In ways eerily analogous to the years after World War I, the intermission between two world wars, national policymaking in all the major powers—the United States, Great Britain, France, Germany, Japan, China, Russia—is principally preoccupied by affairs at home. But when serious rethinking begins about American interests, American capabilities, and American policy, hard questions should be asked not only in Model I terms but also from Models II and III perspectives. Analysts must reexamine not only trends in international conditions but also the appropriateness of Cold War institutions (from the Department of Defense and intelligence community to the IMF).

Fifth, an admonition we have offered to students in our courses in which this book has been used has wider application: *When considering abstract or theoretical claims or arguments, translate them into common sense.* Commonsensical analogues in one's own direct experience will never be precise equivalents. But commonsense counterparts can help dispel the fog that clouds too many minds when students and others attempt to come to grips with abstractions or theories.

One strength of Model I is that when considering the Chinese or Mexican choice about human rights or trade, one can imagine being in that government's shoes and asking what one would do. Students who find Model II mysterious should think about their own direct experience, for example, in dealing with the college registrar, or the phone company— particularly when one is frustrated by forms and procedures that feel ill-suited to one's own specific case. Model III becomes more credible as one thinks about analogous group decision-making processes, from a couple deciding where to vacation (when one prefers the ocean and the other the mountains) to clubs' choices about the location, music, and refreshments for a party. Similar commonsense analogues can help one appreciate both the insights and the limits of the prisoner's dilemma in game theory; alliance formation or defection; or liberalism's claim that the character of a state's government matters. . . .

Notes

1. For the purpose of this argument one of the authors (Allison) accepts Carl G. Hempel's characterization of the logic of explanation: an explanation

"answers" the question "*Why* did the explanandum-phenomenon occur?" by showing that the phenomenon resulted from certain particular circumstances, specified in *C1, C2, . . . Ck, in accordance with the laws L1, L2, . . . Lr.* By pointing this out, the argument shows that, given the particular circumstances and the law in question, the occurrence of the phenomenon *was to be expected*; and it is in this sense that the explanation enables us to "*understand why* the phenomenon occurred." Carl G. Hempel, *Aspects of Scientific Explanation* (New York: Free Press, 1965), p. 337. While various patterns of explanation can be distinguished (e.g., Ernest Nagel, *The Structure of Science: Problems in the Logic of Scientific Explanation* [New York: Harcourt, Brace & World, 1961]), satisfactory scientific explanations exhibit this basic logic. Consequently, prediction is essentially the converse of explanation. The other author (Zelikow) does not believe that this paradigm from the philosophy of science carries over into the philosophy of history. It is history—not replicable scientific experimentation on objective phenomena—that provides the empirical base for explaining the human choices aggregated in government actions. Critiquing Hempel's logic, see the essays by Isaiah Berlin, Maurice Mandelbaum, and especially William Dray conveniently compiled in *The Philosophy of History*, ed. Patrick Gardiner (Oxford: Oxford University Press, 1974). History can usefully draw attention to plausible possibilities, suggesting scrutiny and questions, but cannot provide laws of government behavior. Empiricism "ekes out the narrowness of personal experience by concepts which it finds useful but not sovereign; but it stays inside the flux of life expectantly, recording facts, not formulating laws." William James, *Some Problems of Philosophy* [1911], ed. Henry James, Jr. (New York: Longman's, Green & Co., 1948), pp. 98–100; see also John Dewey, *The Quest for Certainty: A Study of the Relation of Knowledge and Action* (New York: Minton, Balch & Co. 1929), pp. 207–208, 228; John Ziman, *Reliable Knowledge: An Exploration of the Grounds for Belief in Science* (Cambridge: Cambridge University Press, 1978), pp. 42–56, 158–86; Hilary Putnam, *Pragmatism: An Open Question* (Cambridge: Blackwell, 1995), pp. 7–23 (defending William James); and the concept of "colligation" in Clayton Roberts, *The Logic of Historical Explanation* (University Park: Pennsylvania State University Press, 1996), pp. 55–88.

2. Hereafter in this book we will generally follow convention in using "men" and "he" generally to refer to *homo sapiens*, females and males alike.

3. In attempting to understand problems of foreign affairs, analysts engage in a number of related but logically separable enterprises: (1) description, (2) explanation, (3) prediction, (4) evaluation, and (5) recommendation. This study focuses primarily on description and explanation and, by implication, prediction.

4. For a fundamental account of why, see Ludwig Wittgenstein, *Philosophical Investigations*, trans. G.E.M. Anscombe, 3rd ed. (New York: Prentice-Hall, 1973).

5. See Report of the Commission on America's National Interests, "American National Interests," Belfer Center for Science and International Affairs, Harvard University, Cambridge, MA, 1996.

Middletown 3

*A Study of Modern American Culture**

Robert S. Lynd and Helen Merrell Lynd

editor's introduction:

Methodological Significance

In some situations, the significance or special nature of your case study may depend entirely on your theoretical framework. Under this condition, the theoretical issues even may drive the selection of your particular case.

In this third selection of the anthology, the authors deliberately chose a medium-sized city in the Midwestern United States as an *average* city, as "representative as possible of contemporary American life." The authors are careful to note, however, that the study's findings can "only with caution" be applied to other cities or to American life in general.

The case study is primarily a descriptive case, taking 550 pages to present the social life in this community. What interest could there be in such an average case? Here, the authors' theoretical perspective focuses on a significant development in all of American history: the transition from an agricultural

*Editor's Note:** Excerpted, with light editing, from Chapters I and II, "Nature of the Investigation" and "The City Selected," from *Middletown: A Study of Modern American Culture*, by Robert S. Lynd and Helen Merrell Lynd. Harcourt Brace, Orlando FL, 1957, pp. 3–9; Copyright © 1957. Originally published in 1929. Reprinted with permission.

to an industrial economy that occurred in the average American city as part of the industrial revolution. Thus, another significant choice made by the authors was to have their case study compare contemporary life (at that time, around 1924) in this average city with life in 1890—an approximately 35-year period also coinciding with the passing of a generation.

Although the excerpt chosen for this selection is of modest length, the excerpt contains the authors' complete discussion of the criteria used to select their single case, their rationale for these criteria, and their rationale for describing the city's social life in terms of six topics.

Substantive Note

Middletown is one of the most famous case studies of all time in American social science. The authors and three other staff members lived for up to 18 months in the city being studied, during the mid-1920s. (The city is not named in the book, but virtually every sociologist knows its identity, which now also appears on the back cover of the paperback version of the book—Muncie, Indiana).

The book was pioneering because no one had tried to provide such detailed and comprehensive coverage of American life in a medium-sized city. The research covered six major topics ("getting a living," "making a home," "training the young," "using leisure," "engaging in religious practices," and "engaging in community activities"). The resulting work was so well-received that the authors returned to the city 10 years later, eventually producing a follow-up book of similar length, *Middletown in Transition* (1965). The second book describes how the original city was adapting to the Great Depression of the 1930s. Together, the two books capture a major slice of American life in the early half of the 20th century. *Middletown* was first published in 1929 and is still in print, some 75 years later. Not many case studies enjoy such an extended life. How long do you think your case study will continue to be of interest to your field?

Nature of the Investigation

The aim of the field investigation recorded in the following pages was to study synchronously the interwoven trends that are the life of a small American city. A typical city, strictly speaking, does not exist, but the city studied was selected because it has many features common to a wide group of communities. Neither fieldwork nor report attempted to prove any thesis; the aim has been, rather, to record observed phenomena, thereby raising questions and suggesting possible fresh points of departure in the study of group behavior.

The stubborn resistance that "social problems" offer may be related in part to the common habit of piecemeal attack upon them. Students of human behavior are recognizing increasingly, however, that "the different aspects of civilization interlock and intertwine, presenting—in a word—a continuum."[1] The present investigation, accordingly, set out to approach the life of the people in the city selected as a unit complex of interwoven trends of behavior.

Two major difficulties present themselves at the outset of such a total-situation study of a contemporary civilization: *First*, there is the danger, never wholly avoidable, of not being completely objective in viewing a culture in which one's life is imbedded, of falling into the old error of starting out, despite oneself, with emotionally weighted presuppositions and consequently failing to get outside the field one set out so bravely to objectify and study. *Second*, granted that no one phase of living can be adequately understood without a study of all the rest, how is one to set about the investigation of anything as . . . [complex as] Schenectady, Akron, Dallas, or Keokuk?

A clue to the securing both of the maximum objectivity and of some kind of orderly procedure in such a maze may be found in the approach of the cultural anthropologist. There are, after all, despite infinite variations in detail, not so many major kinds of things that people do. Whether in an Arunta village in Central Australia or in our own seemingly intricate institutional life of corporations, dividends, coming-out parties, prayer meetings, freshmen, and Congress, human behavior appears to consist in variations on a few major lines of activity: getting the material necessities for food, clothing, shelter; mating; initiating the young into the group habits of thought and behavior; and so on. This study, accordingly, proceeds on the assumption that all the things people do in this American city may be viewed as falling under one or another of the following six main-trunk activities:

Getting a living.

Making a home.

Training the young.

Using leisure in various forms of play, art, and so on.

Engaging in religious practices.

Engaging in community activities.

This particular grouping of activities is used with no idea of its exclusive merit but simply as a methodological expedient.[2] By viewing the institutional life of this city as simply the form which human behavior under this particular set of conditions has come to assume, it is hoped that the study has been lifted on to an impersonal plane that will save it from the otherwise inevitable charge at certain points of seeming to deal in personalities or to criticize the local life. . . .

It [also] is commonplace to say that an outstanding characteristic of the ways of living of any people at any given time is that they are in process of change, the rate and direction of change depending on proximity to strong centers of cultural diffusion; the appearance of new inventions; migration; and other factors that alter the process. We are coming to realize, moreover, that we today are probably living in one of the eras of greatest rapidity of change in the history of human institutions. New tools and techniques are being developed with stupendous celerity, while in the wake of these technical developments increasingly frequent and strong culture waves sweep over us from without, drenching us with the material and nonmaterial habits of other centers. In the face of such a situation it would be a serious defect to omit this developmental aspect from a study of contemporary life.[3]

The further device has, therefore, been adopted in this investigation: Wherever the available data permitted, we use as a groundwork for the observed behavior of today the reconstructed and, in so far as possible, objectively observed behavior of 1890. The year 1890 was selected as the baseline against which to project the culture of today because of the greater availability of data from that year onward. Also, not until the end of 1886 was natural gas struck in the city under study and the boom begun—which was to transform the placid county seat during the 1890s into a manufacturing city. This narrow strip of 35 years [from 1890 to 1924, the year that the Middletown study was started] signifies for hundreds of American communities the industrial revolution that had descended upon villages and towns, metamorphosing them into a thing of Rotary Clubs, central trade councils, and Chamber of Commerce contests for "bigger and better" cities.

Had time and available funds permitted, it obviously would have been desirable to plot more points in observed trends between 1890 and the present. But the procedure followed enables us to view the city of today against the background of the city of a generation ago—out of which it has grown and by which it is conditioned—to see the present situation as the most recent point in a moving trend.

In summary, the following pages aim to present a dynamic, functional[4] study of the contemporary life of this specific American community in the light of the trends of changing behavior observable over the last 35 years.

So comprehensive an approach necessarily involves the use of data of widely varying degrees of overtness and statistical adequacy. Some types of behavior in the city studied lie open to observation over the whole period since 1890; in other cases, only slight wisps of evidence are obtainable. Much folk talk, for instance—the rattle of conversation that goes on around a luncheon table, on streetcorners, or while waiting for a basketball game to commence—is here presented, not because it offers scientifically valid evidence, but because it affords indispensable insights into the moods and habits of thought of the city. In the attempt to combine these various types of data into a total picture, omissions and faults in proportion will appear. But two saving facts must be borne in mind: No effort is being made to prove any thesis with the data presented, and every effort is made throughout to warn where the ice is thin.

Since the fieldwork aimed at the integration of diverse regions of behavior rather than at the discovery of new material in a narrowly isolated field, it will be easy to say of much of the specific data presented, "We knew that already." Underlying the study, however, is the assumption that by the presentation of these phenomena—familiar though some of them may be, in their interrelatedness in a specific situation—fresh light may be thrown upon old problems and so give rise to further investigation.

The City Selected

The city will be called Middletown. A community as small as thirty-odd thousand affords at best about as much privacy as Irvin Cobb's celebrated goldfish enjoyed, and it has not seemed desirable to increase this high visibility in the discussion of local conditions by singling out the city by its actual name.

There were no ulterior motives in the selection of Middletown. It was not consulted about the project, and no organization or person in the city contributed anything to the cost of the investigation. Two main considerations guided the selection of a location for the study: (1) that the city be as representative as possible of contemporary American life, and (2) that it be at the same time compact and homogeneous enough to be manageable in such a total-situation study.

In line with the first of these considerations the following characteristics were considered desirable: (1) a temperate climate;[5] (2) a sufficiently rapid rate of growth to ensure the presence of a plentiful assortment of the growing pains accompanying contemporary social change; (3) an industrial culture with modern, high-speed machine production; (4) the absence of dominance of the city's industry by a single plant (i.e., not a one-industry town); (5) a substantial local artistic life to balance its industrial activity— also a largely self-contained artistic life (e.g., not that of a college town in which the college imports the community's music and lectures); and (6) the absence of any outstanding peculiarities or acute local problems which would mark the city off from the midchannel sort of American community. After further consideration, a seventh qualification was added: The city should, if possible, be in that common denominator of America, the Middle West.[6] Two streams of colonists met in this middle region of the United States: "The Yankees from New England and New York came by way of the Erie Canal into northern Ohio. . . . The southern stream of colonists, having passed through the Cumberland Gap into Kentucky, went down the Ohio River."[7] With the first of these came also a foreign-born stock, largely from Great Britain, Ireland, and Germany.

In order to secure a certain amount of compactness and homogeneity, the following characteristics were sought: (1) a city with a population of 25,000–50,000. This meant selection from among a possible 143 cities, according to the 1920 Census. A city of this size, it was felt, would be large enough to have put on long trousers and taken itself seriously, and yet small enough to be studied from many aspects as a unit; (2) a city as nearly self-contained as is possible in this era of rapid and pervasive intercommunication, not a satellite city; and (3) a small minority and foreign-born population. In a difficult study of this sort it seemed a distinct advantage to deal with a homogeneous, native-born population, even though such a population is unusual in an American industrial city. Thus, instead of being forced to handle two major variables, racial change and cultural change, the field staff could concentrate on cultural change. The study thus became one of the interplay of a relatively constant native American stock and its changing environment. As such it may possibly afford a baseline group against which the process of social change in the type of community that includes different racial backgrounds may be studied by future investigators.

Middletown, selected in the light of these considerations from a number of cities visited, is in the East-North-Central group of states that includes Ohio, Indiana, Illinois, Michigan, and Wisconsin. The mean annual temperature is 50.8°F. The highest recorded temperature is 102°F. in July and the lowest is –24°F. in January, but such extremes are ordinarily of short duration, and weather below zero is extremely rare. The city was in 1885 an agricultural county seat of some 6,000 persons; by 1890 the population had passed 11,000, and in 1920 it had topped 35,000. This growth has accompanied its evolution into an aggressive industrial city. There is no single controlling industrial plant; three plants on June 30, 1923 had between 1,000 and 2,000 employees on the payroll, and eight others from 300 to 1,000; glass, metal, and automobile industries predominate. The census of 1890 showed slightly less than 5 percent of the city's population to be foreign-born[8] and less than 4 percent Blacks, as against approximately 2 percent foreign-born in 1920 and nearly 6 percent Blacks; over 81 percent of the population in 1890 and nearly 85 percent in 1920 was native White of native parentage. In the main, this study confines itself to the White population and more particularly to the native Whites, who comprise 92 percent of the total population.

The nearest big city, a city under 350,000, is 60 miles away, nearly a two-hour trip by train, with no through hard-surface road for motoring at the time the study was made. It is a long half-day train trip to a larger city. Since the 1880s Middletown has been known all over the state as "a good music town." Its civic and women's clubs are strong, and practically none of the local artistic life was, in 1924, in any way traceable to the, until then, weak normal school on the outskirts.

The very middle-of-the-road quality about Middletown would have made it unsuitable for a different kind of investigation. Had this study sought simply to observe the institution of the home under extreme urban conditions, the recreational life of industrial workers, or any one of dozens of other special "social problems," a far more spectacular city than Middletown might readily have been found. But although it was its characteristic rather than its exceptional features which led to the selection of Middletown, no claim is made that it is a "typical" city, and the findings of this study can, naturally, only with caution be applied to other cities or to American life in general.

Notes

1. A. A. Goldenweiser, *Early Civilization*, Knopf, New York, NY, 1919, p. 31.

2. W. H. R. Rivers in his *Social Organization*, Knopf, New York, NY, 1924 sets forth a sixfold classification of social groupings identical with the six types of activity employed here. Clark Wissler presents a ninefold culture scheme, in *Man and Culture*, Crowell, New York, NY, 1923, chaps. V and XII. Frederick J. Teggart criticizes Wissler's use of a universal culture pattern, but himself implicitly recognizes certain activities as common to men everywhere, in *Theory of History*, Yale University Press, New Haven, CT, 1925, p. 171.

3. Cf. Rivers' closing sentence in *The History of Melanesian Society*, Cambridge University Press, Cambridge, 1914: "It is because we can only hope to understand the present of any society through a knowledge of its past that such historical studies as those of which this book is an example are necessary steps toward the construction of a science of social psychology."

4. "Function" as here used denotes a major life activity or something contributing to the performance of a major life activity.

5. The relation of climate to the elaborate equilibrium of activities that make up living is suggested by the late James J. Hill's motto to which he is said absolutely to have adhered: "You can't interest me in any proposition in any place

where it doesn't snow," or, more picturesquely, "No man on whom the snow does not fall ever amounts to a tinker's dam." (Quoted in J. Russell Smith's *North America*, Harcourt, Brace and Company, New York, NY, 1925, p. 8.)

6. "The 'Middle West,' the prairie country, has been the center of active social philanthropies and political progressivism. It has formed the solid element in our diffuse national life and heterogeneous populations. . . . It has been the middle in every sense of the word and in every movement. Like every mean, it has held things together and given unity and stability of movement" (from John Dewey, "The American Intellectual Frontier," *The New Republic*, May 10, 1922).

7. Smith, *op. cit.*, pp. 296–297.

8. The census of 1890 shows 62.1 percent of the foreign-born in the state to have been of German-speaking stock and 24.5 percent British and Irish. Belgian glass workers were prominent among Middletown's foreign-born population in the 1890s.

Yankee City

4

The Social Life of a Modern Community*

W. Lloyd Warner and Paul S. Lunt

---

editor's introduction:

Methodological Significance

As with the previous selection, the case study of *Yankee City* (the pseudonym for a real jurisdiction located just north of Boston, MA) also represents a classic in the sociological literature. Again, the case (another community) was chosen to be average, not special. What made the case study special was the authors' choice of a topic having great theoretic value for their entire academic field.

The topic concerns the documentation—some might say "discovery"—of social class structure within American society. *Yankee City* described the life of the people in the different classes, also showing how a person's class designation was independent of his or her economic condition. Although the class jargon is readily accepted today, the case study was one of the first to use and give operational meaning to such terms

---

*Editor's Note: The selection is excerpted, with light editing, from Chapters IV and V of Volume I of a six-volume study, by the same authors, with the permission of the publisher. The subtitle of this selection was the title of Volume I of the original work, *The Social Life of a Modern Community* by W. Lloyd Warner and Paul S. Lunt, Yale University Press, New Haven, CT, 1941, pp. 81–91. Copyright © 1941. Reprinted with permission from Yale University Press.*

as "upper-upper class," "lower-upper class," and so on. The case study is, therefore, remembered not because it is about any special "case," but because, as with Chapter 3 of this anthology, the data pertain to a topic of central concern to the entire discipline of sociology, if not also the related fields of political science and psychology. The selection suggests that, even if you do not have access to a special "case," you can nevertheless set your goals high in designing a special "case study."

Also to be noted is the authoritativeness of the investigation—established by its methodological range and depth. The enormous data collection activity that was undertaken involved interview data covering nearly the entire community of 17,000 people; extensive observations in the community; case histories of individuals and families; genealogies and kinship charts; the use of newspapers and other documentary and written materials; and an airplane survey to conduct a photographic survey of houses. The result is possibly the longest case study in social science annals, consuming five (!) separately published volumes published over an 18-year period.

Substantive Note

Research on social class or stratification, also embracing differences among ethnic and racial groups, remains of great interest to this day. A key part of the stratification process may be the continued influx of newcomers from foreign countries. Research studies can help uncover the desired and less desired patterns of change. Research also can examine potential inequities among the social classes (e.g., inquiring about the role of communities, school systems, and places of employment in dealing with any inequities).

Whether social classes (again, independent of people's economic conditions) matter, and how they might matter, form the heart of the five-volume series on *Yankee City*. Volume I, from which the present selection comes, describes the overall social life of the case study community. Subsequent volumes cover the "status system," the social systems of ethnic groups, the social systems in a modern factory, and "the living and the dead." The case study came at a watershed period in American history, when the "newer" ethnic groups were the Irish, Jews, Greeks, and Italians. Do you think a contemporary community study might produce equal or even greater insights?

General Description of Yankee City

Yankee City is situated on a harbor at the mouth of a large river in New England. The pilot of an airplane looking down some 10,000 feet might see the harbor as the dark hand of a giant with its five fingers reaching for the sea, and the river flowing through the brown land toward the white sandy shores as an arm extended straight back from the hand and then bending sharply some few miles from the sea. The streets of the town run along the banks of the river for a few miles up from the harbor until they almost reach the bend in the river.

In shape the town is a long, thin rectangle which bends at each end. Near the center of the rectangle at the bank of the river is a square around which the business district is located. The residential area covers the two ends of the rectangle as they extend up and down the river. From the two ends of the town square a highway runs out along the waterfront for the full length of the town. This river street is paralleled, on the other long side of the rectangle, by another broad street that runs along a ridge of high ground from one end of the city to the other. In the center of the city, the residential area projects beyond the outline of the rectangle for a few blocks, and a number of dwellings are found outside the rectangle at either end. Generally speaking, however, the population is concentrated within the few blocks of streets between the river and the broad street that parallels it on the ridge. The town sits on high ground with a river on one side and flatlands on the other.

The two long avenues are connected by a large number of side streets that cross several short streets as they climb from the river to the summit of the hill. A highway, one of the more important motor roads connecting southern with northern New England, crosses the center of Yankee City and leaves it over a large bridge. A railway line parallels this highway and has a station in the town.

Along the river are a large number of wharves and shipyards that were once employed in the sea trade but abandoned when the town turned to manufacturing. Most of the factory sites are in and near the business district, but a few are situated in each arm of the rectangle. The residences tend to be larger and better kept on the Hill Street than on the River Street side of the town. There are six cemeteries in the community and one fairly large park and a few small ones.

Several smaller towns are situated in the surrounding countryside. Yankee City maintains its own economic life and is not a satellite community to a large city. It does, however, look to Boston as its metropolis. Movement to and from Boston by automobile and train is frequent. Some of its citizens look ultimately to New York, but none of them would admit it; a very few of them look to Europe for their social centers, and all of these citizens will admit that.

Yankee City has some 17,000 people.[1] There are a few more women in its population than there are men. Slightly over 50 percent of the population was born in or near Yankee City; 23.5 percent was foreign-born; and the remainder was born elsewhere in the United States. The first impression one gains of the town is that it has a living tradition inherited from generations of Yankee forebears. Yankee City is "old Yankee" and proud of it.

About one-fourth of the employable population is in the shoe industry. The other principal but smaller economic activities are silverware manufacturing, the building trades, transport, and electric shops. The clamming industry, the only remaining economic activity of the town that depends on the sea, employs about 1 percent of those who work for a living.

The semiskilled workers constitute the largest group (46.2 percent) in our occupational sample. The workers in the factories compose the great bulk of this group. Only 5.3 percent are classifiable as unskilled.[2] The professional,[3] proprietary, and managerial group comprise a seventh of those economically occupied; wholesale and retail store managers and similar proprietors, 7.9 percent; clerks and kindred workers, 14.9 percent; and skilled workers, 11.4 percent. When the unemployment study was made in 1933, 50.7 percent of those who were employable had jobs at which they were working,[4] 30.6 percent were employed part-time, and 18.7 percent were without work. A little over 13 percent of the total population were recipients of relief.

According to ethnic affiliations, the Yankees comprised 53.8 percent (9,030) of the 16,785 individuals represented in our study, and the nine other ethnic groups, 45.6 percent (7,646).[5] There were 3,943 Irish, 1,466 French Canadians, 397 Jews, 284 Italians, 677 Poles, 412 Greeks, 246 Armenians, and 141 Russians. The Blacks, with 80 individuals, constituted the smallest group in the population. The Irish are the oldest ethnic group in Yankee City, other than the Yankees, and the Jews are next in order of age. The Russians, Poles, Greeks, and Armenians are comparatively recent migrants.

Yankee City is one of the oldest Yankee cities in the United States. It was founded early in 1600 and by shipbuilding, fishing, and sea trade grew into one of the most prominent of the colonial New England communities. It quickly became a city of several thousand inhabitants. After certain fluctuations in size, it attained approximately its present population and has succeeded in maintaining but not in adding to it. At one time the town was of sufficient commercial importance to compete on equal terms with Boston in its trade activities. The histories of the state in which it is located tell of its importance politically and socially and of the role it played in the life of New England at a period of its greatest prosperity. While still an important shoe and silverware manufacturing center, Yankee City is no longer of the same comparative importance; with the general growth of population and industry throughout the United States, like many other New England communities it has not grown but maintained a stable population in a stable society.

The city's earlier farming and shipping industries have largely gone. They helped employ the early Irish immigrants, but with the appearance of the factory the Irish and new immigrant groups were recruited for less-skilled jobs in the shoe, textile, and other industries. The, older ethnic groups have moved into varying occupations, and some of them have succeeded in climbing to the top of the occupational ladder.

Economically and socially Yankee City is organized very much like other American industrial towns. Its business district is supported by the residential area that surrounds it, and the residential area is supported, at the base at least, by workers who are largely maintained by the wages and salaries of the factories. The town has a city government with a mayor and council; city officials, boards, and committees direct such activities as the school, police, and fire departments. The mayor, council, and school board are elected by the voters.

There are a number of grade schools, parochial and public, and one public high school. There are a large number of Protestant churches, the principal ones belonging to the Congregational, Presbyterian, Unitarian, Baptist, Methodist, and Episcopalian denominations. The two Catholic churches are staffed primarily by Irish and French-Canadian priests and nuns; the congregation of the larger Catholic church is Irish, and the other, French-Canadian. The Jews have one synagogue in the community and the Russians and Greeks have remodeled a Protestant church into a Greek Orthodox house of worship. There are thousands of members of lodges, secret societies, and fraternities, and of organizations such as the Rotary, Kiwanis, and Chamber of Commerce.

Yankee City is an American town. Its people live a life whose values are in general as understandable to Midwesterners as they are to people from the Pacific and Atlantic coasts. Specific differences are present; certain kinds of behavior are more definite and more highly developed than else-where in the United States, and other ways of life are not quite so heavily accented in Yankee City as in the South or in the West. But although it is important, for a full understanding of the community, to know these differences, it would be erroneous to emphasize them and forget the fundamental similarity to other American towns.

How the Several Classes Were Discovered

When the research on Yankee City began, the director wrote a description of what he believed was fundamental in our social system, in order that the assumptions he held be explicitly stated and not become unconscious biases which would distort the fieldwork, later analysis, and ultimate conclusions. If these assumptions could be stated as hypotheses, they were then subject to criticism by the collection of data that would prove, modify, or disprove them. Most of the several hypotheses so stated were subsumed under a general economic interpretation of human behavior in our society. It was believed that the fundamental structure of our society, that which ultimately controls and dominates the thinking and actions of our people, is economic, and that the most vital and far-reaching value systems which motivate Americans are to be ultimately traced to an economic order. Our first interviews tended to sustain this hypothesis. They were filled with references to "the big people with money" and to "the little people who are poor." They either assigned people high status by referring to them as bankers, large property owners, people of high salary, and professional people, or they placed people in a low status by calling them laborers, ditchdiggers, and low-wage earners. Other similar economic terms were used, all designating superior and inferior positions.

All our informants agreed that certain groups, of whom we shall soon speak, were at the bottom of the social order. However, many of the members of these groups were making an income that was considerably more than that made by people whom our informants placed far higher in the social scale. It seemed evident that other factors contributed to their lower societal positions.

Other evidences began to accumulate that made it difficult to accept a simple economic hypothesis. Several persons were doctors; and while some of them enjoyed the highest social status in the community and were so evaluated in the interviews, others were ranked beneath them although some of the latter were often admitted to be better physicians. Such ranking was frequently unconsciously done and for this reason was often more reliable than a conscious estimate of a person's status. We found similar inequalities of status among the ministers, lawyers, and other professional people. When we examined the business and industrial world, we discovered that bankers, large manufacturers, and corporation heads also were not ranked equally but were graded as higher or lower in status. An analysis of comparative wealth and occupational status in relation to all the other factors in the total social participation of the individuals we studied demonstrated that, although occupation and wealth could and did contribute greatly to the rank-status of an individual, they were but two of many factors that decided a person's ranking in the whole community. For example, a banker was never at the bottom of the society, and none in fact fell below the middle class, but the banker was not always at the top. Great wealth did not guarantee the highest social position. Something more was necessary.

In our efforts to find out what this "something more" was, we finally developed a class hypothesis which withstood the later test of a vast collection of data and of subsequent rigorous analysis. By class is meant two or more orders of people who are believed to be, and are accordingly ranked by the members of the community, in socially superior and inferior positions. Members of a class tend to marry within their own order, but the values of the society permit marriage up and down. A class system also provides that children are born into the same status as their parents. A class society distributes rights and privileges, duties and obligations, unequally among its inferior and superior grades. A system of classes, unlike a system of castes, provides by its own values for movement up and down the social ladder. In common parlance, this is social climbing, or in technical terms, social mobility. The social system of Yankee City, we found, was dominated by a class order.

When we examined the behavior of a person who was said by some to be "the wealthiest man in our town," to find out why he did not have a higher position, we were told that "he and his family do not act right." Their moral behavior was "all right," but they "did not do the right things." Although they were Yankees by tradition and not members of any ethnic group, we were told that "they did not belong to the right families" and that "they did not go around with the right kind of people." Our informants further said that the members of this family "didn't know how to act," and that they were not and could not be members of the "right" groups. The interviews clearly demonstrated, however, that all the members of the family were regarded as "good people," and their name was always a lure when marriage was contemplated for a young woman "of good breeding," even though there was some danger that she would be looked upon as "lowering herself" by such a marriage. Similar analysis of the industrial and businesspersons who occupied lower positions brought forth the same kind of information.

Interviews about, and with, people who were ranked socially high by our informants but had little money or occupational status brought out the opposite kind of information, supplying further confirmatory evidence for our first tentative theory of a class system. These interviews revealed that "you don't need but a little money in Yankee City to do the right thing," or as it was sometimes said, "you have to have a little money but it is the way one uses it which counts." Questions about such people often brought out such statements as: "John Smith belongs to the X group," followed by remarks to the effect that "Henry Taylor and Frank Dixon and other prominent men who are at the top also belong to it." These same people, we were informed, "went around with the Fred Brown clique" or "went with the Country Club crowd," which were small groups of close friends.

In these interviews certain facts became clear which might be summarized by saying a person needed specific characteristics associated with his/her "station in life" and needed to go with the "right kind" of people for the informants to be certain of the person's ranking. If a person's education, occupation, wealth, income, family, intimate friends, and clubs, as well as manners, speech, and general outward behavior were known, it was not difficult for citizens to give a fairly exact estimate of the person's status. . . .

While making these observations on the criteria of class and attempting to locate people in the class hierarchy, we made a valuable discovery. In the expressions about wealth and occupation to which higher and lower valuations were attached, we noticed that certain geographical terms were used not only to locate people in the city's geographical space but also to evaluate their comparative place in the rank order. The first generalization of this kind which we noticed people using in interviews was the identification of a small percentage of the population as "Hill Streeters" or people who "live up on Hill Street." These expressions were often used as equivalents of "Brahmin," the rarer "aristocrat," or the less-elegant "high mucky-muck," or "swell," or "snoot." The term "Hill Streeter," we soon learned, was employed by people both within and outside of this classification. Whenever an individual was called a "Hill Streeter," all of our evidence showed that he/she was near or at the top of the hierarchy.

Another geographical term with a strong evaluative class meaning was "Riverbrook." When a person was said to be a "Riverbrooker" or to live in Riverbrook, he/she was felt to be at the bottom of the social hierarchy. Interviews showed this generalization to be true regardless of the informant's place in the social scale. Riverbrookers were contemptuously referred to by all, their sexual morals were considered low, and their behavior was usually looked upon as ludicrous and uncouth. . . . The Riverbrooker was often a good and highly skilled worker in the shoe factories, [frequently earning] a good wage by clamming, usually a good family person, and one of the many variants of what is called the typical Yankee. The "low" behavior was attributed . . . because of low social position. . . .

With the acquisition of the terms "Hill Streeter" and "Riverbrooker" as designations for the two extremes of class, our next problems were (1) to find out to whom the expressions did and did not refer, (2) to learn what distinctions, if any, were made to differentiate other groups than these two, and (3) to discover who used any or all of these terms.

A descriptive expression which appeared with considerable frequency in our interviews was "the classes and the masses." This expression was seldom used by the people referred to as "the masses" but quite frequently by those who considered themselves "the classes." The lower members of the community sometimes spoke of those in the higher statuses as "the upper classes," and when this expression was used by them it was ordinarily synonymous with Hill Streeter. We soon found, however, that when "the masses" was used, not all the people who were so designated were

Riverbrookers, and that most of them were believed to be higher in status. A distinction was made within the masses between Riverbrookers and people of somewhat higher status.

Another geographical expression which frequently appeared in the interviews was "Side Streeter," used in contradiction to Hill Streeter. In some contexts a Side Streeter was anyone who was not a Hill Streeter, but more careful interviewing indicated that to a Hill Streeter a Side Streeter and a Riverbrooker were different. Frequently, the better informants stated, "People who live in Riverbrook are at the bottom," and "Of course Side Streeters are better than Riverbrookers." A Side Streeter was one who was not on the social heights of Hill Street nor in the social depths of Riverbrook. The individual was somewhere in between. Living along the streets connecting the river area with Hill Street, the Side Streeters were socially as well as territorially intermediate.

All Side Streeters were not the same, we discovered. Some were superior and others inferior, the former being commonly called by another geographical term—"Homevillers." The Homevillers were "good people," but few of them were in any way "socially acceptable." Certain informants placed all of them in "the classes." Homeville is a well-defined area in Yankee City at the northern end of the community. The Homeville people, we roughly estimated at the time, were people in the midsection of the social scale but on the whole nearer the top than the bottom. The term "middle class" or "upper-middle class" was often used as equivalent for Homeviller. The Homevillers and their like, it developed through our later associational analysis, were graded ordinarily into two groups (upper-middle and lower-middle classes) and separated from a lower stratum of Side Streeters who were too much like the Riverbrookers in many of their characteristics to be classed with the Side Streeters of high status. The distinctions between the lower group of Homevillers and this lowest group of Side Streeters were not so clearly marked as the others.

At this point we saw that Hill Street was roughly equivalent to upper class, Homeville to at least a good section of the middle class, and Riverbrook to the lowest class. We perceived, too, that these geographical terms were generalizing expressions by which a large number of people could be given a class designation but which nevertheless did not define class position explicitly. When the people classed as Hill Streeters were located on a spot map it soon developed that not all of them lived on Hill Street and that not all the people living on Hill Street were Hill Streeters (upper class). Many of the people who were by class Hill Streeters lived elsewhere in the city, and some of them were fairly well concentrated in two areas other than Hill Street. We found a similar generalization to be true of the Riverbrookers and Homevillers. This discovery further demonstrated that these designations were terms of rank employed by the members of a "democratic" society to refer obliquely to higher and lower social statuses in the community.

Careful interviewing among people who were called Hill Streeters showed that the members of this group divided the general upper class into a higher and a lower subdivision. Our informants made frequent references to people of "old family" and to those of "new families." The former were individuals whose families, it was believed, had participated in upper-class behavior for several generations and who could trace this behavior through the father or mother's line or both for three or more generations. An upper-class genealogy of this kind has been called a lineage for the purposes of this report. Long residence in Yankee City was very important, but length of residence by itself did not establish a family at the apex of the class system, because in all of the six classes later established we found families with written and attested genealogies which went back two hundred and in some cases even three hundred years to the founding of the community. Some of the lower members of the upper class could also trace their genealogies well back, but their recent mobility upward if they had "come up from below" was enough to prevent an immediate claim to such a lineage. Their recent ancestors, unlike those of the uppermost members of the upper class, had not participated for a sufficient period of time in the forms of behavior and the social position that were ranked as upper class by the community. With the separation of the upper-upper from the lower-upper class, and the upper-middle from the lower-middle, we had distinguished five classes clearly and a sixth less definitely. We knew at this time that the sixth class fell somewhere in between the middle and the lowest class, but it was still possible that it might be not one but several classes. Eventually, however, we were able to establish the existence of six classes—an upper-lower and a lower-lower class in addition to the upper and lower subdivisions of the middle and upper classes.

The amount of membership in associations is comparatively larger than that in most of the other social structures of Yankee City. Despite their size, associations tend to segment the society into separate groups, and some of them help to maintain higher and lower ranking in the community. With this knowledge, we were able to place with greater exactness than we could by the use of the geographical classification a large sample of the members of Yankee City society (see Exhibit 4.1).

Certain clubs, our interviews showed, were ranked at such extreme heights by people highly placed in the society that most of the lower classes did not even know of their existence, while middle-class people showed that they regarded them as much too high for their expectations. A very few of them, indeed, were looked upon as so exclusive that some of the Hill Streeters might be excluded on family grounds. Of other clubs, whose members were mainly Hill Streeters, it was felt that any Hill Streeter was eligible for membership if the individual had the other necessary qualifications (such as being of a certain age or interested in certain kinds of hobbies). These clubs, however, were considered too high for the vast

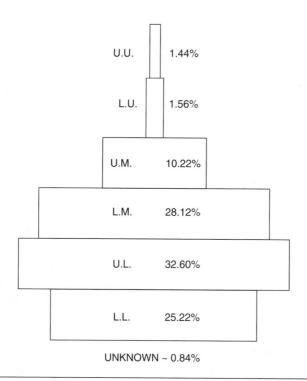

U.U.   1.44%

L.U.   1.56%

U.M.   10.22%

L.M.   28.12%

U.L.   32.60%

L.L.   25.22%

UNKNOWN ~ 0.84%

Exhibit 4.1   The Class Hierarchy of Yankee City

majority of the people in Yankee City to aspire to, and it was clear that many, if not most, of the lower classes did not know of their existence. It was also felt that others did aspire to them but were not chosen because "they did not belong socially."

Below this last level of clubs were other associations which included Hill Streeters but also had members "from further down" who were "not acceptable socially." There were still other associations where these same individuals who were not accepted socially were members and were considered to be at the top of the membership, and all other members were felt to be below them. Some associations of this kind were sufficiently high so that there were members of the community who were too low to do more than aspire to membership. There were other associations too low for Hill Streeters to join and still others which the two middle classes refused to enter. While interviews demonstrated that certain associations or clubs were believed to contain only the "best people," others mostly the "best people" but with additions, and still others only the "lowest people," some associations did not seem to be graded in class; people "of all kinds" were said to belong to them.

From a later understanding of associations, we discovered that members of the three higher classes belonged to associations which we named social clubs. The three lower classes did not. All three of the upper classes belonged to associations organized for charitable purposes. Certain of these clubs had only female members, others only male, and still others were mixed. Several female clubs included women of the three uppermost classes, but interviews showed that their lower members had some difficulty in entering them. Some female clubs refused to admit "ordinary better-class people," and some members said, "We will have only our own kind."

Ordinarily Hill Streeters did not belong to occupational associations, but Homevillers did. Hill Streeters tended to avoid fraternal organizations, secret societies, insurance orders, and associations with formal age grading. Members of the upper-middle class also tended to stay out of fraternal orders and associations with auxiliaries. On the other hand, members of the lower-middle class favored fraternal orders and semiauxiliaries. The upper-middle people, moreover, were allowed into and favored charitable organizations, whereas the lower-middle members were either excluded from such organizations or refused to join them. The breaks in association behavior of the members of the two middle classes greatly aided us in making our classification and in separating members of the two groups.

Lower-middle-class people did not participate in female and mixed social clubs, and since women were very conscious of class in Yankee City, the knowledge of this fact greatly aided us in our interviewing. If a person was a member of several charitable organizations, a social club or two, and possibly an occupational association, but not of a fraternal lodge, and the person was not considered a member of the new or old families of Hill Streeters, it was more than likely that the individual was upper-middle class. A small amount of interviewing soon demonstrated whether this was true or not. . . .

Associations were of great value in placing large groups of people in a fairly exact status within the class system. But because these people belonged to other social structures, such as the family and clique, which made much finer status discriminations, it was possible to place them with even greater exactness. Our study of family membership demonstrated that the vast majority of families had but one class represented in their membership. Although there were very minor rank differences in family membership, the members of a family ordinarily participated as a unit in their place in the social structure. Ultimately, we estimated that 95.2 percent of the members of the upper-upper class belonged to families in which there were only upper-upper-class people; that 87.3 percent of lower-upper persons belonged to families confined to their own class; and that the corresponding percentages for the other classes were 91.4 for upper-middle; 90.2 for lower-middle; 86.3 for upper-lower; and 96.0 for lower-lower.

Cliques tended to include two or even three classes in their membership, but on the whole they, too, drew fairly sharp class lines. Of the upper-upper class, 36.6 percent belonged to cliques in which there were only upper-uppers; 20.7 percent of the clique members in the lower-upper class, 20.1 percent in upper-middle, 14.5 percent in lower-middle, 15.7 percent in upper-lower, and 24.6 percent in the lower-lower class belonged to cliques confined to their own class.

All of the types of social structure and each of the thousands of families, thousands of cliques, and hundreds of associations were, member by member, interrelated in our research. With the use of all structural participation, and with the aid of such additional testimony as the area lived in, the type of house, kind of education, manners, and other symbols of class, it was possible to determine very quickly the approximate place of any individual in the society. In the final analysis, however, individuals were placed by the evaluations of the members of Yankee City itself (e.g., by such explicit statements as "she does not belong" or "they belong to our club)." Naturally there were many borderline cases. A class system, unlike a caste or any other clearly and formally marked rank-order, is one in which movement up and down is constantly taking place in the lives of many people. At the time of our study, for example, some people were moving into the lower-upper class from the upper-middle. Our interviews showed pressure on these mobile people from those above them and the development of new social behavior and memberships among them. It was a problem in these and similar cases from other classes where such people should be placed. In order to make a complete study, it was necessary to locate all of the people in one of the six classes, and this we did to the best of our ability on the basis of the entire range of phenomena covered by our data. . . .

It must not be thought that all the people in Yankee City are aware of all the minute distinctions made in this book. The terms used to refer to such definitions as are made vary according to the class of the individual and his/her period of residence. The terms "Hill Streeter," "Side Streeter," "Homeviller," and "Riverbrooker" would be known to all classes. Occasionally such terms are used only in their geographical sense, but far more often they are applied as terms of status and rank.

Notes

1. Readers will notice as they go through the pages of this and the following volumes that our samples of the population vary according to the subject under investigation. The census reports for Yankee City give but 15,000 people; however, these reports cover only the incorporated large town of Yankee City and do not include the population of the several areas outside the incorporated community which are a part of the town. In addition to the people who live in nearby areas and who are part of the social system of the community, many people come in from outside communities such as Boston and even New York and are a part of the social system. This volume on the class system includes some 16,785 people

for its largest sample. The volume on the status system includes more people because we were able to add to our list members of families and associations who came into the city for social purposes.

2. This sample is somewhat biased because when we studied occupation we did not get as full a census of the unskilled as we did of those who were semi- and fully skilled, since a smaller proportion of the latter were in the factories which we studied. However, Yankee City, being an industrial town where skill, as it is ordinarily defined, is more useful than elsewhere, has a higher percentage of skilled workers than most communities.

3. U.S. Bureau of the Census, Alphabetical Index of Occupations by Industries and Social-Economic Groups, 1937. Prepared by Alba M. Edwards, Ph.D., for use in the National Unemployment Census, Washington, DC, U.S. Government Printing Office, 1937.

4. The total sample for the unemployment study was 5,005.

5. There were 109 whose ethnic affiliations were unknown.

Implementation 5

How Great Expectations in Washington Are Dashed in Oakland*

Jeffrey L. Pressman and Aaron Wildavsky

---

editor's introduction:

Methodological Significance

Case studies can be on a broad variety of topics. Selections 1 and 2 of this anthology were about government actions at the federal or national level. Selections 3 and 4 were about life in local communities, with the social structure of the community (and not any particular government action) being the main interest. These types of cases commonly serve as the subjects of case studies.

The following selection provides yet another common example: Case studies that are about more abstract topics, such as organizational or other *processes*—in this case "implementation." Although the case study is based on events involving a specific economic development program in a specific city, the case study's main contribution is not about economic development (or about Oakland, CA). Rather, its strength and lasting

---

value have been on the topic of "implementation" and the challenge of putting federally inspired changes into place in a local community. (See also Chapter 8 of this anthology for a related case study.)

The selection comes from the first chapter of this case study, providing an interesting example of how you might begin a case study of an abstract topic. In the chapter, the authors try to show how the *appearance* of events before and after 1968 leave open the issue of whether real programmatic changes actually have occurred. This introduction to the case study is intended to entice you to read on, with "implementation" proposed just briefly, at the end, as the topic of study. An alternative introduction might have started quite differently, with a literature review and conceptual discussion of "implementation," and with the events in Oakland only being inserted later. You might want to think about the advantages and disadvantages of each type of startup.

Substantive Note

Implementation processes have existed for a long time, but they did not become the subject of intense academic study until the late 1960s and early 1970s. Until that period, the problems and challenges of implementing change, especially in complex organizations, had not really been either documented or appreciated. Since then, concern over implementation has become so commonplace that it is taken for granted, even if implementation is not always successful.

Pressman and Wildavsky's case study was one of the first major studies on the topic. Their case study showed both how to collect sound data on an abstract topic and how to simultaneously develop new conceptual insights. One of these insights, into "the complexity of joint action," assumes a major portion of the entire case study and has become a common way of thinking—not only about the study of implementation but also about practical ways of reducing implementation problems.

Appearances

On the morning of April 25, 1966, the *Wall Street Journal* ran the following headline: "Urban Aid Kickoff: Administration Selects Oakland as First City in Rebuilding Program."[1] The *Journal* article expressed surprise at the fact that "the Great Society's first package of aid in its drive to save the cities" would "not go to New York, Chicago, Los Angeles or another major metropolis whose poverty and racial tensions have erupted into public demonstration or riot." Rather, the aid would "go to Oakland, California— a city of high unemployment and racial unrest that federal agents have tabbed a potential powder keg." To help solve the problems of un-employment and racial unrest, the new program would finance public works and business loans that would lead to the creation of jobs for the unemployed, primarily Blacks.

A further surprise, according to the *Journal,* was that the "donor will not be the new Department of Housing and Urban Development. . . . It will be an agency with rural antecedents and primarily a rural jurisdiction: The Economic Development Administration of the Department of Commerce. Eugene P. Foley, the enthusiastic, restless and imaginative Assistant Secretary of Commerce who heads EDA, will make the formal announcement this week."

On April 29, Foley formally announced the program at a press conference held at the Oakland airport. Governor Edmund G. Brown of California introduced Foley as "the Assistant Secretary of Commerce for Economic Development, who has decided to conduct in Oakland a massive experi-ment in solving the principal urban problem, unemployment."[2] Foley then read his statement to the press. After discussing Oakland's prob-lems—including an unemployment rate of 8.4 percent, more than twice the national average—Foley announced that the EDA had agreed to offer public works grants and loans amounting to $23,289,000 for various projects in the city. The following public works projects would receive EDA money:

Airport hangar and support facilities	$10,650,000
(Port of Oakland; to be leased by World Airways)	
Marine Terminal and access roads (Port of Oakland)	10,125,000
30-acre industrial park (Port of Oakland)	2,100,000
Access road to coliseum area (city of Oakland)	414,000
TOTAL	$23,289,000

Foley said that these projects would provide 2,200 jobs when com-pleted, with more jobs following from later "spinoffs." In addition, $1,600,000 for business loans then being considered would create 800 new jobs. Thus, he promised some 3,000 jobs in all.

But how would the EDA make sure that the new jobs would go to the unemployed residents of the inner city who were supposed to be the beneficiaries of the new program? Foley unveiled an innovative procedure: Each employer who wished to receive an EDA loan or lease an EDA-financed facility would have to draw up an employment plan. This plan would project the future employment opportunities that would result from EDA financing and would commit the employer to making a concerted effort to recruit hardcore, unemployed Oakland residents to fill those positions. An employment review board, including representatives of business, labor, and the poor, would have to review each plan before the EDA could provide a loan or rule favorably on a lease agreement. (In each case, the EDA itself would have to give final approval to the plan.) Every employer would submit a monthly report on hiring to the review board. If the EDA made a finding of noncompliance and subsequent negotiation failed to resolve the dispute, then the matter would be settled by arbitration. Thus, EDA financial aid would be conditioned on performance by employers. Hopes in both Washington and Oakland for a successful urban experiment were high.

In 1968, over two years after the initial EDA announcement, a book appeared which suggested that the experiment had resulted in some substantial achievements. Titled *Oakland's Not for Burning*, the book was written by Amory Bradford, the former vice president of the *New York Times* who had served as Foley's special representative in Oakland during the first months of the program. Through a series of moving passages, Bradford painted a picture of the hopelessness and rage he had found in the Oakland ghetto when he arrived there in December 1965. One Black leader told Foley and Bradford at an early meeting that "We hate Whitey because he hates us, thinks us no better than dogs. . . . I have no respect for Whites, because they have no respect for me. I just want to be considered human. I'm not responsible for five hundred years of history, but for getting justice now. If we don't get it we'll have a Watts [neighborhood in Los Angeles and scene of a race riot] here, and kill and bomb."[3]

In countless meetings with ghetto residents, labor and business leaders, educators, and government officials, Bradford and his EDA staff tried to break down the barriers of distrust and suspicion that divided the groups. To each, Bradford argued that the EDA could provide vital help in the effort to create jobs for the hardcore unemployed—the key to solving the urban crisis.

Toward the end of the book, Bradford provided an optimistic evaluation of the EDA experiment. He noted that "so many of the other cities have exploded with serious riots that it is clear we face a national crisis of major proportions. But all through 1966, 1967 and the first half of 1968 Oakland has not suffered a riot. We must then ask: What happened in Oakland that saved it from burning, when most observers thought it would be one of the first to go?"[4] Bradford admitted that "there are no easy answers to that question," and he went on to say that the "EDA's purpose in Oakland was not the prevention of a riot." Rather, the EDA's mission was "to attack one of the main sources of frustration and despair in the ghetto—the inability to get jobs." Still, "the fact that there was no riot in Oakland during those years cannot be ignored, as the country inquires into the causes of riots elsewhere, and seeks to decide on the action needed to prevent them in the future."[5]

Looking back at the social and political situation in Oakland during 1966, Bradford identified two developments that "may have made the difference" in preventing a riot in the city:

> The first was the dramatic, massive EDA program, directed at the central ghetto need, training and jobs. This was an experimental pilot project, something that was not being done on this scale or in this way in any other city. It was carried out with unusual speed, and was more fully coordinated with all related federal, state, and city efforts than is usually the case with a large federal program. The second was the local response to this new federal approach. Following the change in the city administration, the new Mayor, John Reading, and the new City Manager, Jerome Keithley, succeeded in mobilizing first the business community, and then minority groups and labor, to respond with effective local action. . . .
>
> This increasingly effective combination of federal and local action gradually dissolved the deadlock between the ghetto and the establishment.[6]

By the end of 1968, the fame of the Oakland experiment was spreading throughout the country. An article in the *New Yorker* of November 30 cited "the allocation of some thirty million dollars to Oakland by the Economic Development Administration." The article stated that Amory Bradford, in the course of directing the spending of this sum, had "managed to break a longtime deadlock between the Oakland ghetto and the local business and government Establishment."[7] The appearance of success seemed overwhelming.

Appearances, however, can change. On March 16, 1969, a *Los Angeles Times* feature carried the following headline: "Oakland Minority Job Program Labeled a 'Pretty Big Disaster.'" According to the article, the once-heralded EDA program in Oakland had fallen on hard times:

> Today, only 20 new jobs have materialized for minorities and the program is bogged down in a bureaucratic fight over minority hiring. Critics see it as a classic case of big promises and little action. "It's a pretty big disaster," says Percy Moore, executive director of Oakland's antipoverty agency. "A lot of commitments were made, but it never got off the drawing board."[8]

Although an impressive array of public works construction had been planned, only the industrial park and access road had been completed.

The *Times'* disheartening story uncovered disillusionment on the part of both businessmen and poverty groups. Walter Abernathy, assistant executive director of the Port of Oakland, observed that "Our people felt the federal government was going a little too far in telling us how to run our business." Other critics, with a different perspective, felt that most of the EDA money would "help the Vietnam war effort rather than the poor. World Airways gains much of its revenue for transporting cargo to Vietnam and the Marine Terminal would accommodate increased military traffic."

As for Oakland's Black leaders, the article found that the hopes engendered by the 1966 urban experiment were badly dimmed by 1969. Local poverty program director Percy Moore complained that "From the beginning it was business as usual . . . and conditions here are getting worse. The port doesn't particularly care about social issues in the community, and the EDA hasn't used what little muscle it has to get employers to hire from minority groups."

In the same week that the *Los Angeles Times* article appeared, the EDA office in Oakland reported to the City Council that the federal agency had invested $1,085,000 in business loans in Oakland, but that only 43 jobs had been created. The City Council was not pleased by the news.[9]

Written accounts of the EDA experience in Oakland provide two widely differing views of the program. In the optimistic view, the program had succeeded in forging an alliance between minority groups, business, and labor for the creation of new employment opportunities. In the pessimistic view, the urban experiment had raised expectations but had delivered only meager results. As time passed, the latter view became dominant. Four years after the initiation of the program, few jobs had been created and the major public works projects—the marine terminal and the aircraft hangar—had not been built. If despair and disillusionment in the minority community were in any way related to EDA activities in Oakland, these conditions would only have been worsened by the gap between promise and performance.

In this study, we will go beyond the appearance of quick success or abject failure that have characterized most of the previous discussion of the EDA program in Oakland. After tracing the tortuous course of the program from the time of its inception, we will examine those factors that lay behind the program's frustrations: the difficulties of translating broad agreement into specific decisions, given a wide range of participants and perspectives; the opportunities for blockage and delay that result from a multiplicity of decision points; and the economic theories on which the program was based.

Our goal is not to be Monday-morning quarterbacks, to dissect the EDA's mistakes with the clarity that only hindsight can give. Rather, we will search for the lessons—administrative, economic, and political—that can be learned from the experience of the EDA in Oakland.

The experience of this program, which began with laudable intentions, commitment, and an innovative spirit, shows that *implementation* of a large-scale federal project can be very difficult indeed. Money was duly authorized and appropriated by Congress; the federal agency approved projects and committed funds with admirable speed. But the "technical details" of implementation proved to be more difficult and time consuming than the federal donors, local recipients, or enthusiastic observers had ever dreamed they would be.

Promises can create hope, but unfulfilled promises can lead to disillusionment and frustration. By concentrating on the implementation of programs, as well as their initiation, we should be able to increase the probability that policy promises will be realized. Fewer promises may be made in view of a heightened awareness of the obstacles to their fulfillment, but more of them should be kept. That aspiration guides this study.

Notes

1. The *Wall Street Journal*, April 25, 1966, p. 1.

2. Quoted in Amory Bradford, *Oakland's Not for Burning* (New York: McKay, 1968), p. 123.

3. *Ibid.*, p. 4.

4. *Ibid.*, p. 204.

5. *Ibid.*

6. *Ibid.*, pp. 204–205.

7. "The Talk of the Town," *New Yorker*, November 30, 1968, p. 52.

8. *Los Angeles Times*, March 16, 1969, p. 8.

9. "U.S. Invests $1,085,000 to Create 43 Oakland Jobs," *Oakland Tribune*, March 16, 1969, p. 1.

Section II

The Strength of Multiple Cases

Korea 6

*Winning With Microwaves**

Ira Magaziner and Mark Patinkin

editor's introduction:

Methodological Significance

The first section of this anthology contained five selections. All of them were about single-case studies. However, case studies need not be about single cases only. Case studies also can follow a multiple-case design.

The present selection appears at first to be a single-case study. However, it is one of nine case studies appearing in an entire book, thereby helping the book (which is the multiple-case study) to draw cross-case conclusions about world trade, international economic competition, and America's role in the global economy in the 1990s.

The single case—about Samsung, then the largest company in Korea—is specific and concrete. Yet, the case presents a variety of principles that will have echoes in the other cases and become the basis for the authors' cross-case analysis and conclusions. For Third World manufacturing growth and expansion, one strategic focus was, paradoxically, on manufacturing production rather than on marketing. Samsung (in this case) used this innovative strategy to successfully enter markets dominated by U.S. or Japanese companies.

In Magaziner and Patinkin's book, this case study appears as one of three under the broader theme of America's competition with low-wage countries. Two other broader themes in the multiple-case study deal with America's competition from developed countries and its competition involving future technologies, with three cases also provided under each theme. The nine cases and three themes together are then taken to be part of the global battles shaping America's future, or, the "Silent War."

Substantive Note

High on any list of salient political and economic topics during the 1980s and 1990s was the position of the United States in the world economy, and the "globalization" of nearly all industrial affairs. For instance, America's advocates were concerned that, among East Asian countries, Japan was a more competitive and economically aggressive nation (see also Chapter 7 of this anthology), and Korea was not far behind. (Not at all anticipated at that time were the economic woes that were later to befall Japan, leading to the diminishing of its economic power just 10 years later.) If the United States could not compete readily with these two countries, how would it respond to China, as the "sleeping giant," whose economic powers were still to emerge during this time but threatened domination sometime in the 21st century?

Heightening these concerns were the continuation of certain business strategies and trends—not all favorable to America's global position. First, Korea showed that Third World countries could leap to the production of "modern" products, not products that lagged the market by a decade or more. Second, engineering assistance by American firms helped the Third World countries to reduce substantially the time needed to produce sufficiently high-quality products. Third, American consumers continued to be willing to purchase products from foreign countries and therefore to create a viable market for their products. The present selection provides insights into Korean manufacturing strategies with what has now become one of the most prevalent products in every American kitchen—if not office, dormitory, and hotel room—the microwave oven.

The microwave oven, invented in America 40 years ago,[1] just recently became one of the best-selling appliances in the world. It has created a multibillion-dollar industry that's spawned tens of thousands of jobs. Yet today, were you to buy a microwave oven in the United States, the odds are one in three that it was built ten thousand miles away, in South Korea.[2] The odds are one in five that it was designed by a 43-year-old engineer named Yun Soo Chu. His company, Samsung, is now the world's leading microwave oven producer.[3] But it wasn't until 1979, when millions of the new ovens were being manufactured each year in America, that Samsung set up its first crude assembly line. That year, the company made only a few dozen ovens a week. Today, it makes over eighty thousand a week. The story of how Samsung succeeded speaks of the growing sophistication of our competition in the developing world.

When Chu joined Samsung in 1973, it had just taken on a manufacturing challenge new to Korea: making home appliances. He started his company career designing washing machines, soon moving to electric skillets. Then, in 1976, he received an unexpected assignment. That year, on a visit to the United States, a Samsung vice president named J.U. Chung had been intrigued by a new kind of oven, heated not by electricity or gas, but by microwaves.

Chung knew there was no way he could market such an oven at home—few Koreans could afford it—but that wasn't a concern. In Korea, when companies consider a new product, the most common first question is whether they can export it. That same year, for example, Samsung had decided to make color televisions, even though there wasn't a single TV station in the country that could broadcast in color.[4]

Knowing that Americans like convenience, Chung felt the microwave oven was perfect for that market, the world's largest. When he got back to Korea, he asked Chu to form a team to design a Samsung microwave. Chu knew his company was starting well behind Japanese and American producers, but Samsung, he felt, had two advantages: low-wage workers, and a willingness to wait for a payback. The company's first priority, he knew, wasn't high profits; it was high production. Samsung was especially interested in modern products. For Korean industry, that was almost unprecedented.

Traditionally, low-wage countries have been content to let their factories lag a decade behind countries like America, making bicycles in the age of the automobile, black-and-white televisions in the age of color. Samsung was one of the first Third World companies to take a new approach, deciding to compete directly in modern products.

Chu began by ordering a new U.S. microwave model called the Jet 230, made by General Electric, America's leading appliance company. Soon, Chu was looking at his first microwave. He took it apart, but still had no idea how it worked. The plastic cavity seemed simple enough, as did the door assembly and some of the wiring; but there were several complex parts, especially the device that generated the microwaves—the magnetron tube. To build it, he could tell, required expertise Samsung lacked. He began to tinker anyway. His team was given 15 square feet in the corner of an old lab that served the company's entire electronics division, which at the time consisted of three Quonset-hut factories. It seemed absurd that such a place could consider challenging major corporations in America and Japan, and Chu knew it. But he also knew Samsung's executives cared little about marketing at the moment. They'd told him they had only one objective right now—production. They'd worry about selling the oven later.

It was around that time, 1977, that I got my first glimpse of South Korea, at the request of the British government. A few years before, Korean black-and-white televisions had begun arriving in England. At first, British TV producers hadn't been concerned. The Koreans gained only a small market share, and besides, this was exactly what developing countries were expected to do: compete in 20-year-old products. But then something disturbing happened. Korean color televisions began arriving, also available at cheap prices. The British government wanted to know whether the assault would get more serious. I was asked to do a study. . . . [5]

Had I looked in all corners of the Samsung lab that day in 1977, I might have seen Chu, just beginning work on a microwave oven prototype. By then, he too had gathered a number of the world's best models—GE, Toshiba, Litton—and was choosing the best parts of each. One thing that drove Chu was his failure at his last assignment at Samsung—designing an electric skillet. He just hadn't been able to make it work right. This time, he told himself, he had to succeed.

Samsung didn't have all the manufacturing machines he needed to make microwave ovens, so Chu began visiting press vendors, plastic vendors, and toolmakers. When he couldn't find anyone in the country to do the kind of welding he wanted, he chose to seal his oven prototype with caulking instead. Slowly, it came together—brackets, outer panel, and door. But when he got to the magnetron tube, source of the microwaves, he was lost. There was no way Samsung could make it, or even subcontract it locally. At the time, only three manufacturers in the world had that ability—two in Japan and one in Rhode Island. Chu decided to buy the magnetron tube outright, from Japan. As months passed, he drove himself ever harder, often staying in the lab all night. It took him a year of 80-hour weeks to finish the prototype, but finally, he was ready to test it. He pushed the "on" button. In front of his eyes, the plastic in the cavity melted. So much for a year's work.

He spent more 80-hour weeks to rebuild, readjust, and redesign the magnetron tube prototype. And again he turned it on. This time, the stir shaft melted. Even his wife began to question his obsessiveness. "You must be mad," she'd tell him. At times, he agreed with her. The Japanese and

Americans, he knew, were now selling over 4 million microwave ovens a year, and he couldn't even get a single prototype to work . . .

In June of 1978, in the corner of his Suweon lab, Chu finally finished another prototype. He turned it on for a test, ready for the worst, but this time, nothing melted. His bosses were encouraged. They knew Chu's oven was still too crude to compete on the world market, but they told him to make more anyway. Chu himself had few global hopes. At best, he felt, Samsung would find a small, low-priced niche in the United States. But that didn't discourage him. The company's preeminent goal was production; marketing was second priority. Soon Samsung management did send out a few salesmen with the prototypes. They didn't have much success, but headquarters decided to put together a makeshift production line anyway. In case an order came in, they wanted to be ready. It was one of the company's rules: Never, ever, keep a customer waiting.

The production team began making one microwave oven a day, then two. Soon, they were up to five. By mid-1979, when over 4 million ovens were sold around the world, Samsung had finished only 1,460 of them. That's when the company decided to try its first real sales push. They chose to focus on the local market. Unfortunately, their low scale meant they had to charge an exorbitant six hundred dollars each—half the yearly income of an average Korean family. Almost no one bought. But management was upbeat. The machines worked. Having no sales was no reason to stop development.

Still, with the domestic push a washout, Samsung's sales people began to look abroad. They sent out brochures and hired distributors in dozens of countries. They offered to cut prices and were ready to fill the smallest order. The first came in from Panama, for 240 ovens. By the time the ovens were shipped, Samsung had lost money, but there was, nevertheless, celebration in Suweon. The company had broken through. And besides, this would be a good way to learn what customers wanted. Samsung felt it best to refine the product in a few small markets before trying big ones.

The Panama sales gave them confidence to apply for underwriter's laboratory approval, necessary for exporting to the United States. Late in 1979, they got it. For Samsung, America wasn't a totally foreign market. Many of the company's managers had gone to school there; they had American knowledge, knew the American language. And Samsung was ready to do something few American manufacturers did at the time: tailor its product to foreign tastes. If that meant retooling production back in Suweon, Samsung would spend the money. Instead of planning on a single line of ovens for the world, its strategy was to make unique models for unique markets.

At the time, microwave ovens sold for $350–$400 each in America. One of the country's biggest retailers, J. C. Penney, had been searching for a $299 model. They hadn't had any luck with the two countries then producing microwaves—Japan and the United States. Then Penney heard about Samsung. The retailer saw an opportunity—a low-wage country capable of building a modern product. In 1980, Penney decided to ask Samsung if it could build a microwave oven to sell in America for $299.

By then, world sales were up to 4.7 million a year.[6] Samsung was being asked for a few thousand ovens only. On top of that, Penney's order would mean designing a whole new oven and taking heavy losses, all in the name of gaining a fraction of 1 percent of the U.S. market. In Suweon, management was ecstatic anyway, promising Penney anything it wanted. To deliver, Samsung promised Chu any investment he needed. The firm put no pressure on him for profits; all it wanted was production.

Penney's technical people would be helping Chu with product quality, but Chu knew the greatest burden would be on Samsung. The challenge now was to turn a still-primitive assembly room into an efficient factory almost overnight. And Samsung would have to get it right the first time. This wasn't another Panama. These machines would be going to Americans, the most sophisticated consumers in the world.

Chu's boss was a quiet mechanical engineer named Kyung Pal Park. Ask him why he chose manufacturing and he'll tell you of his memory of American soldiers during the Korean War. Everything about them suggested wealth: their clothes, their equipment, and their vehicles. How, Park wondered, had America achieved that? In time, he came to see the answer as production. America was wealthy because it made things. Park wanted that for Korea, too: a nation not of rice paddies, but factories. In 1969, he joined Samsung. In 1980, at age 39, he was named head of home appliances. It was his responsibility to deliver the Penney order.

Soon he came up with his plan for organizing a team. In America, such a team typically would be headed by product designers; factory engineers would come second. At Samsung, production is king. So Park merged his product and factory people, stressing that design should be done with manufacturing in mind. He gave the team one unbreakable rule: No matter what, they would deliver on every deadline, not a day later. That responsibility would fall to Park's chief lieutenant, a production engineer just transferred from Samsung's motor division named I. J. Jang.

Before his transfer, Jang was managing the production of millions of motors a year on four separate lines. Now, he found himself in a division making five or six ovens a day. He didn't see it as a demotion. "There is one thing more valued at Samsung than high production," he explains, "the potential of high production." The best engineers aren't placed with boom products, but products that have yet to take off.

Jang immersed himself in learning the product, spending hours talking with designers like Chu, then journeying overseas to Matsushita, Sanyo, and GE. Once he'd learned world standards, he began to make sure Samsung was living up to them. He studied the prototype test results, pausing on the microwave-leakage numbers, which seemed high. That was a problem. He asked if it could be fixed, and was told the seal design made it hard to weld any better. So Jang, one of Samsung's most senior production managers, personally went to the welding vendor to help upgrade his process. Of the one hundred outside vendors working on the project, he ended up visiting 30 of them himself.

Then he turned his attention to building the assembly line. He started with an empty factory room and a delivery date only months away. His senior people would begin at dawn, often working until 10:30 P.M., then take a few hours' nap before going back to work for the rest of the night. Even Jang's boss, Kyung Pal Park, one of the highest executives in Suweon, kept the same hours. Samsung's executives rarely ask a sacrifice they're not ready to make themselves. Actually, there was one area of privilege. There were a few cots littered around the factory. The executives got those, the others grabbed naps in chairs.

The line took shape, production began, but inevitably, there were dozens of bugs. The Samsung people decided they couldn't afford to lose production though, so they fell into a pattern of manufacturing by day, then running the line all night to fine-tune it. Production improved, up to 10 a day, then 15. Soon, they got it to fifteen hundred a month, enough to meet Penney's order of several thousand.

Penney liked the ovens, and soon asked for more. Could Samsung deliver five thousand in another month? Samsung made that deadline, too, but there wasn't time for celebration. Now Penney wanted seven thousand. There was time only to work. "Like a cow," Jang would say later.

The team felt it would be wise to install more assembly lines and asked management for the money. "It was no problem," Jang said. As long as they got production, they would get the investment. By the end of 1981, Samsung had increased microwave production a hundredfold over the previous year, from just over a thousand to over one hundred thousand. Still, it was only a fraction of the world market. And almost none of the giants in America or Japan noticed. South Korea, they still felt, could never be a serious competitor in such sophisticated technology. . . .

In 1982, Samsung's microwave production topped two hundred thousand, double the previous year. But Mr. Park and his team didn't think it was enough. They knew that Samsung was still a global after-thought. American manufacturers were making over 2 million ovens per year, and the Japanese even more—2.3 million at home, and another 820,000 in their U.S. plants. The giant Matsushita company had 17 percent of the world market. Sanyo had 15 percent, whereas Samsung had less than 3 percent.[7]

One problem was that the big producers were bringing their prices down, narrowing Samsung's key advantage. If Samsung was going to keep growing, it realized it had to lower its own prices even more. The executives looked over their cost structure. The highest item was the magnetron tube, which they were still buying from the Japanese. They began to wonder if they could make it themselves. It would mean millions of

dollars of investment for a new, highly complex factory. They approached
Japan's magnetron producers for technical assistance, but were turned
down. That left only one other company to approach—Amperex, the
Rhode Island firm that was America's only manufacturer. But that plant,
Samsung found, had been unable to compete with Japan and was going
out of business.[8]

About that time, in Louisville, Kentucky, the Head Marketing Manager
for GE's Major Appliance Business Group, Bruce Enders, was beginning to
see warning signs in his microwave oven division. Because GE had come
into microwave ovens so late, it had yet to make money on them. In 1982,
the losses began to get worse. The Japanese were chipping away at GE's
U.S. share, pushing it down from over 16 percent in 1980 to 14 percent in
1982.[9] No one at GE thought of conceding ground, though. Japan's wage
rates were no lower than America's, and GE was just completing a multi-
million-dollar modernization at its microwave oven factory in Columbia,
Maryland. The company was convinced it would turn things around.

Enders knew that GE understood the American consumer better than
any other appliance maker. It had just scored a tremendous success with
the Spacemaker, for example, the industry's first under-shelf model. If
the Maryland modernization could make GE cost-competitive, he was
convinced the company could make the business profitable.

But then, in late 1982, the Japanese began to export a new midsized line
of ovens at an alarmingly low price—it was even below GE's costs at its
modernized plant. GE's manufacturing people insisted that the Japanese
must be dumping. But Enders wanted to know for sure. He asked me to
do a study. . . .

While I was finishing my final report, GE management did decide to
explore a joint-venture factory with the Japanese, though they wanted it
built in the States. They chose to work with Matsushita, the biggest producer. Enders traveled to Japan to negotiate, and seemed to be getting
close. He even got the Japanese to agree that a coventure would be highly
profitable for both. But in the end, the Japanese declined.

When they told him, Enders was surprised. He asked one of
Matsushita's key executives why. If the coventure would make them
money, why wouldn't they agree to it? Because, the executive said, it would
mean losing some of the American market to GE. In Japan, he explained,
foreign market share is a key priority.

"Enders-san," he said, "you have to understand. In Japan, it's our destiny
to export. If we don't export, we don't survive."

"That's what this guy said to me," Enders would say later. "Could you
imagine a U.S. business manager thinking that way? I've never forgotten it."

Matsushita's decision left GE with one other option: sourcing—buying
Japanese products and putting the GE label on them. No one in Louisville
was ready to shut down the new Maryland plant, but maybe it made sense
to source a few lines.

In April 1983, I finished my full report. In it, I raised a Korean option. If GE sourced only with Matsushita, I said, the Americans would be at the mercy of a direct competitor. Korean costs, however, were potentially low enough to undercut the Japanese. And because the Koreans were anxious for volume, it would be easier to negotiate a good deal with them.

Louisville was skeptical. The Koreans? Perhaps they were making a few ovens for Penney, but they were a Third World country. A high-quality firm like GE—selling a million ovens—couldn't risk depending on South Korea.

I showed them the cost differences. In 1983, it cost GE \$218 to make a typical microwave oven. It cost Samsung only \$155.[10] I went on to break it down. . . .

In June 1983, management in Louisville decided to begin sourcing microwave ovens from the Far East, but only small and mid-sized models. GE would continue to make full-sized ovens in America. The company's biggest order was with Japan. But GE did give Samsung a much smaller order, only about fifteen thousand. The Americans wanted to see if the Koreans could deliver.

It was now up to Samsung's appliance director, K. P. Park, to produce high-quality goods at a cost America's biggest appliance maker could no longer match. GE sent technical people to Korea to outline its standards. In GE's thinking, this was simply quality control for a second-rate supplier. In Suweon, Park saw it differently. If he was a good student, he'd learn world-class skills. Once again, he told his people there was one unbreakable rule: Every deadline must be met. He knew he'd have to depend on his foot soldiers as much as his lieutenants . . .

At first, Samsung's ovens were not up to GE standards. But with the help of GE's quality engineers, things soon got better.[11] Enders grew increasingly impressed, and eventually put in another order. Sales steadily improved. It was the GE label customers reached for, but Korean workmanship that satisfied them. On his next trip to Suweon, Enders was surprised at the changes. The assembly line had gone from roller conveyors to automatic-transfer mechanisms. Clearly, Samsung had the capacity to deliver far more than GE had been asking for. Enders put in a still-bigger order. Sales kept improving. It was around that time, mid-1983, that the factory in Suweon made a milestone. Samsung shipped its five-hundred-thousandth oven. For the first time since the company had begun four years before, Park said it was time to celebrate. The Koreans paused for a brief party. When the party was over, they went back to work. . . .

By the end of 1983, Samsung's annual microwave production topped 750,000, and by 1984, it passed 1 million. The Suweon factory expanded, as well. In four years, Samsung had gone from a few prototypes to ten mass-production lines. The product that began with melted plastic in an old lab was now becoming a major performer in America's market. But for Samsung, that wasn't good enough.

The company had grown concerned over some new projections. From 1982 to 1986, U.S. microwave sales were expected to keep growing at a healthy rate, but for the four years after that, the predictions said things would slow. It was time, Samsung decided, to seek out other markets. Europe, which was expected to grow by 20 percent a year, offered the most promise. The U.S. manufacturers were aware of the same trend, but Europe didn't seem a worthwhile market to them. The Americans didn't know those countries. It would take too much money to build a marketing network there, too long to get a profit. Samsung faced the same burdens, but its goal wasn't short-term return on investment, it was long-term growth in volume. Among those assigned to Europe was a young marketing executive named J. K. Kim, soon to be named head of appliance-export sales before he was 40. . . .

In early 1979, Samsung had produced exactly one crude prototype of a microwave oven. In 1987, it made 3.5 million microwaves[12] in 250 separate models for over 20 countries. Samsung had gambled correctly. Its appetite to produce had proven stronger than America's. From now on, GE would be doing the sales and service side of the product, Samsung the manufacturing. Soon, the people in Suweon would be the biggest makers of microwave ovens in the world. . . .

In 1970, Samsung, the largest Korean company, had only $100 million in sales. Its main businesses at the time were insurance, medical services, textiles, and trading. That same year, General Electric had sales of $4.4 billion. Today, GE has grown dramatically into a diversified company with almost $40 billion in sales. Samsung has grown, as well. Today, it is one of the biggest industrial corporations on earth. Today, it too has almost $40 billion in sales. . . .

Today, the company designs and makes its own integrated circuits. In 1985, it began a data-systems division. In 1986, it started in aerospace. That year, net profits were only $182 million, among the lowest of the world's large corporations. It is by design. Samsung's priority for money is to plow it back into the company.

Samsung electronics now has over fifteen hundred engineers. In almost every building, showrooms display what they've done. There are VCRs, personal computers, video cameras, and compact-disc players—products of the future, the kind that boost a nation's standard of living. There was a time when only high-wage countries had the vision to invest in such goods. No longer. Sometimes, even the opposite holds true. Although America invented most of these products, and buys more of them than any other country, we make almost none of them. In the case of VCRs and video cameras, we never manufactured them at all. Today, if an American company decided to start making VCRs, it would have to come to South Korea or Japan to get technical assistance. We remain the world's innovator, but others are challenging us as producers. Too often, the dollars we spend buying our own inventions are boosting the living standard of the Far East.

Samsung is not alone in enjoying its microwave-oven success. General Electric is enjoying it, too. With Samsung's manufacturing help, GE's market share has shot up. Microwave ovens have become one of GE's most profitable appliances. In Louisville, management will say, rightly, that sourcing from the Koreans was good for the company. It allowed GE to leap over its Japanese and U.S. competitors to gain share and succeed.

But there is also the question of country. Over forty thousand Koreans make their living producing microwave ovens. In America, the number is a fraction of that. In 1980, almost 100 percent of every hundred dollars Americans spent on GE microwave ovens stayed in America. Today, well over half flows to South Korea.[13] While over eighty-four thousand microwave ovens are made in Suweon each week, GE's Maryland plant stands idle. . . .

Notes

1. The idea of cooking with microwaves originated with Raytheon managers involved in the production of magnetron tubes for radar installations during World War II. They worked on the concept beginning in 1942 and received their first microwave cooking patents in 1949. Raytheon introduced the first microwave-cooking oven, the Radar-range, in 1953. The original versions were as big and heavy as refrigerators and cost as much as some automobiles. Raytheon licensed its invention to Tappan and Litton, who in 1955 began selling home models.

2. This estimate is based on internal production figures from Samsung and GE internal sources. Publicly reported industry-association data are not accurate in market-share breakdowns, as companies do not necessarily report accurate figures to these associations. Korean-made microwaves are sold under many labels, including GE, J. C. Penney, Montgomery Ward, Whirlpool, Sears, Emerson, Samsung, and Goldstar.

3. In 1988, Samsung surpassed Matsushita, Sanyo, and Sharp in total number of units produced, although its total sales valued in dollars may still be slightly smaller at the retail level due to mix and high retail prices in Japan.

4. Korea did not begin to offer color television transmission until four years after the production of color televisions had commenced at Samsung, Goldstar, and Lucky (now part of Goldstar).

5. The study was commissioned by the National Economic Development Office in Great Britain, an industry-, labor-, and government-sponsored organization with separate councils for a variety of industries. Britain's television makers were suffering and wanted to understand the new competition they were facing from Japan and Korea. They asked for a strategy on what they could do to become competitive again.

6. Almost all of the world market growth from 1975 to 1980 came in the United States. The U.S. market grew from 900,000 units in 1975 to 3.2 million units in 1980. Meanwhile, the Japanese market declined from 1.3 million units in 1975 to 900,000 units in 1980. The competitive battleground clearly shifted to U.S. territory.

7. These figures were derived from a Telesis survey of producers. In addition to Matsushita and Sanyo, Sharp had a 14 percent share, Toshiba 7 percent, Hitachi 2 percent, and Mitsubishi 1 percent. Altogether, Japanese companies had about 60 percent of world production.

8. Amperex is actually a subsidiary of the Dutch electronics giant Philips. Its magnetron facility was relatively new in Rhode Island, but did not have the scale, cost levels, or technology to be competitive.

The prices Amperex needed to be profitable were 30 percent higher than those quoted by their Japanese competitors. GE and other U.S. manufacturers did not want to purchase from their competitors in Japan, but could not suffer the 30 percent price penalty that purchasing from Amperex entailed. They switched to the Japanese, and Amperex had to shut down.

9. Telesis study for GE. GE's share had risen from 7 percent in 1975 to 16 percent by 1980, and had then declined.

10. Telesis analysis.

11. GE sent over a number of quality-control and manufacturing engineers who helped Samsung develop its testing and production techniques. It took well over a year of joint work before GE felt that an acceptable quality level had been met. This assistance probably cut years off of the time Samsung would have required to become a high-quality, high-volume microwave oven producer on its own.

12. Interviews with Samsung management in Suweon in July 1988.

13. The distribution, marketing, and selling elements of the price, as well as part of quality control and engineering and profit, stay with GE in the United States. The exact proportion is confidential, but it is less than half of the selling price.

The Rise of the Pentagon and U.S. State Building

The Defense Program as Industrial Policy*

Gregory Hooks

---

editor's introduction:

Methodological Significance

The definition of multiple-case studies also includes "two-case" case studies—where a case study consists of two cases. With only two cases, such a design can nevertheless form a stronger platform for your findings than if you had relied on only a single case. In the following selection, Gregory Hooks ably demonstrates this "two-case" design. He presents both cases and uses them to build a more general empirical argument.

Hooks's research interest is about the central (federal) government's role in industrial planning. His main hypothesis was contrary to the prevailing conventional wisdom at the

---

*Editor's Note: Abridged and edited from Hooks, Gregory, "The Rise of the Pentagon and U.S. State Building: The Defense Program as Industrial Policy," in *American Journal of Sociology,* September 1990, 96, pp. 358–404. Reprinted by permission of the University of Chicago Press. Due to its original length, large portions of the original text, as well as tables and footnotes, have been omitted, and the selection's lead paragraph comes from the concluding section of the original text.

time, which stipulated that the United States' traditional free enterprise economy precluded a strong role by the federal government. He examines his hypothesis by tracing the course of events in two different industries.

If Hooks had limited his study to a single industry or case, critics might have claimed his findings to be unique to the particular case. Having two industries or cases effectively counters such a claim (and note how having three cases, all replicating similar courses of events, might have produced an even stronger counterclaim).

Substantive Note

Japan's rise as a powerful industrial state in the 1970s sparked great concern within the United States. A global economy was emerging (see also Chapter 6 of this anthology), and observers worried that Japan could become one of the dominant forces in this economy—with a concomitant shift away from traditional centers of power, such as the countries of Western Europe and possibly even the United States. Competition with the United States also drew great attention, with many books being written about the virtues of Japan's work ethic, its ways of organizing productive businesses, and especially the role of its central government in supporting industrial planning and development. An entire Japanese ministry was devoted to this latter role, whereas the United States appeared to have no counterpart.

Hooks's study argues that the needed role was in fact fulfilled by the U.S. Department of Defense (DoD), although its role was less public. His two cases include an industry long dependent on defense spending (aeronautics) and an industry usually considered independent of defense (microelectronics). By documenting DoD's role at critical stages in the development of both industries, Hooks makes a strong argument that the United States' central government, operating through DoD, did and can exercise a centralized role in industrial planning. Furthermore, he distinguishes his interpretation from other prevailing beliefs regarding the functioning of the military–industrial complex in the United States—traditionally seen as serving business consumption and subsidy, but not industrial planning.

As the World War II "arsenal of democracy" and the postwar hegemonic power, the U.S. state has shaped industrial production in strategically important sectors. Society-centered theories of the military–industrial complex view the difference between the pre- and postwar state as essentially a quantitative one. The postwar state purchased a large quantity of weapons, but it remained a consumer, not a planner. [However, the present article on] aeronautics and electronics provides evidence that the hegemonic U.S. state established a qualitatively new relationship with capitalist firms. In Block's terms (1980), the demands of World War II and postwar hegemony pushed the U.S. state beyond a "tipping point" in its relations with private firms. The state in fact did plan the development of sectors that were essential to strategic policy and crucial to U.S. scientific and technological choices, employment, and balance of trade.

. . . This article also challenges the widely shared view that the weak and fragmented U.S. state cannot plan. In the industrial planning implemented by centralized states (i.e., Japan and France), macroeconomic policies and the activities of several agencies have been coordinated with the planning effort. But these extreme cases must not be used to define the concept. That is, industrial planning [can also] refer to sectoral interventions. Planning is more likely among highly centralized states and facilitated when a number of agencies cooperate. But autarkic planning is not only a theoretical possibility; the Pentagon provides a concrete example.

Aeronautics, 1948–64: A Case Study of Industrial Planning

. . . The case study of aeronautics from 1948 to 1964 is of historical interest because this sector was the foremost priority for defense planners and uniquely important to the emergence of the military–industrial complex. The value of this examination is heightened because the aeronautics sector is the extreme case. Not only was it the top priority of defense planners but also the firms in this sector were exceptionally vulnerable to external control. By examining the extreme, this case study highlights "processes that work more subtly, in combination with other determinants, in a range of other situations" (Evans et al., 1985, p. 349). . . .

Policy Tools and Dependent Firms

To shape economic development, the state must wield potent policy tools and private firms must be asymmetrically dependent on the resources at the state's command (Pfeffer & Salancik, 1978). The aviation industry that "emerged from the Second World War provided something of a new phenomena" (Millis, 1956, pp. 306–7). The new phenomenon was a major industry with an interest—a need—for the nation to devote a large portion of the GNP to the production of munitions (see also Rae, 1968, chap. 9). In 1939, the aviation industry produced $244 million and generated $30 million in profits. During World War II, these figures were $8,204 million and $133 million, respectively. However, in 1946 the industry produced only $711 million worth of equipment and lost $13 million (U.S. President's Air Policy Commission, 1948, p. 54).

The air force had an overriding "interest" in maintaining an aircraft industry "that could do aggressive research and development work, produce the military aircraft essential for preserving peace, and expand quickly in case of war" (Snyder, 1956, p. 14). However, if left to their own resources and civilian markets, the struggling aircraft firms could not produce aircraft in quantity, let alone pursue research and development. "Here is a rather different view of the 'military–industrial' complex, for instead of industry insisting on a large air force, the [USAF] planners were insisting on a large aircraft industry to ensure that the anticipated mobilization and development needs in military aviation could be met by the aircraft industry" (Smith, 1970, p. 106). The ascendant military planners not only had an agenda for this industry but also they controlled resources indispensable to the survival of aeronautics firms.

Industrial finance. It is hard to overestimate the importance of federal investments in the aviation industry. In 1939, the gross capital assets in the sector were valued at $114 million. Between 1939 and 1945, the federal government provided $3.5 billion in direct investments and subsidized an additional $317 million in private investments in aviation (U.S. Smaller War Plants Corporation, 1946, pp. 155–56). These wartime investments transformed aviation into the nation's largest industry, and they placed the state in a commanding position. By 1945, the federal government controlled 90 percent of the assets used in the manufacture of aircraft (White, 1980, p. 90). The Pentagon took possession of the most important of these assets at the war's end (Hooks, 1991; see also Rae, 1968; Table 7.1 documents the government's investments in the aviation industry). Only 11 percent of the World War II expansion was privately financed. Even during the Korean War, when the government forced contractors to use the structures already built, the military still financed more than 80 percent of new equipment and provided over 65 percent of all financing.

Dependence on federal financing was so extreme that between 1939 and 1955, "no aircraft company [sought] public financing," and "no airliner program of any size [had] been developed without some military aid" (Quinn, 1960, pp. 324, 330). From 1952 to 1956, the Defense Department owned 63 percent of all plants and equipment. Despite sizable investments by aeronautics firms in the late 1950s, the Pentagon still owned over half of the assets by 1961 (Stanford Research Institute, 1963, p. 44). . . .

Table 7.1 Aircraft Industry Emergency-Facilities Expansion: Cost and Fund Sources, World War II and Korean War

		FUNDS (millions of dollars)		
Total Expansion:		Private	Federal	Federal Funds as a Percentage of Total
1940–45	3,894	420	3,474	89.2
1950–53	3,528	1204	2,324	65.9
Structures:				
1940–45	1,556	212	1,344	86.4
1950–53	1,085	805	208	19.2
Equipment:				
1940–45	2,338	208	2,130	

SOURCE: Stekler (1965, p. 16)

Ensuring demand. Defense contracts commit the government to purchase a specified quantity of munitions in advance of production. Throughout the 1950s and 1960s, nearly 80 percent of aerospace sales were to the federal government (Aerospace Industries Association of America, 1965, p. 8). The postwar procurement program has been built upon the pattern of administration established during World War II, that is, career military officers have enjoyed a great deal of autonomy in contract negotiations (Hammond, 1961, p. 309). While aircraft firms have not been "subject to the vicissitudes of market acceptance" (Stekler, 1965, p. 89), they have been dependent upon military procurement and driven to comply with defense planning (A. D. Little, Inc., 1963, p. 27; Mowery & Rosenberg, 1982).

Research and development. From 1954 to 1964, the military controlled over 70 percent of growing federal research and development (R&D) outlays, and aeronautics was the fastest growing element in the R&D budget. In 1951, the Pentagon spent $758 million for aerospace-related research; by 1967 that figure stood at $7.75 billion (Bright, 1978, p. 114). . . . From 1953 to 1962 at least 30 percent of all research was devoted to aviation, and the government dwarfed the private sector in providing the funds. The military has subsidized aviation R&D throughout this century (Mowery & Rosenberg, 1982, pp. 104–6), but the magnitude of this effort exploded during and after World War II. Following the Pentagon's lead, aerospace firms placed "extraordinary emphasis" on research (Scherer, 1971, p. 361). By 1962, 31 percent of aerospace sales were attributed to R&D contracts; the comparable figure was 20 percent in the weapons industry more generally and only 3 percent for all industries (Stekler, 1965, p. 21).

This overview of the policy instruments at the Pentagon's command and the peculiar structure of aeronautics firms corroborates the argument that this sector has been planned. These resources were made available to aviation firms with strings attached. The relationship has been one of asymmetric dependence: These firms need the Defense Department more than the Pentagon needs any one firm. "The preponderance of bargaining strength in the [relationship] is clearly on the government's side. Its strength comes through control of funds, definition of goals, timing and technique, encouragement of competition, participation in management, the application of political pressures, and power to terminate contacts and retroactively to reduce prices and profits" (Stanford Research Institute, 1963, p. 34). As examined later, this asymmetrical dependence is evident in the performance of aerospace firms and in their inability to diversify.

Planning or Subsidy?

Table 7.2 shows that aerospace firms had on average a modest rate of return when compared to other manufacturing concerns for the 1956–61 period. Table 7.2 may surprise those who associate the defense program with boondoggles and excess. Regardless of the measure—as a percentage of sales, return on assets (including government-owned assets), or return on their own equity—aerospace firms consistently generated a relatively low

Table 7.2   Rates of Return for 51 Aerospace Firms Versus All Manufacturing Corporations (Except Newspapers), 1956–61

| Return Type | NET PROFIT AFTER TAXES (percentage of return type) | | | | | |
	1956	1957	1958	1959	1960	1961
Sales:						
Aerospace	3.7	3.5	2.8	1.9	1.7	2.1
All industry	5.2	4.4	4.9	4.5	4.0	4.8
Return on assets employed:						
Aerospace	—	—	3.9	2.4	2.2	2.8
All industry	8.0	6.4	7.1	6.3	5.5	5.8
Return on equity:						
Aerospace	—	—	7.8	5.0	4.6	5.8
All industry	12.6	9.8	10.7	9.6	8.4	9.0

SOURCE: A. D. Little, Inc. (1963, p. 68)

rate of return. This is largely the result of renegotiation (Stekler, 1965, pp. 158–62). The government compares contractors' risks and costs to profits received. If profits are deemed excessive (and they frequently are), defense firms must return the excess to the government. This retroactive renegotiation of profits is still another anomaly and provides further evidence of the degree to which the government dictates to aerospace firms.

The view that the defense program is primarily a subsidy is also challenged by the Pentagon's intrusion into design and production practices. "[The aircraft] companies were told in brief that they had no choice but to use the Government plant and tools which were furnished to them. The result of this approach was a strait-jacketing of management when it came to planning facilities and tooling requirements for new programs" (Quinn, 1960, p. 314). Not only do Pentagon planners "make the major development decisions," but also they dictate "specific technical features" and modify requirements after the design process has begun (Peck & Scherer, 1962, p. 62). This degree of oversight in military aircraft production is not inevitable. Alexander (1974) makes the case that the Pentagon dictates design and production practices in far more detail than do military planners in France and the Soviet Union.

Defense contractors "complain bitterly" about the Defense Department's intrusiveness, but "for many of the companies [the Pentagon] is the only game in town" (Alexander, 1974, p. 437). No firm left the aerospace field voluntarily (Stekler, 1965, pp. 104–8). Bright (1978, p. 198) cites a large number of severe crises for aircraft firms that failed to secure defense contracts: Curtiss–Wright (1946–50), Martin (1947–49), Fairchild (1958–60), Northrop (1949 and 1956–59), General Dynamics (1947–49), Republic (1964–65), and Douglas (1958–61). Curtiss-Wright withdrew from aircraft manufacture altogether, and Martin only received emergency federal loans on the condition that its chief executive officer be fired. The survivors were severely damaged; the few that recovered needed years to do so. The Pentagon is engaged in the planning of the sector, subsidizing existing firms is a means to that end. The interests of military planners and those of defense firms frequently coincide. But when the interests of the Defense Department and defense firms have diverged, firms have paid dearly.

Diversification into civilian aircraft production is frequently offered as an example of a positive "spin-off" from defense production. The victor in this competition was the Boeing Company. During the early 1950s, Boeing faced an effective tax rate of 82 percent. Instead of permitting its funds to return to the government through renegotiation, Boeing diverted funds to development. The prototype for the 707 was offered to the air force as a jet tanker, but Boeing's "tanker" was painted like an airliner and had passenger seats. The air force accepted the craft as a prototype and subsidized the costs of setting up production facilities and working out the bugs in design and production. In 1962, the U.S. tax court found Boeing guilty of diverting funds and ordered the firm to reimburse the government. By this time, however,

Boeing had established itself in the airliner market and never looked back (see Bright, 1978, pp. 87–92).

This apparent exception actually proves the rule. Nearly all aviation firms dabbled with civilian aircraft; the vast majority lost money in the effort. Martin, Fairchild, Northrop, General Dynamics, Douglas, and Lockheed were brought to the point of financial collapse (Bright, 1978, p. 198). Boeing, the big winner, was only able to succeed by illegally diverting government funds. This is part of a more general pattern in which aircraft firms utilize, for commercial purposes, "technical knowledge developed for military purposes at government expense" (Mowery & Rosenberg, 1982, p. 140).

The most profitable form of diversification has been in the production of missiles and electronic equipment. Over 90 percent of missile sales have been to the federal government (Aerospace Industries Association of America, 1965, p. 8); shifting to missiles has only reproduced dependence on the Pentagon. The aeronautics firms of the 1950s and 1960s lacked the capitalization to succeed in civilian markets on their own or to acquire nonmilitary firms. "Hence, the key resources of the military contractors . . . tend to become locked in and further dependent on the governmental customers. Each additional failure at commercial diversification and equally every successful governmentally contracted undertaking serves to accentuate their locked in nature" (Weidenbaum, 1973, p. 267). The more successful aerospace firms have broadened their defense base, but they have rarely gained ground in civilian markets (see also Gorgol, 1972).

Since World War II, defense production has become increasingly specialized and concentrated (Fox, 1974, pp. 43-44). The Pentagon's increasing dependence on a few large defense firms, which have indispensable research, development, and production capabilities, limits the range of action available to military planners. Admittedly these firms are not always compliant, but they remain client firms and dependent on the Pentagon. They have the means to influence defense planning, but it would be a fundamental misunderstanding to confuse defense planning with a mere subsidy. It is easiest to see who is in a position of power when tough choices are to be made—during crisis periods. During the 1950s and 1960s, when the choice was between the goals of planners and the fate of defense firms, the volatility in the defense sector and failure rate among contractors indicate that the defense firms were sacrificed.

Microelectronics: Defense Planning in a Less Dependent Industry

This second case study emphasizes the decisive role played by the Defense Department in the development and diffusion of semiconductors and integrated circuits. In the early 1950s, although too expensive for many commercial applications, semiconductors provided the military with more durable and energy efficient electronic components. Integrated circuits, which were developed in the late 1950s, combine several elements of a circuit "on one piece of semiconducting material, a chip" (Hazewindus & Tooker, 1982, p. 6); they were at the same time smaller and more reliable than previous technologies. There is consensus that "from 1950 to 1970 the most dramatically growing and ultimately the largest part of the electronics market was defense related" (Utterback & Murray, 1977, p. 9). I provide evidence that this sector was not simply defense related; the Pentagon played a decisive role in developing semiconductors and integrated circuits, making their mass production reliable and inexpensive and ensuring their widespread application. Moreover, this occurred despite the resistance of leading monopoly-sector electronics firms.

Convergence and Divergence Between Aeronautics and Microelectronics

... Whereas it is mistaken to ignore the differences between aeronautics and microelectronics, it is equally in error to obscure important similarities. Tyson & Zysman (1983, p. 422) use the case of microelectronics to argue that the United States lacks an industrial policy. In this view, the incoherence of a weak state leaves decisionmaking to powerful private firms by default (see also Borrus et al., 1982, 1983; Dobbin, 1987). The stress on the decisionmaking of firms underestimates an essential dynamic. This case study provides evidence that, as a patron of R&D and a major customer, the Defense Department revolutionized electronics. Dramatically smaller, more powerful, and more reliable electronic components were developed despite the resistance of leading firms. The Defense Department pursued its own agenda and mobilized resources to shape developments in the sector. The fact that the Pentagon's agenda did not preclude civilian applications does not rule out the possibility that this was an exercise in planning. Nor does the Defense Department's disinterest in maintaining world dominance in chip production by U.S. firms indicate an absence of planning. Rather, it suggests that U.S. planning has been oriented toward military, not commercial, ends.

The Planning of a Relatively Autonomous Sector

In the words of USAF General Schreiver, "The birth and explosive growth of integrated circuits can be directly attributed to a combination of wise policy direction by the Department of Defense; ... and spirited response by industry" (cited in Asher & Strom, 1977, p. 9). This case study provides evidence in support of this general's assertion that the Defense Department shaped the technological choices and path of growth in the microelectronics sector. Although the Pentagon's planning role was not as intrusive as in aeronautics, it was decisive. Conversely, while the leading electronics firms avoided dependence on the Pentagon, they could not prevent the Pentagon from revolutionizing the sector and putting their market position at risk.

The conflict between the Pentagon and large electronics firms was clear on the issue of research. Throughout the 1950s and 1960s, the Defense Department pushed for a sharp reduction in the size of electronic circuitry while improving reliability. The USAF was particularly aggressive; its "molecular electronics" program of the early 1950s sought to develop molecules (probably crystals) that could replace traditional electronic circuits altogether. While molecular electronics proved unrealistic, the military led developments in miniaturization, and the electronics firms, including the largest and most diversified, followed the Defense Department's lead. This development is more remarkable in light of the R&D resources commanded by the leading electronics firms. Together, Western Electric, General Electric, RCA, Sylvania, Philco, CBS, Raytheon, Tung-Sol, and Westinghouse supplied 50 percent of all private R&D spending and captured an even larger share—80 percent—of federal research funds (Tilton, 1971, pp. 94–95). Not only did these firms have a vested interest in the existing technologies, but also the semiconductor was "so radically different . . . in the way it worked, in the way it could be manufactured and sold, and in its apparent potential, that it could not be comfortably accommodated within the existing electronics industry without changes that the industry was . . . unwilling or unable to make [at that time]" (Braun & MacDonald, 1978, p. 71). The diversified firms were equally resistant to integrated circuits, which combine several elements of a circuit on one chip. As late as 1962, most firms shied away from revolutionary integrated circuits, concentrating instead on evolutionary changes and "the extension of well-understood existing technology" (Anthony Golding, cited in Asher & Strom, 1977, p. 53).

Those minimizing the Pentagon's planning role point to the research efforts of established firms. In the late 1950s and early 1960s, the Pentagon funded approximately 70 percent of all electronics research (Asher & Strom, 1977, p. 40). But the Defense Department provided only 25 percent of semiconductor R&D funding in 1958 and 23 percent in 1959, a level of funding much lower than in the larger electronics sector (Tilton, 1971, p. 93). Further, none "of the major innovations in semiconductors have been a *direct* result of defense sponsored projects" (Utterback & Murray, 1977, p. 24; emphasis in original), and defense-supported R&D yielded very few patents and few of these led to commercial applications. "The reason for this is simply motivation. Government-sponsored R&D usually demands production of final devices that might or might not be considered useful (i.e., profitable) for the company involved. If the company chooses to sponsor R&D itself, then it is highly motivated to direct the R&D into products that it feels will be profitable" (Linvill & Hogan, 1977, pp. 23–24).

Although aeronautics firms also sought profits, they rarely succeeded in entering commercial markets. Defense-dependent firms in the electronics sector displayed a similar pattern: There was little "movement of technology into commercial use when a laboratory or firm [was] wholly sponsored or responsive to defense requirements" (Utterback & Murray, 1977, p. 25). However, in contradiction of Melman's (1970) view that the Pentagon captured the military subdivisions of diversified electronics firms, large corporations "with a balance of sales between defense and civilian" markets (Utterback & Murray, 1977) financed research with commercial potential. Beginning with AT&T's rush to publicize the invention of the transistor in the early 1950s (to avoid its classification by the Defense Department) and continuing through the refinement of semiconductors and integrated circuits between 1958 and 1963, electronics firms deliberately maintained their options in commercial markets (DeGrasse, 1984, p. 90).

The Defense Department did not dictate the R&D agenda of large and diversified firms, but it profoundly influenced the research efforts of the smaller, younger, and defense-oriented firms that dominated semiconductor production. New firms, such as Texas Instruments, Fairchild, Transitron, and Hughes, produced 64 percent of all semiconductors in 1957, whereas the much larger diversified firms supplied only 31 percent. The new firms' share of military sales was higher still (Braun & MacDonald, 1978, pp. 68, 82). Conversely, these younger firms were extremely dependent on the Pentagon, sought to expand defense sales, and oriented their research toward the Defense Department's agenda.

Monopoly-sector electronics firms concentrated on evolutionary changes in existing technologies, but these firms could not stop the Pentagon from revolutionizing the industry.

Most important, these firms suffered a "brain drain." Many of the scientists and engineers who pioneered microelectronics left established firms out of frustration: "they resented what they saw as the lackadaisical attitude towards semiconductor work" (Braun & MacDonald, 1978, p. 74). Although newer firms received much less R&D support from the Pentagon than the larger firms, their research efforts led to the major breakthroughs. Texas Instruments developed the integrated circuit in 1959, and Fairchild Semiconductors developed the process that made their mass production possible. Neither of these inventions was directly financed by the Pentagon, but both emerged from defense-oriented firms—not the much larger and well-financed laboratories of the dominant electronics firms. Moreover, once these advances had been made, the

Table 7.3 U.S. Integrated Circuit Production and Prices and Importance of the Defense Market, 1962–68

Year	Total Production (millions of dollars)	Average Price per Integrated Circuit (dollars)	Defense Production (percentage of total production)
1962	4	50.00	100
1963	16	31.60	94
1964	41	18.50	85
1965	79	8.33	72
1966	148	5.05	53
1967	228	3.32	43
1968	312	2.33	37

SOURCE: Tilton (1971, p. 91)

Pentagon energetically financed production refinements (Asher & Strom, 1977, p. 4; Tilton, 1971, p. 93).

At a fundamental level, the agenda for the electronics industry was established by defense policy—not by the firms dominating sales and assets. "This policy not only stimulated the companies contracted to continue in this direction, but it had a similar effect on the others who either could not or would not obtain R&D contract awards. In such a manner, the Government accomplished one of its major objectives: it 'persuaded' the industry to allocate its own funds toward the same goals. . . . The combination of heavy R&D spending and the attendant publicity constituted a steamroller mechanism which the industry found difficult to ignore; it wouldn't and couldn't" (Herbert Kleiman, cited in Asher & Strom, 1977, p. 35). As this quote suggests, the Pentagon directly influenced the research efforts of firms under contract. The momentum toward semiconductors and integrated circuits proved too great for even the large and diversified corporations to resist.

Beyond research and development, the Pentagon voraciously consumed the expensive first generations of integrated circuits. The Minuteman 2 intercontinental missile program of the early 1960s offered the first large-scale use of integrated circuits. Not only did this guarantee a market for costly integrated circuits but it also proved their utility. In addition to applications in weapons systems, NASA relied on integrated circuits (NASA purchases are included with defense purchases in Table 7.3). The large government orders of the early 1960s compressed the time needed to perfect manufacturing and achieve economies of scale (Borrus et al., 1983, pp. 151–52). As the unit price of integrated circuits fell, industrial firms became important customers. By 1967, the military consumed less than half of all integrated circuits, and this share declined further as the sale of consumer goods using integrated circuits (e.g., calculators and watches) exploded. Defense-dependent firms in this sector resembled aeronautics firms—they put forth less effort and had less success in civilian applications. However, the large and diversified firms successfully pursued civilian markets (Tilton, 1971, pp. 96–97). . . .

Conclusion

. . . If the Defense Department's planning had been restricted to dependent aeronautics firms, this article would provide an interesting case study of a unique sector. However, the ability of the Pentagon to shape the revolution in microelectronics provides evidence of the breadth of the Defense Department's influence, including its capacity to shape vibrant industries dominated by monopoly-sector firms. The growing momentum to expand and generalize the Defense Department's influence over scientific (Tirman, 1984, pp. 215–17) and industrial policy (Cushman, 1988) bears witness to the fact that the Pentagon is the sole federal agency with sufficient resources to pursue a distinctive agenda. I have argued throughout that it is a mistake to concentrate solely on planning focused on commercial goals. When implementing a commercially oriented plan, typically designed to increase the competitiveness of national firms, the state imposes a longer time horizon and provides investment and research funds that individual firms may not provide. As Poulantzas points out (1975, p. 169), commercially oriented planning may well serve the interests of the ruling class, offering alternative means for reproducing capitalism and ensuring profits for leading firms. That the Pentagon's goals have been primarily strategic—and not commercial—makes this a topic of greater, not less, theoretical interest.

References

A. D. Little, Inc. (1963). *How sick is the defense industry?* Cambridge, MA: Little.

Aerospace Industries Association of America. (1965). *Aerospace facts and figures.* Fallbrook, CA: Aero.

Alexander, A. (1974). Weapons acquisition in the Soviet Union, the United States and France. In F. Norton, A. Rogerson, & E. Warner III (Eds.), *Comparative defense policy* (pp. 426–43). Baltimore: Johns Hopkins University Press.

Asher, N. J., & Strom, L. D. (1977). The role of the Department of Defense in the development of integrated circuits. Washington, DC: Institute for Defense Analysis.

Block, F. (1980). Beyond relative autonomy: State managers as historical subjects. In R. Miliband & J. Saville (Eds.), *Socialist register, 1980* (pp. 227–42). London: Merlin.

Borrus, M., Millstein, J., & Zysman, J. (1982). *International competition in advanced industrial sectors.* Washington, DC: U.S. Congress, Joint Economic Committee.

_____. 1983. Trade and development in the semiconductor industry: Japanese challenge and American response. In L. Tyson & J. Zysman (Eds.), *American industry in international competition* (pp. 142–248). Ithaca, NY: Cornell University Press.

Braun, E., & MacDonald, S. (1978). *Revolution in miniature.* New York: Cambridge University Press.

Bright, C. (1978). *The jet makers: The aerospace industry from 1945 to 1972.* Lawrence, KS: University Press of Kansas.

Cushman, J. (1988, October 19). Bigger role urged for defense department in economic policy. *New York Times*

DeGrasse, R. (1984). The military and semiconductors. In J. Tirman (Ed.), *The militarization of high technology* (pp. 77–104). Cambridge, MA: Ballinger.

Dobbin, F. (1987). The Institutionalization of the state: Industrial policy in Britain, France, and the U.S. Unpublished doctoral dissertation, Stanford University, Department of Sociology.

Evans, P. B., Ruescherneyer, D., & Skocpol, T. (1985). On the road toward a more adequate understanding of the state. In P. Evans, D. Rueschemeyer, and T. Skocpol (Eds.), *Bringing the state back in* (pp. 347–366). New York: Cambridge University Press.

Fox, J. R. (1974). *Arming america: How the U.S. buys weapons.* Cambridge, MA: Harvard University Press.

Gorgol, J. F. (1972). *The military industrial firm: A practical theory and model.* Prepared for publication by Ira Kleinfeld. New York: Praeger.

Hammond, P. Y. (1961). *Organizing for defense: The American military establishment in the twentieth century.* Princeton, NJ: Princeton University Press.

Hazewindus, N., & Tooker, J. (1982). *The U.S. microelectronics industry: Technical change, industry growth, and social impact.* New York: Pergamon.

Hooks, G. M. (1991). *The battle of the Potomac: The mid-century transformation of the U.S. political economy.* Urbana, IL: University of Illinois Press.

Linvill, J. G., & Hogan, C. L. (1977). Intellectual and economic fuel for the electronic revolution.In P. H. Abelson & A. L. Hammond (Eds.), *Electronics: The continuing revolution* (pp. 23–30). Washington, DC: American Association for the Advancement of Science.

Melman, S. (1970). *Pentagon capitalism: The political economy of war.* New York: McGraw-Hill.

Millis, W. (1956). *Arms and men: A study in American military history.* New York: Capricorn.

Mowery, D. C., & Rosenberg, N. (1982). The commercial aircraft industry. In R. R. Nelson (Ed.), *Government and technical progress: A cross-industry analysis* (pp. 101–61). New York: Pergamon.

Peck, M. J., & Scherer, F. (1962). *The weapons acquisition process: An economic analysis.* Boston: Harvard University, School of Business Administration.

Pfeffer, J., & Salancik, G. (1978). *The external control of organizations: A resource dependence perspective.* New York: Harper & Row.

Poulantzas, N. (1975). *Classes in contemporary capitalism.* London: New Left Books.

Quinn, J. (1960). Aircraft. In L. Plum (Ed.), *Investing in American industries* (pp. 300–341). New York: Harper.

Rae, J. (1968). *Climb to greatness: The American aircraft industry, 1920–1960.* Cambridge, MA: MIT Press.

Scherer, F. M. (1971). The aerospace industry. In W. Adams (Ed.), *The Structure of American Industry* (pp. 335–379). New York: Macmillan.

Smith, P. M. (1970). *The air force plans for peace, 1943–1945.* Baltimore: Johns Hopkins University Press.

Snyder (1956). *History of production problems during the Air Force buildup, 1950–1954.* Wright-Patterson Air Force Base: Office of Information Services.

Stanford Research Institute. (1963). *The industry-government aerospace relationship.* Menlo Park, CA: Stanford Research Institute.

Stekler, H. (1965). *The structure and performance of the Aerospace industry.* Berkeley, CA: University of California Press.

Tilton, J. E. (1971). *International diffusion of technology: The case of semiconductors.* Washington, DC: Brookings Institution.

Tirman, J., (1984). Conclusions and countercurrents. In J. Tirman (Ed.), *The militarization of high technology* (pp. 215–236). Cambridge, MA: Ballinger.

Tyson, L., & Zysman, J. (1983). American industry in international competition. In L. Tyson & J. Zysman (Eds.), *American industry in international competition* (pp. 15–59). Ithaca, NY: Cornell University Press.

U.S. President's Air Policy Commission. (1948). *Survival in the air age.* Washington, DC: Government Printing Office.

U.S. Smaller War Plants Corporation. (1946). *Economic concentration and World War II.* Washington, DC: Government Printing Office.

Utterback, J. M., & Murray, A. E. (1977). *The influence of defense procurement and sponsorship of research and development on the development of the civilian Electronics Industry.* Cambridge, MA: MIT Center for Policy Alternatives.

Weidenbaum, M. (1973). Industrial adjustment to military expenditure: Shifts and cutbacks. In B. Udis (Ed.), *The economic consequences of reduced military spending* (pp. 253–288). Lexington, MA: Heath.

White, G. T. (1980). *Billions for defense: Government financing by the Defense Plant Corporation.* University of Alabama Press.

New Towns-In-Town

The Limits of Centralization*

Martha Derthick

8

---

editor's introduction:

Methodological Significance

This selection provides another example of a multiple-case study, the events taking place at seven locations—the Fort Lincoln neighborhood of Washington, District of Columbia; Clinton Township (in the greater Detroit region), Michigan; Atlanta, Georgia; Louisville, Kentucky; San Antonio, Texas; New Bedford, Massachusetts; and San Francisco, California. All seven were part of the same federal program, and the case study uses the experiences at the seven sites to draw conclusions about the program as a whole.

The design and analysis of the broader case study does not follow any intensive presentation of the individual cases, as in the preceding two selections. Rather, Martha Derthick's selection shows how to cite integrated evidence from multiple cases, while also building an overall explanation for the single federal program's outcomes. The author then tries to generalize her findings about the program as a whole,

---

*Editor's Note: Excerpted with light editing from "The Limits of Centralization," in *New Towns-In-Town*, by Martha Derthick. The Urban Institute, Washington, DC, pp. 83–102. Copyright © 1972. Reprinted with permission of The Urban Institute. For the sake of brevity, several footnotes in the original text have been omitted.

claiming implications for parallel experiences with other initiatives.

Offering such an integrated cross-case discussion, instead of dwelling on the single cases, presents case study authors with a creative option: Your entire case study may be based on a similarly integrated discussion—chapter after chapter—without including the single cases as part of the text. Using this option, a common practice (also followed by Derthick) is to present the individual cases in abbreviated fashion only (e.g., as part of an appendix to the text).

From a design standpoint, Derthick's seven cases happen to reflect a natural variation, and her overall explanation must account for differences among the cases (e.g., Fort Lincoln vs. Atlanta and Clinton Township, vs. the rest). Other multiple-case designs could have selected cases serving as "replications" of each other or as direct contrasts with each other. Whatever the choice, note that the multiple-case designs are analogous to multiple-experiment designs. In neither situation are the results from the selected cases (or experiments) simply tallied to arrive at the general findings. Rather, cross-case findings, as with cross-experiment findings in the natural sciences, depend on building explanations or arguments—with both likely to be strengthened through connections to citing relevant literature and theory.

Substantive Note

The substantive argument, in Derthick's study, is the inability of the U.S. federal government to influence local events, even when the underlying economic principles appear sound. Such inability has become a repeated finding of research on federal programs in local communities—whether the programs deal with housing, education, criminal justice, job, or other functions common to the local public sector. Not all programs fail, but for programs to succeed, they may have to be designed to embrace the political reality of the structural relationship between federal and local governments.

The conclusions from Derthick's study do not differ substantially from those of Pressman and Wildavsky's study of implementation (see Chapter 5 of the anthology). Ironically, the conclusions from both studies might be contrasted with those of the preceding selection by Gregory Hooks (Chapter 7), which suggested a potentially strong federal influence in industrial planning. You might use these three studies as the start of a new set of "cases," now part of a larger, "mega" multiple-case study, to explain the role of the federal government in American life. You also could use these studies as background citations to complement your own original cases on the matter. An interesting research question is whether the amount of funds devoted to a federal program may, in fact, be part of the explanation for its success or failure.

Four years after the start of the surplus lands program, only 120 units of housing had been built. At Fort Lincoln, where this housing stood, no other construction was underway. In Clinton Township, 160 units were being built. In Atlanta, a developer was ready to start, but was being delayed by a citizen's suit. In Louisville, approval had only recently been received from the board of aldermen. In San Antonio, New Bedford, and San Francisco, the projects had been cancelled. This chapter analyzes why the program produced so little.

Failure resulted mainly from the limited ability of the federal government to influence the actions of local governments and from its tendency to conceive goals in ideal terms. Both of these disabilities are associated with its place as the central government in the American federal system.

To achieve many of its domestic purposes, including community development, the federal government relies on local governments. However, because of the division of authority among governments in the federal system, the federal government cannot order these governments to do anything. It gets them to carry out its purposes by offering incentives in the form of aid, which they may accept or not, and by attaching conditions to the aid. To achieve results, federal officials must have enough knowledge of local politics to perceive which incentives are necessary; they must supply the incentives in sufficient quantity; and they must direct the incentives to those holders of local power whose support is required to achieve the federal purpose. In short, they must intervene successfully in local politics. They were unable to do this in the surplus lands program.

Limited Knowledge

The President's distance from local politics made it difficult for him to analyze the housing problem from the perspective of local officials, and to calculate the advantages and disadvantages of housing development as they would. "He did not understand," one of his aides later said, "what a mixed blessing low-income housing was for the cities."

The President [Lyndon B. Johnson] and his staff believed that housing construction for the poor had run into trouble locally because of objections from those who would be displaced by development or from those whose neighborhoods the displaced would invade. If local officials were supplied with vacant land, they could produce housing. This analysis overlooked the extent to which objections arose from persons whose neighborhoods would be invaded by development, and it overestimated the desire of local governments to house the poor. What defeated the surplus lands projects locally was not different from what has defeated other attempts to build low-income housing: the preference of local officials for types of development that will yield more tax revenue; their reluctance to act in the face of specific, intense opposition; and the absence of organized support.

This flaw in conception might have been corrected as the program passed from the White House into the hands of the executive departments. HUD [the U.S. Department of Housing and Urban Development], where experience with urban development programs was concentrated, might have been sensitive to the prospect of resistance or indifference at the local level. However, rather than assessing the effectiveness of the means the program would employ, HUD concentrated on objectives of development; its first act was to prepare development standards. It took the basic means of bringing development about—offers of surplus land at low prices—as given. Federal officials generally assumed that these offers would be very effective.

That HUD formulated the objectives to call for model communities did not significantly alter the local officials' estimate of the federal proposal. It still required a large amount of housing for the poor, and—on top of that—race and class integration, superior public services, and technological innovation. Because development in these cases was to occur on a large scale, often on vacant land in remote parts of the city, local officials were probably more concerned than usual about having to develop public services, especially transportation and education. Otherwise, there was probably nothing that distinguished local resistance to these projects from resistance to other proposals for housing the poor. For the purpose of this account, which is to analyze the failure of a federal program, the main point is that federal officials failed either to anticipate these forces or to counteract them.

Because conditions affecting development (e.g., the availability of federal land, the content of state laws, local experience with development programs, the leadership ability of the mayor, and the responsiveness of the city government to the interests of the poor) could vary greatly from place to place, it might be argued that HUD would have found it very difficult to make in advance a general estimate of the program's prospects. It would have to judge the conditions in each city. In fact, this is what the department did, but even case-by-case it was unable to calculate the prospects of success correctly. It was unable to evaluate accurately the local officials' expressions of interest. It also was unable to anticipate either the development of local opposition or the willingness and ability of local officials to deal with opposition.

Again, distance from the scene and detachment from the conduct of local affairs were handicaps. HUD's central office had to rely for information on what planning teams and regional officials reported. They in turn had to rely on local officials, whose statements were often misleading. If the mayor of New Bedford said that he had the votes he needed in the city council, how were federal officials—those in Washington especially—to know better? To judge the prospects for local success required a very sophisticated system for gathering political intelligence, which HUD lacked. Besides, not even the most sophisticated intelligence system could have forecast accurately the amount, source, and timing of opposition. How could anyone have known that the Atlanta project, which had met no neighborhood opposition in four years, would be stalled at the last minute by a citizen's suit? . . .

The Limited Stock of Aid

That the supply of federal incentives was limited was a second cause of failure. To induce local governments to accept the burden of developing new towns-in-town, the federal government had to give them something of value. The President assumed that low-cost surplus land would be available for this purpose, but this assumption turned out to be wrong.

Under pressure from the White House to put a program together in a hurry, administrative officials had jumped to the conclusion that the federal government could sell surplus land at a low price. However, lawyers from the executive agencies revised this assumption when they studied the question more carefully. In fact, sale at less than fair market value would have required a change in federal law. Having launched the surplus lands program on the assumption that it needed no new legislation, the Administration thereafter would not ask for any. HUD officials had to content themselves in 1968 with submitting one minor amendment for clearance by the Bureau of the Budget, a bill that would have facilitated below-market-value sales in a limited number of cases. The bill was never sent to Congress.

The program still might have been saved if local officials had been much interested in saving it. Even without a reduction in land price, the program gave local governments help with land assembly and relocation.

Also, federal ownership of the land would relieve a developer of the interest charges and taxes normally incurred between the time of site acquisition and construction. If they had wanted to use the federal sites for housing, local officials might have asked Congress to help by authorizing disposal at less than fair market value. As of 1969, they were showing much interest in getting federal land cheaply for industrial development, but not much in getting it for housing. The surplus lands projects had aroused so little interest locally that few ever reached the point of land transfer and thereby encountered the obstacle of land cost.

Even if the federal government had been able to offer the incentives the president thought it could, HUD might not have been able to make the program work. It is not clear that land at a reduced price would have elicited the amount of local support that was necessary to realize the president's or HUD's objectives. A still more powerful incentive would probably have been required—perhaps free land, combined with very large subsidies for housing construction and for public facilities and services.

The Limited Uses of Aid

A third cause of failure was the limited ability of the federal government to use effectively such incentives as it possessed. Because it depended on local officials to be the agents of its purpose, whatever flaws there were in the local officials' ability to act effectively—to gather public support, to overcome opposition, to assemble an administrative organization—were liabilities for the federal government as well.

HUD tried to direct local governments to create their own support. At Steiner's suggestion, planning teams were supposed to urge the mayor to set up an "advocate force" in the city. Political support, however, rarely is generated by pure artifice. Where little support existed, a directive from HUD to the mayor could not create it. Besides, the mayor would do what HUD asked only if he were eager to have its aid. In the surplus lands program, the offer of aid was itself problematic, and the terms—creation of a model new community, containing much housing for the poor—were not very appealing. Local officials, therefore, were not amenable to federal direction. . . .

As the Johnson Administration neared an end, HUD resorted to a threat to withhold funds. . . . That HUD felt it necessary to resort to this technique shows how poor the federal government's stock of influence [can be]. In view of the federal origins of the project, the threat amounted to saying, "We are so anxious for you to hurry with what we want you to do that if you don't hurry, we will prevent you from doing it at all."

In the end, the Administration did not withhold funds; on the contrary, the mayor extracted additional funds from it as the price of producing a groundbreaking by the Administration's deadline. He bought off citizen opposition with federal money.

In summary, one explanation for the failure of the program is that it lacked local support, or, more precisely, enough support to outweigh opposition. The federal government was unable to anticipate this problem or to overcome it once the program was underway. Federal administrators could not control what happened in local politics because they had too little knowledge of it, too little right to intervene, limited resources with which to intervene, and limited ability to manipulate the resources they had.

This explanation applies well to the cancellation of projects in San Antonio, New Bedford, and San Francisco, the delay in Louisville, and much of the delay in Project One in the District of Columbia. Conversely, the existence of local support explains the *relative* success of projects in Atlanta and Clinton Township, which progressed with reasonable dispatch to the point at which construction might be started. These cases taken together suggest the proposition: The greater the local support for a project, the greater the likelihood of success.

In both Atlanta and Clinton Township, organizations with the backing of the municipal government (the Atlanta Housing Authority and MDCDA respectively) were prepared to promote development. In both, especially in Atlanta, the local organizations got strong support from the federal regional office. Local initiative was necessary in both cases to bring about federal as well as local action.

The federal government depends on local initiative to overcome some of its own disabilities, especially lack of coordination. For a local development project to be carried out requires specific contributions of support from various components of the federal government—in an extreme case, from Congress, several executive departments, and several operating units within HUD. At least in the surplus lands program, the federal government was unable to achieve coordination from "the top down"; instead, coordination had to come from "the bottom up," through the appeals of local officials. The lobbying activities of the director of MDCDA illustrate this process, although because they were not very successful, they do not illustrate it very well.

The trouble with the proposition stated thus far—that the degree of success depended on the degree of local support—is that it does not very well fit the leading case, Fort Lincoln. Development in the District of Columbia, with the partial exception of Project One, did not founder on local politics. Local officials as of 1969 wanted to go ahead with the new community project, and, despite the distractions of the citizen participation issue, no local interests were objecting. Some other explanation is required for the failure of Fort Lincoln.

The Inflation of Objectives

A final cause of the program's failure, which had more effect at Fort Lincoln than elsewhere, was that federal officials had stated objectives so ambitious that some degree of failure was certain. Striving for the ideal, they were sure to fall short. Worse, striving for the ideal made it hard to do anything at all.

The Fort Lincoln project got stalled mainly because neither federal nor local officials believed that the development plan was feasible. This plan, however, was quite faithful to the development guidelines that HUD laid down. If the plan would be very difficult to carry out, that was because the goals would be very hard to achieve.

The goals of the surplus lands program were defined by HUD officials and consultants to HUD who were chosen to represent professions involved in urban development. The only local public official among them was the city manager of Tacoma, Washington, who was named because he was president of the International City Management Association. Logue, as principal development consultant for the pilot project, confirmed and elaborated the goals. He was chosen . . . not for any experience with the District of Columbia, but, rather, for skills that presumably were applicable anywhere in the country and commensurate with the demands of the pilot project of a national program. Whereas execution of the projects depended on local politics and administration, conception of the program and the definition of goals were independent of local activity; they occurred at the federal level. The planners of the surplus lands program and particularly of the Fort Lincoln project sought to serve ends that would be of at least symbolic value to the whole society. Their impulse was to create a community that would be a model for urban society in the second half of the twentieth century. They assumed that different social classes and races could be integrated through a shared attachment to a place and the symbols, lifestyle, and activities associated with it. With an emphasis on "participation" and "decentralization," they also sought to set new styles in social action. And they sought innovation in every aspect of planning, design, and development. In the end, this freight of social significance proved too much for Fort Lincoln to bear. The effort to achieve integration through community yielded a plan of high cost and great complexity. The quest for innovation further inflated objectives and produced a host of economic, technical, and political problems in the final plan.

Why, it may be asked, was the Fort Lincoln project particularly frustrated by the planners' striving for the ideal?

To some extent, the program as a whole was handicapped. The difference between Fort Lincoln and other projects was simply the point at which frustration occurred. In other places, activity stopped before the planning stage. Learning of the program's goals, especially racial and class integration, local officials decided against participating or, having decided to participate, later had to give up in the face of opposition. Fort Lincoln, as the pilot project, had greater momentum, and got far enough along to embody the general objectives in a specific plan.

A second explanation is that, outside of the District of Columbia, HUD proved willing to compromise its objectives for the sake of achieving action. This was what happened in Atlanta. But in the District, Logue was pursuing HUD's objectives with independent commitment, and the high visibility of the project made compromise difficult.

Comparing the Fort Lincoln and Atlanta cases, it is tempting to assert that the closer local adherence was to HUD's objectives, the less likely it was that development would actually occur. However, this proposition ignores the case of Clinton Township, where MDCDA, fully sharing HUD's goals, progressed to the point of construction.

The optimum situation, from HUD's point of view, was that which was obtained at Clinton. There, a development agency—a private, nonprofit corporation in this case—had a high degree of autonomy at the local level and shared HUD's goals. In effect, MDCDA was a local "model new communities" agency, committed to technological innovation, provision of housing for the poor, and other leading elements of HUD's guidelines. If such agencies had existed in all local places, and if they had had much authority and scope for action, the prospects for the surplus lands program would have been much better.

Federal Disabilities: The Federal Government as Social Activist

In summary, the surplus lands program failed both because the federal government had limited influence at the local level and because it set impossibly high objectives. Its goals exceeded by far its capacity to achieve them.

These causes of failure cannot be dismissed as peculiarities of the program. To be sure, it was peculiar in its impulsive origin and improvised character, but it arose because President Johnson and his aides in the White House believed that other federal programs, especially public housing, were failing. It was designed to make them work better. The failure of the surplus lands program probably reveals something about the failure of the other programs.

Fundamentally, the program failed because of characteristics of the federal government that are associated with, and to a degree are inherent in, its central position in the governmental system. These characteristics are the scale of its jurisdiction and its separation from the actual execution of domestic programs. Separation, in turn, results from the division of authority among governments in a federal system and the distance between the "top" and the "bottom" level of government hierarchy in a large, complex society. . . .

If the flaws described here are inherent in the federal government, it may be asked why all federal domestic programs do not fail. How do any survive and achieve their purposes? What distinguished the surplus lands program from those that succeed?

One answer is that the degree of federal dependence on local government varies from one domestic function to another. Community development is extremely dependent on local initiative and thus extremely vulnerable to the vicissitudes of local politics.

The peculiar origins of the surplus lands program did handicap it. More than most federal programs, it was centrally conceived. Not only did it originate exclusively at the federal level, but also within the federal government, it received no consideration from the legislature, where local interests are formally represented. Within the executive branch, federal officials at the regional level did not participate in the planning of it, nor were local officials invited to do so. Those officials in the White House and HUD who did plan it did so in great haste, without themselves making a careful attempt to take local interests into account. . . .

Federal programs often [can] "work" at the local level—that is, they survive and make progress toward federal goals—because in the usual case an adjustment between the federal program and local interests is worked out. This is an elaborate process, beginning when a federal legislative proposal is formulated and continuing as it gets enacted and administered. Often it is a very time-consuming process. Some federal programs—urban renewal, for example—start very slowly, and pick up momentum only after the original enactment has been amended many times to make it of use to local interests. Years may pass before the program develops a local constituency whose supporting activity will help it to flourish.

No federal programs succeed totally. In the process of adjustment to local interests, purely "federal" purposes are compromised: Ideals expressed at the federal level are revised to suit local realities. Yet the adaptation is not on the federal government's part alone. Federal action does influence what happens on the local level, with the net result that domestic programs are neither "federal" nor "local," but a blend of the two.

The surplus lands program failed because it was too centralized; it did not incorporate the necessary adjustments to local interests. Perhaps no federal program that seeks to build housing for the poor through the agency of local governments can succeed on a large scale. The federal purpose in this case may be so at odds with the prevailing local interests that no compromise can be worked out that will satisfy the federal purpose very well.

Granting that the surplus lands program suffered from federal disabilities at the local level and from inflated objectives, it might be argued—contrary to the position taken here—that these handicaps are not inherent in federal action. For instance, some might say that the failings were those of the federal chief executive or of a progressive administration. Still others might say that failure occurred not because the program was too centralized, but because it was not centralized enough.

Within the federal government the program was purely presidential, and it suffered from the inability of the president to elicit the necessary support from other elements of the government—Congress and the executive agencies—and then to coordinate them so as to make federal action as effective as possible at the local level. If these other parts of the government had been more responsive to the president's direction (Congress, of course, was not even asked to respond) the program would have had a better chance. . . .

Section III

Quantitative Evidence and "Embedded" Units of Analysis

Implementing an Education Innovation* 9

Neal Gross, Joseph B. Giacquinta, and Marilyn Bernstein

editor's introduction:

Methodological Significance

The case study method is not limited to any single type of evidence (or data). Both qualitative data (e.g., categorical or nominal data) and quantitative data (e.g., ratio and ordinal data) may be relevant and may come from different data-collection techniques (e.g., surveys, use of archival records, documentary evidence, direct observations in the field, focus groups, and ethnographies). Your own case study may call upon a combination of these techniques and a combination of qualitative and quantitative data. In fact, the

*****Editor's Note:** Abridged and edited from Chapter 5 of *Implementing Organizational Innovations: A Sociological Analysis of Planned Educational Change*, by Neal Crasilneck Gross, Marilyn Bernstein, and Joseph B. Giacquinta. Basic books, New York, NY, 1971. Copyright ©1971. Reprinted with permission of Basic Books, a division of Perseus Book Group. To make the selection clearer, the summary from the original chapter has been moved to the beginning of the text, and the verb tense of a few words changed so that the summary now serves as an introduction to the rest of the selection. Similarly, to make the text easier to follow, the material on quantitative findings originally appeared in a later portion of the chapter and has been moved forward in this selection, but with no substantive changes.

more that your case study relies on different types of evidence that triangulate or converge on the same findings, the stronger it will be. Doing case studies therefore requires you to be familiar with the techniques for collecting different types of data.

The present selection illustrates the use of detailed observational evidence in an educational (classroom) setting. The observations cover both qualitative and quantitative dimensions. Similar observational evidence can be an important part of any case study, not just education research. The desired procedures include having: (1) an observational instrument; (2) a scheme for coding the resulting observations; and (3) most often neglected in case study field methods, an awareness of the representativeness (or nonrepresentativeness) of the sample of times and places when the observations are being made. The care with which the selection describes its observational procedures and data deserves to be emulated by others who do case studies.

The selection represents but one chapter from a single case study, which covers an entire book. The other chapters in this book, not reproduced here, report about additional types of evidence and help to create a strong evidentiary base for the case study.

Substantive Note

The case study is about a new instructional practice or "innovation" (the *catalytic role model*) that was tried in a single elementary school (the "case"). The selected material covers a key part of the case study—the extent to which teachers were implementing the innovation. The evidence shows that they were not. The chapter therefore contains the critical data for addressing the book's central finding—that implementation was not occurring, even though other chapters show that the school had a history of successful innovation.

The findings and the book contributed substantially to the then-newly-emerging study of "implementation." Since then, scholars have come to recognize that uncertainties in the implementation process may lead innovations to fail or succeed.

This contrasts with the earlier research that only focused on the presence or absence of organizations' active resistance to change. Such an insight may seem obvious today. However, at the time that the book was published, scholars had overwhelmingly attended only to the initial adoption of innovations, overlooking how they were actually implemented in organizational settings. As a result, the case study may be considered a major contribution to the study of the implementation of innovations.

Summary

We [find] in this chapter that the educational innovation, the catalytic role model, announced in November was not being implemented in May despite a set of apparently positive antecedent and prevailing conditions in the school system, community, and school. After a brief discussion of the rationale underlying the evaluation methods employed, we [present] the data-collection and data-reduction procedures used to determine the extent to which the teachers had changed their performance in the classroom from a traditional role definition in November to behavior that conformed to the catalytic role model in May. Analysis of the evidence gathered [shows] that the staff, in May, was still behaving for the most part in accord with the traditional role model, and was devoting very little time to trying to implement the innovation; moreover, we [present] evidence that showed that the staff's performance, when efforts were made to conform to the catalytic role model, was of low quality. These findings [lead] us to conclude that the degree of implementation of the innovation in May was minimal.

Evaluation Rationale

... Our definition of the degree of implementation of an organizational innovation ... has reference to changes in the organizational behavior of members. We contend that even for the most technological of organizational innovations—for example, closed-circuit television—their introduction and presence in a school provides no evidence about the degree of their implementation. We maintain that teachers must exhibit new behavior patterns *before* it can be said such innovations are actually being implemented. Moreover, the implementation of the organizational innovation under examination, the catalytic role model, required not only that teachers perform many new tasks, but also that they no longer behave as they previously did in their classrooms. Therefore, the assessment of the degree of implementation in May [also] required gathering data about the extent to which the teachers no longer behaved in accord[ance] with the traditional role model. . . .

We examined the degree of implementation of the innovation from two perspectives: (1) the *quantity* of time teachers devoted to trying to implement the new role model and (2) the *quality* of their performance during this period of time. The measurement of the quantity of innovative effort required assessing the proportion of classroom time that teacher behavior conformed to the traditional teaching pattern: teacher-directed, group instruction of single subjects in blocks of time. The measurement of the quality of their innovative effort necessitated assessing the extent to which nontraditional teacher behavior conformed to the new catalytic role model as indicated by a set of 12 behavioral indices that are specified later in this chapter. . . .

Before we present and interpret the data it is necessary to specify the kind of evidence that we decided would lead us to conclude that there was a maximum or minimum degree of actual implementation. If the evidence revealed that the classroom performance of all the teachers during the assessment period was consistently high on the 12 behavioral indices, we would then assess the degree of actual implementation as maximum. On the other hand, the degree of actual implementation would be assessed as minimal if we found that most teachers were spending nearly all of their time behaving according to the traditional model. If we found that the quality of effort that was made to conform to the new role model was high, but little time had been devoted to attempts to carry out the innovation, it would be appropriate, we reasoned, to judge such behavior as minimal implementation. Furthermore, if the quantity (of innovative effort of most teachers was high but the quality of their performance was low, this too would represent minimal implementation in most cases, but not in this case. We reasoned that because the innovation involved a major change in role performance that had been proposed only six months prior to the assessment, we could not legitimately expect all teachers to be performing in accord[ance] with *all* the specifications of the new role model. But we reasoned that it would be possible for all teachers to be making maximal efforts to do so. That is, they could be continually trying to behave in conformity with the new, not the traditional, model.

For our purposes, therefore, we would treat such a finding as a successful implementation effort, although we were aware that it would not constitute an example of maximal implementation unless the quality of performance was also high.

Data Collection Procedures

Two general ground rules were specified for the classroom observations in order to minimize the possibility that chance fluctuations in the daily classroom behavior of teachers and systematic observer bias would contaminate the implementation assessment: (1) the fieldworker must spend a number of weeks observing classrooms, and (2) [the fieldworker] must conduct the observations in a randomized and unannounced order. The first was carried out by setting aside three weeks, from April 24 through May 12, for classroom observations related to the assessment. The second could not be carried out as easily. The observations of the classrooms by the fieldworker prior to the period of assessment and statements made by teachers during the formal interviews revealed that many of them were not devoting large blocks of time each day to efforts to implement the new model. Consequently, observations of classrooms on a completely randomized basis during the three weeks' set aside for classroom assessment might not provide the fieldworker with the opportunity to observe adequately the quality of some teachers' performance in connection with the innovation.

To minimize this possibility, the fieldworker asked each teacher for his/her weekly schedule in order to obtain some indication of when the teacher planned to make efforts to implement the innovation. This information allowed [the fieldworker] to rearrange [the] schedule of classroom visitations. . . .

These procedures and the observer's presence in classrooms did not appear to have any significant influence on the performance of most teachers. This is not to say that [the fieldworker's] presence in the school had no influence on teacher behavior. That it did is evidenced by the following situations: (1) one teacher informed the fieldworker that another teacher told the pupils days in advance of the observer's classroom visit, "an important visitor will be coming in, and when he/she does you should be quiet, do not move around too much, and no fighting!"; (2) a teacher-in-training told [the fieldworker] that one teacher gave her pupils explicit instructions to remain at what they were doing when the fieldworker visited the class unless they received permission . . . to do other things. Moreover, during [the fieldworker's] visit, this teacher insisted on talking continually to the fieldworker rather than interacting with the pupils; and (3) another teacher revealed to the fieldworker, after [visiting] the class several times, that she told the children about his probable visits and asked them to be "extra nice the next time he came." Evidence to be presented later indicates, however, that minimal implementation existed in each of these three classes; therefore, whatever the bias caused by the observer's queries and presence, they did not materially influence the teacher's performance, and, therefore, did not materially influence the findings of the assessment.

The following procedures for collecting data were used during the three-week period of observing classrooms. To assess the *quantity* of innovative effort, the observer monitored all classrooms daily to determine whether teachers were making any efforts to alter their traditional role performance. This involved making daily rounds throughout the building to observe classrooms. Each round included a "spot check" for each class and usually took two to three minutes. The number of daily spot checks varied for each class; their frequency was determined by the activity in which the teacher was requiring the class to engage and the extent to which the fieldworker sensed it would continue before a possible shift might occur. As many as 15 checks were made on some classes and as few as five for others; overall during the three-week period nearly 500 spot checks were made.

To determine the quantity of innovative efforts made by teachers, we observed whether teachers were making "traditional or innovative efforts" during the spot check; we employed the following ground rules: If the teacher was directing the group as a whole, or requiring the students to sit at their desks and to engage in the same activity, this was interpreted as evidence that the teacher was behaving according to the traditional role, and thus was not trying to implement the catalytic role model. Any time it was apparent that the teacher was permitting the children to work individually, or in small groups on different subjects, or allowing them to move freely about the room, this was interpreted as teacher effort to implement the new role model, and thus, as "innovative effort." The fieldworker noted on a daily record . . . whether the teacher's behavior at the time of observation reflected performance in conformity with the traditional or the new role model.

Extended observations in the classrooms were conducted to measure the *quality* of the implementation effort. Since the observer's very presence might have influenced teacher or student behavior, the following steps were taken to minimize this possibility. When entering a room the fieldworker made himself as inconspicuous as possible by finding the most obscure corner from which to observe. In taking notes he jotted down key phrases or events to help him remember afterwards what had happened during the class period. When the observation ended he would go to a quiet place in the building to complete the observation schedule . . . First, he would write down as much as he could remember about the physical arrangement of the room and the interpersonal activities that had taken place in it; then, after reviewing all of the evidence, he reported his observations on the teacher's behavior on each of the 12 behavioral criteria listed below, using a five-point scale (from "not at all" to "completely"). Did the teacher:

1. Make the materials existing in the room available to students?
2. Arrange the room into work areas?

3. Utilize the room according to these work areas?
4. Permit students to choose their own activities?
5. Permit students to decide whether they want to work individually, in pairs, or in groups?
6. Permit students to move freely about the room?
7. Permit students to interact with each other?
8. Permit students to decide how long they want to remain at a particular activity—that is, move freely from one activity to another?
9. Move about the room?
10. Work with (as) many individual(s) or groups (as possible)?
11. Try to act as a guide, catalyst, or resource person between children?
12. Try to act as a guide, catalyst, or resource person between children and the materials?

These 12 behavioral indices used in evaluating the extent to which teachers were making efforts to behave in accord with the catalytic role model deserve further comment.

Since teachers could vary on how well they performed different role requirements, they were assessed on each of them. They, therefore, could vary in the number of the 12 criteria to which their behavior would or would not conform; for example, a teacher could "permit students to move freely about the room" and "arrange the room into work areas" but not meet any of the remaining criteria; another could conform to five or all of the 12 criteria. . . .

. . . Observations were conducted in eight classrooms: four primary classrooms, two regular intermediates, one special intermediate, and the art room. The fieldworker visited one primary, one intermediate, the special, and the art room three times each, spending on the average two hours of observation time in each class. Observations were carried out four times in another primary room and the second intermediate room; nearly three hours of observations were carried out in each of these rooms. In the remaining two primary rooms, it was possible to schedule visitations that lasted an hour in one case, and one-and-a-half hours in the other. In total, over 21 hours were spent observing, in-depth, the quality of staff performance with reference to its conformity to the new role model. During the three weeks devoted primarily to this aspect of the assessment, most of the fieldworker's remaining time was spent monitoring classrooms to assess the quantity of the staff's performance.

To obtain a measure of the reliability of the fieldworker's data would have required that another observer be present in classrooms during the period of assessment. This was not done for two reasons. First, at the time of the assessment visitors were continually in the building and classes; another observer would have added to the already high degree of resentment that we noted teachers had toward outside visitors. Second, we reasoned that an additional observer would interfere with the high degree of rapport that the fieldworker had established with the teachers during the earlier part of the school year. To check on the accuracy of the fieldworker's observations, we decided to use data from other sources, namely, data that we would obtain during formal and informal interviews with the teachers, teachers-in-training at the school, and subject specialists.

Findings

... The *quantity* of innovative effort made by each teacher was calculated in the following manner: the amount of time recorded in minutes that [was] spent each day performing according to the traditional model was divided by the total minutes of classroom time that were available to the teacher. ... The data are summarized in daily, weekly, and overall per-centages in [Exhibit 9.1] ... for the total staff. [Ed.'s Note: The original text also included individual tables, with similar breakdowns, for each individual classroom that was observed.]

... If we view percentage scores of 76–100 percent as very high innov-ative effort, 51–75 percent as moderately high, 26–50 percent as moder-ately low, and 0–25 percent as very low effort, the findings [in Exhibit 9.1] reveal that: (1) general overall teacher innovative effort, quantitatively, was

By Class and by Week	Minutes Available	Minutes Monitored	Traditional Role Model Behavior (in Minutes)	Traditional Role Model Behavior (in Percent)	Catalytic Role Model Behavior (in Percent)
By Class:					
Primary #1	3250	3090	2350	76.05	23.95
Primary #2	3000	2880	2820	97.92	2.08
Primary #3	2750	2690	2330	86.62	13.38
Primary #4	3250	3180	2870	90.25	9.75
Intrmdt #1	3250	3250	1945	59.85	40.15
Intrmdt #2	3250	3190	3000	94.04	5.96
By Week:					
April 24–28	7250	7165	6145	85.76	14.24
May 1–5	4500	4355	3710	85.19	14.81
May 8–12	7000	6760	5460	80.73	19.22
Grand Total	18750	18280	15315	83.73	16.22

Exhibit 9.1   Amount of Classroom Time Devoted by the Staff Performing in Accord With the Traditional Role Model and the Catalytic Role Model (by Class and Week)

very low (16 percent); (2) the weekly overall school efforts were very low (14 percent, 15 percent, 19 percent); (3) with one notable exception (Intermediate #1) overall individual classroom efforts were very low; (4) a few daily (and fewer weekly) efforts in individual classrooms were moderately low [Ed.'s Note: The referenced data for this and the next point are from the tables for individual classrooms, not presented in this text]; and (5) only four daily efforts, all in Intermediate #1, could be judged moderately high. No daily classroom effort was ever very high. . . .

The evidence thus reveals that during the three-week assessment in May the staff as a whole was devoting most of its time (84 percent) to behavior that tended to conform to the traditional role model and that it was giving minimal time to efforts to implement the catalytic role model.

. . . To demonstrate how the *qualitative* assessment was made for teachers, we will present abstracts of two in-depth observations made by the fieldworker of the Intermediate #1 teachers, who exhibited the greatest quantity of innovative effort in their classroom . . . :

April 24 observation (11 A.M. to 12 noon): The general overview Two teachers were in the room with 24 children. The classroom was quite noisy, and small group and individual activities were in evidence. The two teachers allowed a number of children to work with microscopes on such things as human skin, hair, and saliva, permitting some to remain all period, others to leave early, and others to join later; up to eight children were involved at one time, at other times only two. [One teacher,] Stan visited the group four times. [The other teacher,] Linda, for a large part of the period (about 25 minutes), coordinated the efforts of four girls drawing a large map in connection with a social studies unit; at other times she "talked" to the two or three children who were either reading independently or working on math problems. Stan also walked among students to some extent, but did not make contact during the period with a large number (10–13) of the 24 children in the room. Along with the use of microscopes, reading, working on math, and map making, teachers allowed a noticeable number of children to engage in "gaming"—for example, playing cards, Peggity, and Clue were several of the activities. Neither teacher approached a hard core of seven to eight children who became involved in this sort of activity, and who did not switch from it while I was there during the observation. There were four boys who did not use any of the materials in the classroom and created a number of disturbances by playing tag, punching and shoving each other, and then running close to either Stan or Linda to avoid being caught by the others. However, neither teacher tried to encourage them to become interested in doing other things. Stan, losing his temper twice, did send two of the four downstairs to the office the second time. The lunch bell ended the period.

April 24 observation (11 A.M. to 12 noon): The specific evaluation[1]:

1. Neither teacher placed any restrictions on using materials available in the room; both teachers were therefore rated as high on permitting use of available materials.
2. The room was arranged into science, reading, and drawing areas, so both teachers were rated as high on room arrangement.
3. Both were rated as moderate on utilization of room. The science area was being used for science; however, both teachers allowed children who were playing cards there to remain. The teachers also permitted the reading area to be used for playing games and for children to talk about TV programs. The art area was in fact not used as such; the teachers permitted everything to be pushed back to make room for some of the card players.
4. Both were rated as high on permitting student choice of subjects. Neither placed restrictions on the children other than those who were "horsing around" and even then they were not stopped by Stan, except for two students who began to fistfight.
5. Both were rated as high on permitting students to choose with whom they wanted to work. However, Stan was slightly more restrictive than Linda; he talked to a number of students, admonishing them to "do your own work," "don't ask him for help, do your own thinking." Linda, more passive, allowed the children to do what they wanted to do without comment. Neither encouraged children to interact in order to learn from each other.
6. Stan was rated moderate on permitting movement and Linda was rated high, since Stan stopped a number of students whom he thought "weren't doing much" and were "bothering others" from moving about, whereas Linda did not say anything with respect to these matters.
7. Because Linda did nothing to inhibit interaction among the children while Stan actually admonished a number of children who were interacting by demanding that they do their own work, and restricted others who were in his eyes "fooling around," Linda was rated as high on permitting students to interact with each other and Stan, moderate. Neither encouraged children to interact.
8. Again, Linda did nothing along these lines to inhibit the children while Stan wanted quite a few (7) of the children to start working, especially those of whom he would say "they're flitting about from one thing to another" or "they're doing nothing to settle down to get some work done, this isn't just a play period"; Linda was rated as high and Stan, moderate.
9. Both teachers spent about half the time during the observation moving about the room. But neither attempted to get to all children. The other half of the time they simply stood and watched unless some child came to them and initiated the interaction with a question or a plea for help. Both were rated "moderate."

10. Of the time spent moving about, Stan interacted more with different groups and individuals. Linda did very little. Stan was, therefore, rated "moderate," Linda as "low."

11. & 12. Stan was very restrictive; for example, at the microscopes he would issue directives such as "That's enough with the hair; put the slide with saliva on," "It doesn't take all day for you to look at the skin." He asked questions, but they were not of a probing nature. Linda was much more passive and didn't ask any questions to which children could react or which led them to ask additional questions. The teacher interaction with children did not indicate efforts to act as catalysts either between children, or between children and materials. Both teachers, therefore, were rated low on their efforts to act as catalysts between children and materials or between children.

The numerical equivalents for these ratings are presented in the first and second columns of Exhibit 9.2. Stan is coded as "A" and Linda as "B." Exhibit 9.2 also summarizes the performances of Stan and Linda at three other points in time; it reveals that the behavior of each of these teachers was highly consistent at each of these points in time. [A similar tally of the ratings for all the observed individual teachers suggest] . . . two findings of special interest. . . . The first is that during those periods when the teachers did make some attempt to implement the innovation, most engaged in activities that required them to expend little effort, permit[ting] their pupils to use all materials in the classroom, . . . permitting students to interact, [and] allowing students to move freely in the classroom. . . .

The second finding is that most teachers did not try to act as catalysts or guides during the period when they were making innovative efforts. . . . The data . . . thus reveal that during the time when teachers made efforts to implement the innovation, they generally did little more than allow their pupils to do what they wanted to do, short of physical harm to each other, or directed the children in multi-activities. The majority (six out of 10) paid little attention to the room arrangement, and most were unconcerned about how they could maximize space in their rooms (eight out of 10), or about steps they could undertake to serve as catalysts to pupil learning (nine out of 10). In short, the staff exhibited, qualitatively speaking, a minimal degree of implementation of the catalytic role model. . . .

Our assessment of the overall *quality* of innovative effort thus revealed that it consisted primarily of the teachers' insertion into traditionally scheduled, self-contained classrooms varying "chunks" of free time for their pupils each week. During these periods we found little evidence of behavior reflecting the basic notion of teachers serving as "catalysts." Most teachers used these periods essentially as "free play" sessions, periods when children were free to do as they wished, short of harming each other; they did little more than see to it that their pupils did not get hurt and when

Criterion	April 24 (60 min.)		April 28 (60 min.)		May 1 (45 min.)		May 12 (60 min.)		Overall Rating	
	A	B	A	B	A	B	A	B	A	B
1. Make available all materials	3.00	3.00	3.00	3.00	3.00	3.00	3.00	3.00	3.00	3.00
2. Arrange room into areas	3.00	3.00	3.00	3.00	3.00	3.00	3.00	3.00	3.00	3.00
3. Utilize the areas	2.00	2.00	—	3.00	1.00	1.00	1.00	1.00	1.36	1.36
4. Permit choice of subjects	3.00	3.00	3.00	3.00	3.00	3.00	3.00	3.00	3.00	3.00
5. Permit choice in number of learning mates	3.00	3.00	3.00	3.00	3.00	3.00	3.00	3.00	3.00	3.00
6. Permit free movement	2.00	3.00	3.00	3.00	3.00	3.00	3.00	3.00	2.73	3.00
7. Permit student interaction	2.00	3.00	3.00	3.00	3.00	3.00	3.00	3.00	2.73	3.00
8. Permit shift in activities	2.00	3.00	3.00	3.00	3.00	3.00	3.00	3.00	2.73	3.00
9. Teacher movement in room	2.00	2.00	1.00	1.00	1.00	1.00	1.00	3.00	1.62	1.62
10. Interact with students	2.00	1.00	1.00	1.00	1.00	1.00	1.00	3.00	1.62	1.00
11. Try to act as a catalyst between children	1.00	1.00	1.00	1.00	1.00	1.00	1.00	1.00	1.00	1.00
12. Try to act as a catalyst between child and materials	1.00	1.00	1.00	1.00	1.00	1.00	1.00	1.00	1.00	1.00

Exhibit 9.2 Profiles of Ratings for Intermediate #1 Teachers (A and B) for Each Period of Observation and Their Overall Ratings

a. Blanks in April 28th observation due to insufficient data. Code: 1 = low, 2 = moderate, 3 = high

b. Average score adjusted for differences in lengths of observations.

activity time ended, they resumed their traditional schedules. Teachers, in short, tended to behave as guards rather than guides. They failed to use this time to enrich a child's educational experience. . . . Therefore, we conclude that the quality, as well as the quantity, of the innovative effort of teachers in May was minimal.

Evidence from other sources supports our two major assessment findings: (1) that teachers devoted only a small proportion of their time to efforts to perform in accord[ance] with the new role model, and (2) that their performance when they made such efforts was of low quality. . . . In light of this body of evidence that corroborates data obtained by systematic techniques used in the classroom observations by a trained observer, we feel confident in the findings and conclusions of our assessment.

Note

1. The original five-point rating scales were collapsed for this analysis: "1" and "2" were set equal to "1"; "3" equal to "2"; "4" and "5" equal to "3." Therefore, in the discussion and statistics that follow, 1 = low, 2 = moderate, and 3 = high.

Union Democracy

10

The Internal Politics of the International Typographical Union*

Seymour Martin Lipset, Martin A. Trow, and James S. Coleman

---

editor's introduction:

Methodological Significance

Case study evidence can involve more than multiple types of data and data-collection techniques. In addition to including both qualitative and quantitative data, the evidence can cover two different levels of analysis—a main unit (the "case") and a subunit (embedded within the overall case). In the present selection, three well-known social scientists show how a single unit of analysis (an organization) can be the main subject of study but also contain subunits (a random sample of 434 employees in the organization) that also are important parts of what may be called an "embedded" case study. How to deal with analyzing data and generalizing about the collective unit can pose far greater challenges than analyzing data and

---

generalizing about the subunits. A further challenge is to connect the findings between the larger unit and the subunit as part of the same case study.

The three investigators first describe how they conducted a case study of a single trade union, over a four-year period (1950–54). Although occurring over 50 years ago, the experience still provides a solid, concrete example of how a major organizational study itself needs to be organized. The selection begins by describing the origins of the study in relation to the investigators' earlier work and interests. You may derive some insight into how research topics "germinate" from this description.

A second part of the selection then goes into an extensive methodological discussion of the problem of dealing with a single-case study along with its subunits. The issues raised and the strategies used by the investigators continue to be appropriate for contemporary case studies. For example, the authors discuss having a tentative *model* of the organization's political system as one alternative for organizing the entire case study (a strategy not different from the use of "theory" highlighted by Selections 3 and 4 of this anthology) or of "logic models" (see Selection 11). Thus, even 50 years later, this case study has invaluable lessons for anyone wanting to do a similar kind of case study.

Substantive Note

This chapter is about the organization of a single trade union, the International Typographers Union, chosen because of its distinctive, internal democratic structure—in this case taking the form of a unique, two-party system within the organization. The case study's central objective is to explain the origins and workings of this two-party structure.

As a large organization, such a democratic structure differs from the more commonly found bureaucratic oligarchy that, at the time, marked other unions but also to this day mark all large corporations and bureaucratic offices. The case study therefore serves, in the authors' words, as a "deviant" case that demonstrates the viability of a very important, alternative form of organization.

This book is a detailed study of democracy in a single trade union, the International Typographical Union. This union, alone among North American labor organizations, has maintained a two-party political system (much like that existing in national politics) for over half a century. The study deals with many aspects of the political life of the ITU: the history of the unique two-party system; the behavior of the union members, in and out of the shop; the way in which leaders are recruited; the reasons why their power over the union does not become absolute; the way members become interested in union politics, and the reasons why they are sufficiently concerned about the government of their union to keep it democratic. Basically this book is designed to explain why the ITU has managed to maintain a system of democratic self-government for generations.

But an understanding of the democracy of the ITU is only the proximate aim of the study. The workings of democracy in a union, in other voluntary organizations, or even in the state itself are not so dissimilar that the understanding of democracy in one situation will not help us to understand it (or its absence) in another. A larger objective of this book, therefore, is to illuminate the processes that help maintain democracy in the greater society by studying the processes of democracy in the small society of the ITU.

History of the Study: Research as Process

The study is based on data gathered over a long period of time, by diverse methods, and from many sources. Chronologically, it has moved through four phases, each marked by different concerns and characterized by different methods of collection and treatment of data.

Phase I: Definition of the problem and initial explorations. The study first began to take shape in 1949 and early 1950. The senior author for various personal and professional reasons had for some years been interested in the ITU's unique two-party system and internal democracy. As early as 1943, while still a graduate student, he had written a term paper on the subject, and in 1949, while a member of the faculty of the University of California at Berkeley, he began to study the union in greater detail and more systematically.

His preliminary investigations involved an examination of the literature on printing unionism, together with an inspection of the publications and voting records of the ITU itself. He also held some exploratory interviews with informed members of the ITU locals in the San Francisco area. It was in this period that the basic problems of the study crystallized: on the one hand, to explain the unique characteristics of the ITU's internal politics, as they appeared in sharp contrast to the internal politics of other trade unions here and abroad; and on the other hand, to consider these democratic internal processes in the ITU as a crucial deviant case challenging the powerful body of organizational theory stemming from Michels' development of his "iron law of oligarchy" in private organizations.

During this period, a critical review of various hypotheses which had been put forward by students of trade-unionism to "explain" the ITU's unique internal political arrangements indicated that no one of the factors so far cited was adequate to account for the phenomenon. At the same time certain other factors in the union, occupation, and industry emerged which had been ignored, up to that time, but which appeared to better explain the persistence of the union's internal democracy than many of the factors cited earlier. Among these new elements was the large and important role played by the printers' "occupational community." The preliminary formulation of hypotheses that might account for the ITU's internal political system—hypotheses based on a qualitative analysis of union documents and exploratory interviews—was particularly reported in an article written at the time.

Phase II: Elaboration and respecification of the problem through qualitative analysis. In the second phase, beginning in the fall of 1950, when the senior author came to Columbia University, through the fall of 1951, the exploratory work begun at Berkeley was extended and deepened. During this period a systematic study of the history, and especially the political history, of the ITU was undertaken, based largely on primary sources. This work was facilitated by the existence of a special collection of primary materials on printing and printing unionism in the library of Columbia University. In addition, the fact that New York City is the center of the printing industry in the United States and home of the ITU's largest local, Big Six, which has had a long and lively political life of its own, made available large numbers of active and informed union members for exploratory interviews.

Aside from long exploratory interviews with key informants in the union, members of the research team . . . familiarized themselves in every way possible with the actual political life of the union, attending union meetings, party caucuses, and chapel meetings, while paying particular attention to the events preceding the local union election held in May 1951.

The additional knowledge and insight gained during this period led to a sharpening and respecifying of hypotheses. This thinking was reported in an article dealing with the historical origins and the contemporary structural supports of the union's political system. These ideas formed the study design that was carried out in the next phase.

At this point it seemed that certain crucial aspects of the internal political process of the ITU could best be studied through survey research methods, and moreover, that such a study could be feasibly carried out among the members of the New York local. A proposal to that effect was written, setting forth the problems on which such an effort would focus. The outlines of a study design were also included in the proposal. Financial support was gained for this additional major effort of field research.

Phase III: Design of the study and the field problem. During the fall of 1951 the important task of gaining the consent and at least tacit support of both political parties active in the New York local was accomplished. Simultaneously, an interview schedule embodying the major theoretical and substantive ideas that had emerged to date was constructed, tested among members of Big Six, revised, tested again, again revised, and finally administered to a sample of Big Six members. . . .

This schedule had built into it questions designed to produce quantitative data bearing on most of the factors and variables which the preceding years of preliminary and exploratory work had suggested might be relevant to an understanding of the nature and processes of the union's unique political system. Thus we asked questions not only about the respondent's sentiments and loyalties in union politics but also about his/her attitudes toward a variety of extra-union social and political issues. . . .

At the time the schedule was designed we did not by any means anticipate all of the implications and findings that would and did flow from the data we were aiming to collect. Nevertheless the inclusion of many questions bearing on the printer's informal relations with other printers, both at work and during leisure time, was not a happenstance. Besides our previous sensitization to the importance of the union's "occupational community" for its politics, several lines of theory and research in sociology and social psychology had already given clear evidence that knowledge of . . . informal social relations is a prerequisite to any clear or adequate understanding of . . . behavior in any of the formal organizations to which [people] belong or in which they are employed. The classic studies by Roethlisberger and Dickson in the Hawthorne plant of Western Electric had been followed by many other studies in industrial sociology which also emphasized the importance of primary-group relations and the "informal organization" to the workings of a formal organization. In other traditions the work of Moreno and his followers and of Kurt Lewin and the "group dynamics" school he fathered had produced much evidence on the crucial importance of small primary-group relations to an understanding of the actual processes that go on within formal organizations. And just about the time we were considering the relevance of these factors for our study, George Homans's *The Human Group* summarized and reanalyzed a number of studies bearing on the same general problem.

So far as we knew, a systematic concern for small-group processes and informal social relations had not been incorporated into any studies of trade-union organization or behavior. But at the time we designed our study, the small group and informal social relations as special areas of focus were clearly prescribed by the considerable body of recent solid empirical work done on related subjects, and they became integral parts of our research design and analysis. And if the directive of contemporary research and theory in other fields had not been enough, our own preliminary explorations, and especially the identification of the printers' "occupational community" as a crucial element in the union's political life, were additional reasons for incorporating related questions into the schedule.

While the interview schedule was being constructed, we decided on a stratified random sampling method, with shop size defining the several strata, as the best way of choosing an accurate representative sample of Big Six members. At the same time it was decided to interview an additional sample of shop chairpersons, in order to have comparative data on a larger number of these especially important men than would be included in a wholly representative sample. Interviewing these shop chairpersons also provided better information on the structure of the union as a whole than would a simple random sample. A total of 500 interviews was projected, of which 434 constituted the representative sample, and 66 the added sample of chapel (shop) chairpersons.

During the winter of 1951–52 the interviews were conducted with the aid of the facilities and technical assistance of Columbia's Bureau of Applied Social Research. In addition, it was decided at that time to carry through a separate and independent series of intensive, "focused" interviews with substantially all of the active political leaders in Big Six. These included both party and nonparty persons, in and out of office. An interview guide for this series was constructed, and these interviews, some 35 in number, each taking from two to five hours, were conducted during the winter and spring of 1952.

Phase IV: Follow-up studies, the analysis of data, and the writing of the report. With the bulk of the fieldwork completed, the interview data were coded . . . and preliminary analysis of the quantitative data began in the spring of 1952. At that time, the forthcoming election of ITU international officers in May suggested the possibility of the conversion of our sample into a "panel" for the collection of data bearing on certain crucial aspects of the union's political process. Reinterviewing of the whole sample was out of the question for many reasons, but a short mail questionnaire with two follow-ups, aimed particularly at learning how our respondents voted in that international election, elicited a response of over 70 percent of the original sample. These data were also . . . [coded] in the summer of 1952 while preliminary analysis of the interview data proceeded. Finally the national presidential election in November 1952 suggested an effort to gain additional comparative data on the voting behavior of our sample (or panel members) in a national election. Three mailings of a post-card questionnaire elicited a 55 percent response.

The period from the fall of 1952 through the spring of 1954 was devoted to the intensive analysis of a great part of the qualitative and quantitative data gathered in earlier phases, and to the writing of this report. During this period, special problems arising in the course of analysis and writing required the collection of certain additional data—for example, a detailed breakdown of voting in past ITU elections by locals. But the only adequate summary of this final phase of the work is this book itself.

Methodology

The methodological aspects of this study are challenging. Some are problems that will recur with increasing frequency in social research, and in view of this fact are worth discussing in some detail. . . .

When an empirical analysis of a single case (in this instance, the typographical union's political system) is to be carried out, it can be of either of two general types, as follows:

(a) Description and explanation of the single case, to provide information concerning its present state, and the dynamics through which it continues as it does. This may be called a *particularizing* analysis.

(b) The development of empirical generalizations or theories through the analysis of the single case, using it not to discover anything about *it* as a system but as an empirical basis either for generalization or theory construction. This may be called a *generalizing* analysis.

The crucial element that distinguishes these two types of analysis is the way they treat general laws and particular statements about the single case. The first kind of analysis uses general laws or regularities to carry out the analysis of the particular case, much as a metallurgist utilizes his knowledge of general chemical properties in analyzing a sample of ore. That is, particularizing analysis uses previously known generalizations to help make particular statements. Generalizing analysis is the reverse of this: Much as a biologist focuses his microscope on a living and growing fruit fly to make generalizations about processes of growth, the social scientist in this kind of analysis attempts to utilize the particular case in developing general statements. The particular statement and the general law trade places in these two types of analysis. In the former, the law is used to aid in making particular statements; in the second, the particular statements are used to develop the law.

Both types of analysis have long and honorable traditions in the social sciences, as they have in the natural sciences. . . .

The present analysis is not clearly in either of these categories; it always attempts to be in the second, though it sometimes goes no further than the first. Many statements refer to the ITU rather than to organizations in general; however, at the same time there is usually implicit extension to organizations other than the ITU.

Because it is the second kind of analysis that is attempted here (though not always with success), [three] problems specific to this kind of analysis arise in the study.

1. Multiple-level analysis: The problem of units and properties. In an analysis of the second kind, a generalizing analysis, several requirements arise that a particularizing analysis need not meet. An important one is the necessity of delineating *units* of analysis and characterizing the units according to certain general *concepts* or *properties.*

If, as is possible in a particularizing analysis, nothing more than a vivid picture is to be given of the system being analyzed, this problem need not arise. A faithful recording of events as they occur can fulfill the task of the particularizing analysis, much as a documentary film does, without once using general sociological concepts. But to make generalizations that may be applied to other organizations, general sociological concepts must be used. In the present analysis, this means characterizing several different "sizes" or "levels" of units. The employee; his/her immediate social environment (e.g., . . . shop), the local, and the ITU as a whole comprise a minimum set of units. In this study, the union as a whole was characterized in terms of certain structural and environmental properties: for example, the degree of stratification in the occupation, the political structure of the union, the issues that have existed at various times, the union's policies, and the kind of employer attitudes toward the union.

It was necessary to characterize the New York local by these same kinds of variables. For example, the difference in types of policy problems at the local and international levels was documented. This was related to an important difference in voting behavior . . . (i.e., the predominance of wage-scale problems in local politics leads to interest voting which often unseats the incumbent). . . .

The kinds of observations made and the properties by which the various units were characterized are indicated in Exhibit 10.1, which summarizes the aforementioned discussion. The kinds of properties by which these units were characterized are listed in the cells of the table. This table suggests the complexity of the analysis, for properties in each cell must be related to those in other cells in propositions or generalizations.

This complexity raises a number of problems in the design of a study. Some of the most important of these, in the present study, were those related to the interview data. These data were perhaps the most important in the study. It was a primary means of characterizing at least three of the units in the analysis: (1) The population of the New York local union as a whole, in order to make statements like: "X percent of the members are good friends with other printers off the job;" (2) the immediate social environment of the individual . . . ; and (3) the individual. . . .

KINDS OF DATA

UNIT BEING CHARACTERIZED	Total System	Intermediate Units		Individuals	
	Issues, Data on Occupation; Union Laws; Policies; Historical Data; Convention Reports	Locals' Histories and Voting Records; Issues on Local Level; Size of Locals	Shops' Voting Records; Shop Size	Interviews With Leaders	Interviews of the Sample of Man
ITU as a whole	Structural, environmental, behavioral properties	By inference: communication network (structural)			
Locals	Behavioral properties (militancy, etc.)	Behavioral properties, size	By inference: communication network (structural)	Structural, environmental, behavioral properties	
Shops			Behavioral properties, size		Distribution of individual properties
Other immediate social environment of men	The social climate, by inference from dominant issues and election outcome	The social climate, by inference from dominant issues and election outcome			Chapel chairman's attributes; friends' attributes
Men	By inference: dominant values and interests	By inference: values, interests, and loyalties (e.g., local over international)	By inference: values, interests, loyalties (e.g., to shop over local)	By inference: values	Behavior, background, values, attitudes

Exhibit 10.1 Types of Data Gathered, Types of Units Being Characterized, and Types of Resulting Properties

This study is weakest in its characterization of the immediate social environment. We could have attempted explicitly to characterize shops by interviewing all or almost all the persons in them. . . . But such concentration would have been made at the expense of other gains: Interviewing more people in each shop would have meant interviewing each person less thoroughly or covering fewer shops, thus gaining knowledge about shops at the expense of knowledge about either individuals or the union as a whole.

What this really means is that not all values can be maximized at once. Also, studies such as the present one must include in their design a decision as to which of the units is the most important to characterize with the interview data . . . the experience of the study suggests that in a single case analysis like this, it is more important to characterize the individual and his/her immediate social environment than to characterize the union itself, that is, the single case being analyzed. . . .

2. *Multiple-level analysis: Relations between different units.* The second major problem concerning units at different levels is the problem of relating them by means of generalizations. This problem is an important one, for it is such generalizations that are the fruits of the analysis. The problem in its simplest aspects may be posed in this way: Certain properties of one unit (e.g., the total union) are determinants of behavior at another level (e.g., the individual). Yet how is it possible to really bridge the gap between the units? For example, to say that a certain political climate characterizes the union does not mean that this climate is felt by all printers. The climate makes itself felt more strongly by some people than others, depending on their social and political locations. . . .

We previously noted that relating two different levels is the simplest case of the general problem. This certainly is true, for even if we succeed in relating properties of diverse social units to a person's vote decision, this is not the end of the analysis. The aim of this study is to be able to make statements about political systems as wholes, not statements about the determinants of individual vote decisions.

What we have done in focusing on this individual vote decision has been to enter the system at a particular point and to work outward. . . . But is this the best strategy for analyzing a social or political system? The point at which we entered is probably a very important one in the system, but would it have been better to proceed differently? For example, by having a tentative *model* of the political system, . . . the way is pointed toward certain *variables* or concepts (which are simply the properties as outlined in Exhibit 10.1) and certain *processes* that seem important in the operation of the system. Only one of these processes concerns the vote decision; others concern the policy decisions of the administrative leaders, and the decision of the oppositionists or potential oppositionists.

Perhaps the best mode of analysis, given that the aim is to analyze the system as a whole, would be to start with a crude model . . . and to focus on each of the processes postulated in that model. An example of the way that such an analysis would be of aid is the following: The model indicates that one important decision point in the system is the president's policy decisions. In particular, it suggests that to know the constraints placed by the organization on the president is important. Thus it directs one to ask such questions as: What restrained Scott (the ITU president) from sending in strikebreakers to New York in 1919? And why was George Berry, the pressmen president (who did send in strikebreakers for the same strike by the printing pressmen) not restrained in the same way?

If we had focused in this study on the several decision points, and on the communication processes, rather than entering the system at a particular point, the results might have been far superior to those obtained. However, this is a matter as yet unresolved, and we intend only to raise the question: What is the most advantageous way to carry out a study of the dynamics of a social or political system?

3. *The paradox: How to generalize from a single case.* Another difficult problem arises in studies of organizations or social systems rather than individuals. Often, only a single case is analyzed, as is done here. This is in strong contrast to the usual statistical procedure with studies of individual behavior, where the number of cases is relatively large. The fact that the present study includes a sample of individuals from the union, and that part of the analysis is one of individual behavior, must not be allowed to confuse this issue. Clearly in this study these individuals are not themselves the focus of the analysis; it is the union as an organization that is the center of interest. This focus on a single case rather than the statistical study of individual behavior implies a quite different kind of analysis [an internal analysis rather than a comparative analysis]. . . .

A comparative analysis seeks to develop . . . generalizations in the obvious manner, by comparing occupations that differ with respect either to the independent or the dependent variable and then testing whether they also differ with respect to the other variable. The "internal analysis" attempts to establish the same generalization in one of two fashions:

1. It uses variations that occur *within* the system, either (a) over a period of time (e.g., at one time, there was stratification between a politically important group of Mailers and the majority, typographers; at the same time, rigid cleavage between these groups occurred); or (b) between different parts of the system (e.g., while there is little stratification within the union as a whole, there is economic stratification between officers and employees; this creates issues between the membership and the administration. . . . The internal analysis thus substitutes variations within the one system for variations between systems). . . .

2. An internal analysis can operate in a different way. By going behind the overall generalization to the processes through which it is presumed to exist, the internal analysis may validate the generalization by validating these processes. For example, the previous generalization, relating economic stratification to the rigidity and intensity of political cleavage, can be either observed to hold true statistically or built up through more fundamental generalizations, to wit: (a) the economic motivation is an overriding one, which will be a very strong determinant of one's decision if economics are involved; (b) the policy decisions in a stratified union involved economic matters which will differentially affect persons at different economic levels. By proving that these two statements are true, one can prove, by inference, the original statement about stratification and rigidity of cleavage. Thus internal analysis, which, in some cases, cannot directly prove a generalization, may prove it by indirection through proof of the generalizations underlying it.

An internal analysis will not ordinarily be as exhaustive of the important elements that affect a particular variable as will a comparative analysis—simply because certain things are invariant for the single system as a whole. Certain kinds of issues may never occur in this union, though they occur in others; certain aspects of the particular system are so invariant that situations common in other systems are simply absent in the ITU. These invariances can lead to overgeneralization. . . .

But except for these difficulties, it seems that internal analysis has no great disadvantages with respect to comparative analysis. It may, in fact, have one important advantage: By taking simple comparative correlation out of the reach of the investigator, it focuses his attention on the underlying processes that operate within the system. In this way the internal analysis may lead to a deeper explanation of the phenomenon and to generalization of a more fundamental kind.

But regardless of whether an internal analysis has more advantages or disadvantages with respect to a comparative analysis, it is important to realize that these two kinds of analysis of organizations both exist in social science, and a choice must be made between them in any research. The problem that begs for resolution here is the problem of spelling out the two different logics of analysis for these two methods, and of providing diagnostic indicators that will tell the relative merits of the two methods for a particular research problem.

These three problems discussed here seem to be of increasing importance as social research moves from description into analysis, and as it moves from focus on individuals to a focus on social units: voluntary organizations, the social system of communities, industrial plants, and so on. We have not attempted to give answers to the problems, but only to state them, in the hope that this will stimulate a search for the answers.

Testing the Basic Logic of the Chicago School Reform Act*

Anthony S. Bryk, Penny Bender Bebring, David Kerbow, Sharon Rollow, and John Q. Easton

---

editor's introduction:

Methodological Significance

This selection demonstrates how case studies can even include rather advanced quantitative analyses. In so doing, it reinforces the definition that a case study can rely on qualitative or quantitative data, calling upon any number of analytic techniques. The definition is to be contrasted with other renditions of the case study method, which tend to limit case studies to either qualitative data or a subset of field techniques.

Essential to understanding the methodological importance of this selection is that, again as with other chapters in this

---

*Editor's Note: Excerpted, with minor edits, from "Testing the Basic Logic of the Chicago School Reform Act," in *Charting Chicago School Reform: Democratic Localism as a Lever for Change*, by Anthony S. Bryk, Penny Bender Bebring, David Kerbow, Sharon Rollow, John Q. Easton. Westview Press, Boulder, CO, pp. 195–211. Copyright 1998 by Perseus Books Group. Reproduced with permission of Perseus Books Group in the format Textbook via Copyright Clearance Center.

anthology, the selection comes from a book whose entire subject is a single-case study (reforming the Chicago public school system). Other parts of the book include qualitative data about the district and also about the individual schools in the system, which are an embedded unit of analysis within the larger case study. (A large public school system such as Chicago's has hundreds of schools.) Analyzing the data about such embedded units also can create a need for using quantitative techniques.

The analysis presented in the present selection—structural equation modeling—is based on school data. The resulting "path analysis model" is a quantitative counterpart to qualitative "logic models." Important to note is that, had the selection been the entirety of the original study, it would have been but an example of a quantitative study, not a case study. The advanced nature of the quantitative analysis also should suggest how case study investigators (or teams) should have a diverse methodological capability.

Substantive Note

The reform and improvement of large urban school systems has been a major challenge for the past two decades. The urban systems enroll a large proportion of all students in the country's public schools. However, the systems tend to have fewer resources even though they serve students with greater needs, compared to suburban or smaller school systems.

In Chicago, a major change occurred in the 1980s when a new law (PA 85–1418) was passed to implement local school councils, embracing school-level community participation and governance. The case study (represented by the entire book) is about the initial years of the reform effort. The selected portion of the case study focuses on the main hypothesized sequence whereby reform is claimed to produce the desired outcomes, investigating the presumed linear relationship among: (a) expanded democratic participation, (b) systemic organizational changes in the school system, and (c) instructional improvement.

A First Look at Testing the "Logic of Reform"

We now turn to formally testing the key propositions embedded in Chicago's school reform. Our first approach involves descriptive comparisons across the types of school governance, organizational change, and instructional innovations introduced [elsewhere in the original book]. With this background, we then employ a path analysis as a final test of whether expanded democratic participation in Chicago leveraged systemic organizational changes that focused attention on instructional improvement.

School Politics and Organizational Change. Based on results from the case study synthesis [not presented in this selection], we anticipated three salient connections between the nature of school governance and organizational change.[1] First, we posited that adversarial politics would inhibit systemic school restructuring and lead to an unfocused approach to organizational change. This connection is based on the observation that sustained conflict within a school over basic issues of control tends to dominate the activity of all involved. This diminishes the opportunities for the cooperative efforts necessary to carry out meaningful school improvements.

Second, the case study synthesis also provided several examples in which consolidated principal power inhibited systemic improvements and led to unfocused changes. In the most extreme cases, principals blocked efforts to significantly alter the status quo. In other schools, with more reform-minded principals who "ran the show," teachers and parents tended to remain largely uninvolved in school reform and unengaged in collective discussion about change. Although principals can play a key role in catalyzing local initiative, ultimately more professionals and parents must be drawn in and remain involved if broad-based institutional change is to occur. In these case study sites, at least, this did not happen.

Finally, we found in the case study synthesis that in schools where strong democratic practices emerged, there was greater likelihood of systemic restructuring. This connection, the key premise of PA 85-1418, suggests that a political practice that engages a broad base of people, who have a stake in the local school and who sustain discussion about educational issues, can create valuable human and social resources to support meaningful school change.

Using the type classifications for school governance and organizational change identified [elsewhere in the original book], we now examine the linkage between a school's political practice and its organizational change efforts.[2] . . . Of the schools with adversarial politics, 70 percent reported unfocused approaches to school improvement. Only 9 percent of these schools reported systemic initiatives. Given the extent of conflict present in these schools during the first phase of reform, these results are not surprising. It is difficult to imagine how systemic efforts could emerge under such circumstances.

The results . . . also support the second hypothesized connection. Among the schools with consolidated principal power, 43 percent had an unfocused organizational approach. Another 31 percent of the schools reported some features of both unfocused and systemic activity, and the remaining 26 percent of the schools with consolidated principal power schools indicated systemic restructuring efforts.

The prevalence of systemic efforts reported here is actually somewhat greater than we had expected based on the case study synthesis. Two possibilities seem likely to account for these findings. First, in every indicator system, there is some measurement error that causes misclassification. Less-than-candid responses on the school surveys tend to inflate reports about the extent of desirable activities, such as how well developed the reform efforts may be. This results in a more favorable organizational change classification than a school might deserve.

Second, some of these schools are probably making a transition toward a strong democracy focused on emergent restructuring, and, as a result, the data reports are uneven. For schools that are at an early stage in the transformation from a hierarchical, control-oriented system to a commit-ment-oriented learning organization, principals may well use their con-siderable role authority to pull their institution toward more broad-based initiatives. . . . It is important to remember that school change is a process that occurs over time. The survey data only captured a snapshot of the process at a particular moment.[3]

Finally, we turn to the key premise of Chicago reform: that increased participation will promote systemic restructuring. The data . . . provide strong support for this idea. By far the greatest number of the schools with strong democratic politics, about 60 percent, report systemic restructuring efforts. An additional 24 percent show at least some features of systemic restructuring. In contrast, only 17 percent of the strong democracies indi-cate unfocused school improvements. These results provide our first broad-based evidence supporting the logic of Chicago school reform—enhanced democratic participation can be an effective lever for systemic organizational change. We note that the corollary is also true. Our evidence indicates that if school politics do not engender broad-based participation, fundamental changes in organizational roles and responsibilities are much less likely. . . .

A More Rigorous Test

On balance, it might still be argued that perhaps some factors other than school reform may account for these observed patterns. As noted earlier in the chapter, for example, some schools were making improvement prior to reform. Could this account for the aforementioned results? In particular, schools that began the restructuring process before reform, or introduced instructional innovations prior to reform, may have been in a better position to take advantage of the additional autonomy and resources connected to the legislation. It could be argued that the prior initiative of some schools had more influence on subsequent developments than the reform itself. Specifically, to evaluate adequately the contributions of strong democracy to systemic restructuring, and the contribution of both of these in turn to innovative instruction, it is essential that we take into account the level of pre-reform activity in the schools.

Another potential explanation for observed differences is that some schools served more advantaged student groups, and this accounted for the relative progress of these schools. We have already explored this topic [and] . . . found that [although] school background factors, such as racial composition or the percentage of low-income students, had some impact, they were not powerful predictors of strong democratic practices or systemic organizational change. Nonetheless, before we conclude that the Chicago School Reform Act actually catalyzed broad-based change efforts, it is important to take a closer look at all of these factors simultaneously in a single analysis.

A Path Analysis Model. For this purpose, we turn to a statistical technique called path analysis. This procedure allows us to separate out the effects of background characteristics and pre-reform restructuring activity from the key relations of interest in this study. The path analysis thus provides a more rigorous test of the linkages posited in the logic of reform. The aim of a path analysis is to identify the direction and magnitude of "paths," both direct and indirect, by which one factor is related to another, such as the connection between strong democratic practices and systemic restructuring. Importantly, path analysis allows us to take into account the fact that any relationship of interest sits within a network of many other relationships. For example, the emergence of a systemic restructuring approach is influenced both by the extent to which the school has adopted strong democratic practices and by other basic characteristics of the school, such as racial composition or school size. Path analysis permits us to assess the unique contribution of each factor, while simultaneously taking into account the other relationships that are also present in the data. Exhibit 11.1 displays the model used in our analysis.

Each numbered arrow in the figure represents the direct effect of a particular school attribute or some key aspect of Chicago's reform. Arrow 1, for example, depicts the relationship between basic school characteristics, such as a school's student mobility rate and the percentage of low-income students, and the adoption of strong democracy in the school. In parallel fashion, Arrows 2 and 3 represent the influence of these school

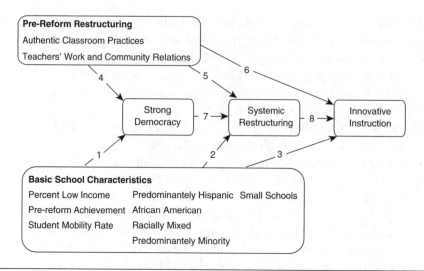

Exhibit 11.1   Analytic Model to Probe the Logic of Reform

characteristics on systemic restructuring and instructional innovation, respectively.

In parallel, a school's level of restructuring prior to reform may directly influence the extent that the school progresses in developing productive political relationships among the principal, teacher, and parent community. This potential effect is represented in Arrow 4. The nature of the pre-reform activity may also be a factor in the approach that the school takes to organizational change under reform. For example, a school that had established more collaborative work among teachers prior to reform should have more social resources to draw upon to pursue systemic restructuring under reform. Arrow 5 depicts this expected relationship. Similarly the degree of instructional innovation since reform is likely to build on the extent of such activities prior to reform. Arrow 6 portrays this relationship.

Our primary interest in the model, however, is with Arrows 7 and 8, which link strong democracy, systemic restructuring, and instructional innovation. It is here that we represent the key logic of Chicago school reform—strong democracy facilitates systemic restructuring, which in turn promotes the introduction of innovative instructional practices. Notice that we have not posited a direct relationship between strong democracy and instructional improvement. Instead, we argue that this relationship is indirect, mediated through the effect of school politics on organizational change. (The path analysis also allows us to test the validity of this proposition.) The key point is that the impact of basic school characteristics and pre-reform restructuring levels are taken into account in the model. Thus, not only are we able to judge the strength of the separate influences of these characteristics and levels, but also to control for any confluence that either may have with the relationships of primary interest. . . .

Results of the Path Analysis

Exhibit 11.2 presents the results. All of the [original] variables . . . are included in the model; however, only those with significant associations are actually joined by arrows or "paths." The numbers associated with each arrow are "standardized regression coefficients," and reflect the relative importance or magnitude of influence for each path.[4] We also note that, like analyses in previous chapters, the base for our examination is the 269 elementary schools whose test scores in 1989 were below national norms.

First, we consider the associations between basic school characteristics and the three key concepts of Chicago reform—strong democracy, systemic restructuring, and innovative instruction. As expected . . . , the prevalence of strong democratic politics is equitably distributed among the various types of elementary schools in the city. As the lack of significant paths indicate, basic background characteristics are only weakly predictive of strong democratic politics. In general these results reinforce [earlier] findings . . . where we found that strong democratic activity had emerged in almost every neighborhood of the City.

The only significant exception is in predominately Hispanic schools where strong democratic practices are more prevalent than average [see the path in Figure 11.2 whose coefficient is .190]. The case study

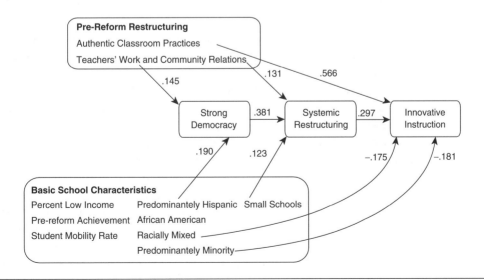

Exhibit 11.2 Path Analysis Model for the Logic of Reform

synthesis offers a possible explanation for this relationship. At several of the case study sites, which were Hispanic schools, an extensive array of productive ties existed among community-based organizations, churches, and other religious groups. The presence of these social resources in the school community appeared to contribute to the emergence of strong democratic governance. A base of positive social relations acted to strengthen participation in these schools and provided a supportive context for discussion of educational issues.

Next, we examine the direct influence of basic school characteristics on the adoption of a systemic restructuring approach. . . . Schools pursuing this approach were also quite diverse in their characteristics. . . . The extent of systemic restructuring is significantly related to only one basic characteristic: school size [see the path in Exhibit 11.2 whose coefficient is .123]. Small schools (with fewer than 350 students) were more likely to have a coherent approach to school improvement. Although school size does not have a direct effect on the nature of local school politics, it does appear to facilitate systemic organizational change. In general, smaller school size facilitates more informal social interactions among teachers, the principal, and other staff. In such a situation, it is much easier for a professional community to emerge that is committed to deep organizational changes. Here too, these statistical results are highly consistent with observations from the case study synthesis.

The direct impact of basic school characteristics on instructional innovation contains two significant "arrows." Both racially mixed and predominately minority schools tend to have fewer new instructional initiatives [−.175 and −.181]. . . . The internal diversity within these schools makes them more problematic contexts for reform and restructuring. Although these compositional factors were not significantly related to the likelihood of strong democracy and systemic change in the path model, they are directly linked to instructional innovation. In general, our case study synthesis suggests that the diversity of culture and language found in these schools creates organizational environments where even basic issues of social control can become challenging. Thus, the findings documented here, that these school communities engage in less instructional improvement, are not surprising.

We now turn our attention to the influence of pre-reform restructuring activity. As expected, we find strong positive effects for schools' initiatives taken prior to the formal implementation of the reform legislation. Elementary schools that had developed more dense ties with their parent community, as well as more cooperative working conditions among their teachers prior to reform, were more likely to pursue strong democratic practices under reform [.145]. Positive social relations at a school provide a foundation for the continued discussion of educational issues and for the facilitative leadership that is characteristic of strong democracy. Schools with previously established values and norms of inclusion are thus advantaged as they pursue a more collective and open approach to school decisionmaking. This does not imply, however, that schools that had not begun this process prior to reform were unable to establish strong democratic practices. Rather, they were just somewhat disadvantaged as they began.

This pattern is also evident as we focus on the impact of pre-reform activity on the nature of organizational change in an elementary school under reform. Positive social relationships in the school prior to reform contribute significantly to a systemic approach toward school improvement [.131]. In particular, the expanding roles for teachers, and the development of a more professional community that are key characteristics of emergent systemic restructuring, are supported by the pre-existing level of social capital in the school community. Thus, schools that had stronger social relations prior to reform were able to move further in their efforts toward focused organizational change under reform.

The final relationship of note, between an elementary school's pre-reform activity and instructional innovation, reveals a very strong association [.566]. Not surprisingly, schools that had begun to adopt more authentic classroom practices prior to reform expanded these practices after reform. Consequently, four years into reform, "best" instructional practices were more broadly employed throughout these schools than in those that had only begun the adoption process after 1988. In general, introduction of new classroom approaches requires time to diffuse throughout a school. Again, this does not imply that schools that did not address these aspects of instruction prior to the reform made insignificant changes. It only means that the level of implementation in those schools was not likely to be as extensive as in those that began at a more advanced starting point.

Of greatest importance, even after adjusting for these differences in school characteristics and pre-reform activism, the results in Exhibit 11.2 firmly support the primacy of the central connection between school politics, organizational change, and instructional improvement. The statistical link between strong democracy and systemic restructuring is especially strong [.381]. Constructive school politics play a central role in the school's adoption of a more focused approach toward organizational change. More specifically, strong democracy creates an environment in which all participants are able to voice their concerns. Subsequently, decisions are more likely to have a collective character that supports systemic change.

Similarly, the path analysis results indicate a strong influence of a systemic restructuring approach on adoption of innovative practices in the classroom [.297]. Elementary schools that approached organizational change in a systemic fashion—through altered roles, relationships, and broad strategic planning—were much more likely to have introduced classroom practices that make students active participants in the learning process. Even after controlling for pre-reform restructuring activities, systemic organizational change continues to be quite influential on the degree to which a school pursues instructional innovation. These results indicate that, even in schools with a disadvantaged starting point, positive organizational efforts created vital links to new classroom practices.

The nature of a school's political activity also played a role in the instructional improvement process; although, as the path analysis indicates, these effects work indirectly through the impact on organizational change. No direct linkage was found between strong democracy and instructional improvement.[5] To be clear, strong democratic politics is an important resource for school change. The actual impact on instruction, however, depends more directly on the development of a systemic restructuring that includes such key features as strategic planning, professional community, and strong school–community ties. Absent such organizational developments, strong democratic practice does not by itself stimulate greater instructional innovation.

Interestingly, the level of student achievement prior to reform did not have a direct effect on democratic practices, systemic restructuring, or the introduction of instructional innovation under reform. Although there is a significant correlation between pre-reform achievement and instructional innovation, this relation works through the amount of restructuring occurring in schools prior to reform. That is, prior to reform, authentic classroom practices were more likely to be found in higher-achieving schools.[6] After the reform, however, school-improvement efforts were more equitably distributed. Significant reform activities occurred in all levels of schools—both very low-achieving and relatively higher-achieving.[7]

In summary, the path analysis supports the general logic posited in Chicago's school reform. These results add further credibility to basic descriptive evidence presented in the earlier . . . case study synthesis . . . . Expanded local participation can be a very productive lever for systemic organizational changes that focus attention on instructional improvement.

The actual nature of these linkages, however, is quite complex. The fact that a systemic restructuring approach to school improvement is associated with the adoption of instructional innovations serves, at least, a dual role. First, a systemic change initiative leads schools away from simply adding peripheral programs. It encourages attention to the organizational core, which naturally leads to focus on instruction.

Second, a systematic change initiative also creates an environment in which more fundamental changes in teaching practice can take deep root. . . . Innovative practices take time and require substantial support to be implemented properly. These practices require significant new learning by teachers; they demand change not only in what is taught but also in how it is taught. In addition, they entail altering classroom management to fashion new roles and relationships among students as well as between teachers and students. As teachers move to transform their classrooms, they initially often experience frustration and failure. Support from colleagues, parents, and outside assistance groups is critical in sustaining teachers through this uncertainty. The emergent community among local school professionals, coupled with more positive school–community ties, can be a major resource in this regard.

Notes

1. Actually, we had a further hypothesis about maintenance politics being at least moderately linked to unfocused initiatives. However, because we were unable to develop a measure of maintenance politics, we could not test this directly. Many of the mixed-politics schools had some features of both consolidated principal power and strong democracy. In terms of the statistical connections between "mixed politics" and the organizational change types, 41 percent showed systemic improvement strategies with another 31 percent showing features of both unfocused and systemic efforts.

2. A Chi-squared test of independence was significant at the .0001 level. Thus, there was strong evidence of a general relationship between the type of political activity at the school and the school's organizational change efforts.

3. That these schools were in transition is at least partially supported by our data. In this sub-group of schools, a disproportionate number of principals (more than 50 percent) were new hires, who were at their school three years or less. Thus, many of these schools were experiencing a leadership transition and, perhaps, a change in their political and organizational arrangements as well. In contrast, for schools classified as having consolidated principal power and an unfocused organizational approach, only 38 percent had hired principals since reform.

4. The following table contains the full statistics for the path analytic model that appears in Exhibit 11.2:

Complete Path Model: Standardized Regression Coefficients

	Model 1 Strong Democracy	Model 2 Systemic Restructuring	Model 3 Innovative Instruction
Percent low income	.008	−.101	.102
High student mobility (>45%)	−.025	−.004	−.015
Racial Composition:			
Predominantly Hispanic	.190*	.020	−.080

(Continued)

(Continued)

	Model 1 Strong Democracy	Model 2 Systemic Restructuring	Model 3 Innovative Instruction
Predominantly African American	.023	−.053	−.147
Racially mixed	−.096	−.098	−.175**
Predominately minority	−.021	−.020	−.181*
Small school (<350)	.050	.123*	−.023
Pre-reform achievement (IGAP)	.036	−.139	.115
Pre-reform restructuring of teachers' work and community relations	.145*	.131*	−.056
Pre-reform authentic classroom practices	—	—	.566**
Likelihood of strong democracy	—	.381***	.061
Likelihood of systemic restructuring	—	—	.297***
R-squared	.068	.210	.461

N = 269 schools in the analysis.
*significant at .05 level; **significant at the .01 level; ***significant at the .001 level.

Models that regressed the endogenous variables of basic characteristics on the pre-reform restructuring measures also were run. Only two statistically significant relationships emerged. The percentage of low-income students was predictive of restructured school relations (at the .05 level, standardized coefficient = .235). A school's pre-reform achievement was statistically associated with the adoptions of authentic instructional practices (at the .05 level, standardized coefficient = .215).

5. The variable for the likelihood of a school being strongly democratic was included in the final equation. However, it was not statistically significant, even at the .10 level. The standardized regression coefficient for this variable in predicting innovative instruction was only .061. . . .

6. The correlation between pre-reform authentic classroom practices and pre-reform achievement is .112, which is significant at the .05 level.

7. The achievement level of a school prior to reform also has a marginally significant relationship (at the .10 level with a standardized coefficient of .115) with the introduction of innovative practices. Schools with higher average test scores prior to reform were more likely to report classroom innovation. Schools with lower achievement scores prior to reform, however, made significant changes in their instructional practices under reform. For example, prior to reform, 21 percent of the higher-achieving schools . . . reported extensive use of authentic classroom practices. The comparative percentage for lower-achieving schools . . . was only 10 percent. After reform, this percentage rose to 39 percent for higher-achieving schools and to 25 percent for the lower-achieving schools. This relationship was also evident for "best" instructional practices. At the outset of the reform, the higher-achieving schools had more of these practices in place. Nevertheless, lower-achieving schools reported significant movement in this direction since reform. Thus, although the gap still remained, the proportional gains for lower-achieving schools were, in fact, greater.

Section IV

More Illustrations of Case Study Evidence

Winning at the Game 12

Intel and Silicon Valley Fever*

Everett M. Rogers
and Judith K. Larsen

---

editor's introduction:

Methodological Significance

Another type of observational evidence deals with the observation of a facility, and not just human beings at work. This selection reports on a high-tech manufacturing production facility.

The first half of the selection places the importance of high-quality production within a two-part competitive framework: first is the occurrence of a "learning curve," whereby facilities must learn how to make their products with fewer errors and hence lower the rejection rate of defective products; second is the importance of sustaining a corporate climate of "continuous technological innovation, based on major inventions and

---

*Editor's note: Excerpted, with light edits, from Chapter 6, "Intel," from *Silicon Valley Fever: Growth of High-Technology Culture*, by Everett M. Rogers and Judith K. Larsen, Basic Books, New York, NY, pp. 96–121. Reprinted with permission of Basic Books, a division of Perseus Book Group in the format Other Book via Copyright Clearance Center. Another aspect of the Silicon Valley case study is presented in Chapter 14 of this anthology.

industry breakthroughs."** The second half of the selection describes the actual manufacturing process and the critical role of line-operators, whose skilled work nevertheless appears to be quite monotonous.***

These excerpts show how case study investigators can present observational evidence and also place such evidence within a meaningful context, both from the standpoint of a company and its goals and the perspective of workers on a factory assembly line.

Substantive Note

High-tech firms combine advanced technological developments with rigorous manufacturing processes. Because human resources are at the center of both situations, high-tech firms must therefore put great energy into finding, recruiting, and retaining talented human beings. The challenges are enormous, ranging from the recruitment of leading scientists to the training of workers who will be paid little more than the minimum wage. Successfully motivating such a range of employees has been a large part of the Intel story (see Chapter 14 of this anthology, for a related selection from a case study of the broader community known as "Silicon Valley"). Intel grew from a start-up company to a bellweather firm whose performance is now part of the exclusive Dow-Jones composite stock index. Partly because of Intel's success, computer chip technology and manufacturing are now central to the U.S. economy, if not culture.

**The excerpt presented here omits a lengthy description of the invention of the microprocessor by one of Intel's early scientists. (He was Intel's twelfth employee.)
***Similarly, the excerpt omits a lengthy description of how layers of circuitry are built up on a wafer's surface through the process of photolithography.

It is one thing to be innovative, quite another to get rich from innovation. Fortunately for Intel, technological innovation equals profit in the semiconductor industry, thanks to what is called the "learning curve." In the semiconductor industry, the learning curve means that the price of a chip typically declines 20 to 30 percent for each doubling of its total production during the years of its life cycle. This downward sloping trend is called a learning curve because the lower price is made possible as a firm gradually

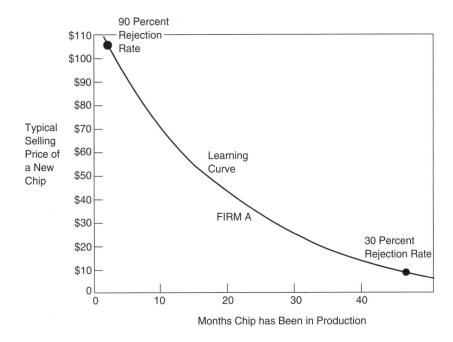

Exhibit 12.1 The selling price for a new semiconductor chip decreases rapidly after its introduction as the firms producing it learn to fabricate the chips with fewer rejects, and thus at lower cost per chip. A competitor introducing a chip a few months later is at a considerable disadvantage, due to lost time on the learning curve.

learns how to produce a chip with higher and higher degrees of quality, thus lowering the rejection rate of defective chips (see Exhibit 12.1). Because more saleable chips are produced for the same amount of manufacturing effort, the firm can afford to charge a lower and lower price for each chip.

Because of the learning curve, unless a firm gets an early start in producing a chip, it is difficult to compete. The sooner a company gets on the learning curve, the greater its advantage over competitors. It is this law that rewards technological innovation and punishes laggardliness in Silicon Valley. The only sure route to survival in the Valley is via continuous innovation, and the model for this strategy is Intel. Indeed the learning curve behavior in the semiconductor industry was most clearly enunciated in 1964 by Dr. Gordon Moore, Intel's co-founder, who formulated Moore's Law, the principle of the learning curve.

An example of the learning curve in action is the cost of pocket calculators. When they first became available around 1972, a four-function (add, subtract, multiply, and divide) calculator averaged $250. There was a tremendous demand for this product and a large number of firms began producing them. The vital component in each calculator was a semiconductor chip. Due to the learning curve, the cost per chip began to decrease precipitously and the cost of pocket calculators also began to drop—from $250, to $100, to $50, to $20, and, around 1977, to $10 or less. Meanwhile, as price competition sharpened, the smaller firms, who had not benefited from the learning curve, dropped out of the race, and soon only Texas Instruments, Hewlett-Packard, Casio, and a few others were left. Such an industry shake-out occurs because of the learning curve.

A consequence of the learning curve for semiconductor chips is a long-range decrease in the cost of computing. The more years that a chip, say the 4K RAM, is produced, the cheaper it becomes. And as the electronics industry moved from the 4K to the 8K to the 16K and on to the 64K RAM, the cost per thousand bits of computer memory dropped very sharply. Cost per bit has been decreasing by about 28 percent per year since 1973. In order to put increasing amounts of electronic circuitry on a smaller and smaller chip, extremely fine patterns must be etched on the silicon wafers. The present width of an electrical connection is only 4 to 6 microns (a micron is 1/25,000 of an inch). In contrast, a human hair is 100 microns in diameter. Objects smaller than 25 microns cannot be seen by the naked eye.

In the mid-1960s, the complexity of a chip was comparable to the network of streets in a small town. Today's chip is comparable to the streets of greater Los Angeles. And an ultimate complexity like that of the quarter-micron chip is similar to a street map covering the entire North American continent.[1]

As chips become cheaper and smaller in size, they are utilized as components in more and more new and redesigned products for the consumer. A major advantage is that the number of moving parts in a consumer product can be greatly reduced by using microelectronic components. For instance, a new model sewing machine can use a single microprocessor to control the stitching pattern in place of 350 gears, cams, and other mechanical parts. The microprocessor not only simplifies the sewing machine and lowers its selling price, but also gives the electronic model greater reliability.

Intel is successful because it turns this growing demand for new semiconductor chips into sales. Technological innovation has provided the boost for the company's success. Growing at about 25 percent per year, Intel now has over 20,000 employees in locations around the world. After its founding in 1968, Intel grew rapidly.

How Intel Does It

Intel got off to *a very fast start*. Soon after its founding, Ted Hoff, a young Intel engineer, invented the microprocessor (a computer on a chip). Since then the inventions have kept on coming, creating a confidence that Intel could out-invent competitors. As Hoff stated, "Intel has its image, its policy of maintaining its position as a leading-edge firm. So we invest heavily in research and development (R&D). We have lots of new products and we try to pick carefully which innovations to produce, and which to drop, on the basis of what is interesting and leads to a sound future."[2]

Early successes in technological innovation provided Intel with *the resources and the reputation* to stay ahead. Intel has one of the highest ratios of R&D to sales of any semiconductor firm.

Intel has faith in the *quality of its personnel,* and is reluctant to let any of them go, even in times of economic downswing. Intel's second-priority goal is to recruit the best people in the microelectronics industry (its number one goal is to lead the industry in innovation; profitmaking is well down the list of official corporate goals). A continuous stream of high-caliber, young engineers flows into Intel's R&D labs, most of them directly out of university engineering schools. College recruiting gets lots of attention at Intel, and personnel recruiters say they don't only go for the 4.0 student. Instead, they would rather hire the individual with 3.0 grades and a strong goal orientation toward innovation—someone who has completed a really creative student project.

Intel brings it all together with *a management style* that is highly structured and thorough. CEO Andy Grove is an intense individual, intimidating to most Intel employees. He feels it is better to bring up failures and discuss what's gone wrong, rather than to compound a problem by allowing it to continue. A lot of executives' time—at least 70 percent of working hours—is spent in meetings. About 100 standing councils at Intel meet regularly to make monthly reviews of such topics as marketing, customer service, facilities, human resources, and so forth. The structure of these review committees provides a close monitoring of the innovation process at Intel. The stream of new products emanating from Intel is carefully managed.

The top managers at Intel are Bob Noyce, Gordon Moore, and Andy Grove. Each has a say in key *decisions,* which are made by consensus. Noyce is the outside man who deals with government and the rest of the industry; Moore, the thinker, focuses on planning; and Grove is the man of action. All three are technical men who hold Ph.Ds. As Bob Noyce pointed out, "Our three top officers have grown up in technical positions—not as lawyers, not as accountants, not as paper-pushers, but as doers. That signals that the way to get ahead at Intel is to make a technological contribution."[3]

Long-range planning at Intel is integral to its success. Over a decade ago, the firm's leaders realized that the housing costs in Silicon Valley would force them to locate new plants elsewhere. They found locations in the United States with conditions similar to Silicon Valley and then purchased future plant sites in Phoenix, Portland, Sacramento, Livermore (California), Texas, and Florida. In addition, Intel has offshore production facilities in Penang (Malaysia), Manila, Barbados, Puerto Rico, and Israel. Thus, the company became an international empire.

Intel chooses to avoid certain areas. Noyce said, "We *build on strength* and try to stay out of competition where we're weak." A few years back, the company learned a lesson the hard way about digital watches. It looked simple to put an Intel chip in a watch and sell the chip along with the watch. But that involved marketing to consumers, rather than to other electronics firms. "We thought it was a technology game, and it turned out to be a merchandising game. That's not our game," said Noyce.[4]

The challenge for Intel today is to stay on top of the microelectronics industry. That's a pretty tough act, as recent events show. Some cracks in Intel's vaunted reputation appeared during 1981, when profits dropped to $27 million, down 72 percent from the year before. Because of the continuing recession in 1982, Intel's profits stayed down. Company executives expected the recession to lift during 1982 and hired 3,000 new employees, anticipating higher production in the face of economic recovery. Their strategy backfired when the recession did not end. As 1982 drew to a close Intel found itself short of cash; it cut salaries by up to 10 percent and froze them for 1983. Then in December 1982 Intel sold 12 percent of its stock to IBM for $250 million, and in 1983 IBM bought additional shares, bringing its total ownership to 15 percent; IBM got one seat on Intel's board of directors. Things became worse for Intel in January 1983 when the Intel employees at the Portland plant defected to launch a new startup. Problems were compounded the following month when Ted Hoff, Intel's star inventor, resigned to go to Atari. But thanks to an upturn in the economy later in the year, Intel's star brightened.

If a single individual personifies Silicon Valley fever, it is undoubtedly Bob Noyce. Any understanding of microelectronics entrepreneurship would have to include the career of this talented man.[5]

Dr. Robert N. Noyce was born in 1926, the son of a smalltown Iowa minister. He attended nearby Grinnell College, an institution which he later endowed with Intel stock estimated to be worth $10 million today. Noyce's physics professor at Grinnell interested him in transistors and when Noyce went on for his Ph.D. in physics at MIT he studied transistor technology. After three years at Philco Corporation in Philadelphia, Noyce arrived in Palo Alto in 1956 to work at Shockley Semiconductor Laboratory as one of the original Shockley Eight. He left the firm a year later as the leader of the "Traitorous Eight," as Shockley dubbed them, to found Fairchild Semiconductor.

By his own description, Bob Noyce was a somewhat reluctant participant in the Shockley walkout; the other seven Shockley dissidents had already lined up their connection with the Fairchild Camera and Instrument Company. However they needed a leader and approached Noyce, who was still in the good graces of Shockley. As Noyce tells it, "Suddenly it became apparent to people like myself, who had always assumed they would be working for a salary for the rest of their lives, that they could get some equity in a start-up company. That was a great revelation, and a great motivation too."[6] Indeed, seven years later when the parent, Fairchild Camera and Instrument, bought out its Semiconductor Division, Noyce and the other seven members of the Shockley Eight each were paid about one-quarter of a million dollars.[7]

While director of R&D at Fairchild, Noyce developed the integrated circuit. The same concept had been invented by Jack Kilby at Texas Instruments (TI) a few months before. In July 1959 Noyce filed a patent for his conception of the integrated circuit. Jack Kilby's employer, TI, filed a lawsuit for patent interference against Noyce and Fairchild, and the case dragged on for some years. Today Noyce and Kilby are generally regarded as co-inventors of the integrated circuit, although Kilby alone was inducted into the Inventors' Hall of Fame as the inventor.[8] Noyce is credited with improving the integrated circuit for industrial purposes.

Relationships deteriorated between Fairchild management on the East Coast and their Semiconductor Division in California. Noyce stayed on as Fairchild's talent dribbled away to start competing firms. Gordon Moore began to agitate for a spin-off. Finally, in June 1968, Noyce resigned from Fairchild to launch Intel with Moore. The price of Fairchild stock dropped sharply on the day Noyce's resignation was announced.

In order to replace Noyce, Sherman Fairchild pulled off one of the most sensational recruiting deals in the history of Silicon Valley when he snared Les Hogan from Motorola. Hogan was an ex-physics professor at Harvard, who had been heading Motorola's semiconductor work. Fairchild gave him a starting salary of $120,000, a 33 percent increase over his Motorola wages and part of a three-year contract totaling $1 million. Hogan also got 10,000 stock shares at the cut-rate price of $10 each; the market price was $60. Thrown in was an interest-free loan of $5.4 million to exercise an option on 90,000 shares of Fairchild stock. Hogan also insisted that the corporate headquarters for Fairchild Semiconductor be moved to Mountain View, in order to avoid the conflicts with the East Coast that had bedeviled Noyce.[9] The Hogan package was so sweet that it serves as the ultimate measure for other job offers in Silicon Valley, as in: "I was offered half a Hogan." When Hogan's move was announced, Fairchild stock shot up seven points, and Motorola's dropped eight points on the same day.

The millions Noyce needed to found Intel came mainly via venture capitalist Arthur Rock. Rock had been impressed by Noyce since the 1950s, when Rock helped arrange the financing for Fairchild Semiconductor. Noyce stated, "It was a very natural thing to go to Art and say, 'Incidentally, Art, do you have an extra $2.5 million you would like to put on the crap table?'"[10] Noyce and Moore indicated their willingness to invest about $250,000 each of their own money, amassed from their original investments of $500 in Fairchild. Rock got on the phone, and in 30 minutes he had lined up the $2.5 million (and became a legend in the process).

In 1982 Noyce's net worth in Intel, with 3.4 percent of the company's stock, was estimated at $36.6 million.[11] Like many others in Silicon Valley,

Noyce invests his earnings in other startups, thus continuing to convert his inside knowledge of Silicon Valley goings-on into yet more money. Noyce presently serves on the board of directors of about seven firms and spends only part of his time at Intel.[12] In 1975 Noyce stepped down from chairman to vice-chairman of the board at Intel in order to pursue his many outside activities.

From the outset Intel concentrated on memory chips, and it was almost accidental that it got a big boost from microprocessors, invented at Intel in 1971. Just as invention of the planar process and the integrated circuit had made Fairchild a commercial success for Noyce, the microprocessor boosted Intel into the big time. . . .

Fab 3: Producing Semiconductor Chips

Fab 3, Intel's largest wafer-production facility, is located in Livermore, California, about 40 miles east of Intel's headquarters in Santa Clara. Fab 3 was built in 1973 outside Silicon Valley to escape the skyrocketing housing prices of the Valley and to tap the cheaper labor force available at Livermore.

Fab 1 and Fab 2, located in Santa Clara, were built soon after Intel's founding in 1968. Intel's practice is to identify their plants on the basis of function and when they were constructed. Intel's newest wafer-fabrication plant, Fab 7, has just begun production in Israel, the first Intel wafer-fab facility outside the United States. Other fabrication takes place in Portland, Phoenix, and Albuquerque. Many of the wafers produced at Fab 3 in Livermore go to "A 2," assembly plant #2 in Manila, where the tiny gold leads are bonded to the semiconductor chips by young Filipino women. Because an assembly plant requires lots of labor, most operations are located where labor is relatively cheap: Puerto Rico, Barbados, Mexico, and Malaysia.

The wafer-fab plant in Livermore is a one- and two-story affair that from the outside does not look large enough to produce 1,200 wafers per workday. Not counting rejects, there are about 160 or so good chips on each wafer, so Fab 3 turns out an average of 200,000 chips daily. If each chip is worth an average $10 after assembly and testing, almost $2 million of chips go out the door of Fab 3 each workday.

Fab 3 is actually a factory within a factory. The "outer factory" contains offices, receiving and shipping facilities, a training room, a cafeteria, bathrooms, and other facilities. The inner factory is the "cleanroom," a particularly antiseptic area that looks like a hospital operating room. Except that it is cleaner—a wafer-fab cleanroom contains fewer than 100 dust particles of one micrometer or more in diameter per cubic foot, while the dust level in a modern hospital is about 10,000 particles per cubic foot.[13]

Ordinary clean air contains about one million dust particles per cubic foot, which is actually not so clean, when looked at from the viewpoint of a semiconductor chip.

The cleanroom is used to manufacture wafers. Each wafer is a 4-inch flat circle of silicon on which from 8 to 10 layers of intricate electronic circuitry are painstakingly built up through a complex series of chemical and electrical processes. The basic idea of creating chips by laying down layer after layer of circuitry, called the "planar process," was developed by Jean Hoerni when he worked for Fairchild in 1960.

Dust specks are anathema to semiconductor production as they short-circuit the miniaturized electronics, thus leading to rejection of the chip. Great care is taken to ensure that the cleanroom is entirely closed off from its external environment. Workers must wear "bunny suits" of lint-free cloth, all of the report forms used in the cleanroom are made of lint-free paper, and only ballpoint pens are used, as pencils are great dust-generators. One enters and leaves the cleanroom through airlocks (there is a negative vacuum inside). Intel requires its employees and visitors to read and sign a 13-page manual of cleanroom procedures. A violation, such as wearing makeup if one is a woman, or not wearing a face cover if a bearded man, can result in a written warning. Fab 3 has a "yield" of about 70 percent, meaning that only 30 percent of the chips are rejected because they do not pass quality tests, which is high relative to the rest of the semiconductor industry. Bob Wigger, manufacturing manager at Fab 3, does not intend to let this standard slip; Intel's profits rest directly upon yield, and Wigger is proud of the quality standard that his 370 employees have set at Fab 3.

Each square foot of cleanroom space is extremely expensive to build and maintain; therefore, the density of workers is high. An impression of Fab 3's cleanroom is that of a surrealistic world, as if it were located on the moon. The bunny suits make everyone look like bulky spacemen; indeed, it is often difficult to distinguish men from women until one learns that all of the 300 or so line operators are female; the only men in the cleanroom are 30 engineers and 40 maintenance men. The workforce is crammed into the rather constrained area of the cleanroom along with several million dollars of equipment. And the main object of everyone's attention is the silicon wafer.

An equivalent of the expression "womb to tomb" in the semiconductor industry is "beach to customer." The wafers come from plain old sand, which is purified chemically, then heated to 1,420 degrees Celsius, after which it crystallizes and is sliced into wafers, each about half a millimeter thick. The raw silicon wafers arrive at Fab 3 from Monsanto, one of several vendors who supply Intel. Each wafer costs about $10, and by the time it leaves Fab 3 two months after it arrives, it will have a thin epidermis of complicated circuitry built up through several basic processes that take place in the cleanroom: photolithography (or masking), diffusion, and thin films. About 200 different operations involving one or another of these processes will occur. If we could follow a particular wafer through this manufacturing process, it would require about four hours just to walk through the labyrinthian sequence of steps as each layer of circuitry is built up on the wafer followed by another layer. To add further to the difficulty of understanding the birth of a chip, a variety of different kinds of wafers are produced. Some will be RAMs (random access memory), others ROMs (read-only memory), PROMs (programmable read-only memory), EPROMs (erasable PROMs), EEPROMs (electrically erasable PROMs), and so on. A variety of chips are manufactured at Fab 3 at the same time by different sequences of basic operations.

The masks come to Fab 3 from a corps of design engineers at Intel 4, a large R&D building adjacent to Intel headquarters in Santa Clara. Designers are the uninhibited free spirits of the microelectronics industry who combine artistic creativity with the precision of electrical engineering. Designers are often called "witches" by others in the semiconductor industry, implying that they combine their engineering skills with a special brand of black magic. Design engineers are one of the highest paid and loftiest prestige occupations in the industry, somewhat akin to brain surgeons in a hospital. An Intel team of designers may have worked for several months or several years, depending on the complexity of the chip being designed, to produce the set of master masks that they send to Fab 3 at Livermore. Each mask is made of glass and is about 4 inches square. It is the negative, in a photographic sense, of one layer of circuitry to be placed on the silicon wafer at Fab 3. If a wafer with 10 horizontal layers of circuitry is to be built up in the wafer-fabrication process, then at least 10 different masks are involved—in most cases, two or more masks are used to imprint one horizontal layer of the chip's architecture. Each of these 10 layers is connected with tiny electrical circuits passing vertically through the three-dimensional structure of the wafer, adding to the complexity of wafer fabrication.

Back at Intel 4 in Santa Clara, design engineers have labored over a chip blown up 500 times. The tricky task here is to position and reposition thousands of component parts of the circuitry so as to maximize efficiency of production and to minimize the size of the chip, as tinier chips mean more of them can be manufactured on a wafer. Much of this design work is done with computer simulation, in which various combinations of the components are arranged and rearranged. A magnified version of the chip is then drawn on an oversized drafting board. This blueprint is then reduced by photography, assisted by a computer, to the miniaturized actual size of the semiconductor chip. Then this tiny blueprint is reproduced several hundred times through a "step and repeat" process to produce each of the 10 or so masks, each a template for the identical chips that are to be soulmates on a silicon wafer. The set of 10 masks are mounted in the photolithography machines at Fab 3, where they are used to clone thousands and thousands of semiconductor chips.

Each of Intel's masks is guarded very carefully; employees are reminded that the world of Silicon Valley contains lots of industrial spies who would love to steal them. . . .

The real heroes of Fab 3, and, more generally, of the entire semi-conductor industry, are the line operators. Most are women, representing a wide cross-section of age and ethnicity. Many are young, fresh out of high school with perhaps a few months' experience working at McDonald's or Burger King. Others are middle-aged mothers, whose children have grown up. Almost all live within a few miles of the wafer-fab plant at Livermore, which means that in this part of California, the majority are Caucasians. They are attracted by a starting salary of $4.10 per hour, low compared to skilled manual jobs in other U.S. industries, but better than alternatives in the Livermore area. The base salary is little more than the legal minimum. On the basis of good work performance, a line operator at Fab 3 can climb to as much as $9.00 per hour after about five years. All of the line operators we talked to at Fab 3 complain about the endless monotony of their work, performing routine operations hour after hour. They cannot dawdle under the watchful eyes of their supervisors, but the women talk almost constantly with nearby peers (although Intel policy discourages such conversation).

Most line operators are women. When we asked a Fab 3 worker why, she replied: "Because our fingers are faster than men's. And we can better cope with the monotony of this work." Further, men won't work for such low wages. Females, because they're glad to have a job, may also be less likely to join a labor union, the nemesis of Silicon Valley executives.

When looking through a microscope at a wafer during a plant tour of Fab 3, one of the authors exclaimed to the female operator at this station, "What beautiful circuitry." She replied, "Not if you look at it hour after hour, day after day, week after week." How do the line operators cope with such monotony? Some don't—they simply quit after a few months or a year. In 1982, Fab 3 expanded its workforce by 150 additional workers—2,000 women applied in response to a local newspaper ad. Six months later, 17 of the new employees had already quit. But most operators stay on the job, or at least in the industry. Within months they develop a skill that is in demand and are assured of having a job when other industries are laying off workers.

Most line operators cannot realistically look forward to becoming a trainer or a supervisor, as there are few job openings. But there are exceptions. One woman was hired as a line operator at Fab 3 when it opened in 1973 and set an outstanding performance record in the cleanroom. By 1976 she was promoted to supervisor of a group of 15 line operators. Her unusual ability then led to a further promotion to acting production manager at Fab 3, an "exempt" position. Last year the once line operator was promoted to production manager of Fab 2 at Santa Clara. She was not yet 30 years old.

Line operators can earn a bonus of up to $75 per month if Fab 3 has superior production, although this bonus usually is only about $30–$40 (about 5 percent of the workers' base salary). Nevertheless the bonus plus other incentives like stock-purchase options appear to motivate the line operators to high-quality production.

Most line operators do not simply push buttons. Some of the machines, like the ion-implanters, require considerable skill to operate properly; fine gradations of judgment are required. Intel has a careful training program. An experienced operator provides extensive one-on-one instruction to the novice in learning to use a new machine and a 200-page manual is provided by Intel. This training typically continues for two or three weeks until the trainee demonstrates a high level of proficiency in performing an operation. The success of the training period, however, rests on the trainer, a peer who has had several years' experience on the machine. Even then there are failures. At Fab 3 one day, an ion-implanter was not working and the production of several thousand wafers was backed up. The huge machine carried a plaintive, hand-lettered sign, "Sorry, down for repair." Earlier that day, a trainee with only one week's on-the-job training had panicked and hit the "stop" button, crashing the machine. The trainer said, "Well, she still has a ways to go in learning how to operate the ion-implanter."

About 30 engineers are assigned to Fab 3's cleanroom (another 70 work in an Intel R&D unit also located in Fab 3). Almost all are male, many just out of engineering college. Their main responsibility is to monitor various wafer-fab operations. They also solve unexpected problems when they occur, as happened during our visit to Fab 3. At about 10:30 in the morning, a sudden spurt in the rejection rate was noticed at one of the wafer test stations in the cleanroom. A team of engineers galvanized into action. X-rays disclosed that minute cracks were occurring inside the latticed architecture of the wafer. After following several likely leads the engineers traced the problem to warping of the wafer. When we left Fab 3 at 5:30, the young engineers were still seeking to determine why the warping occurred. Later we learned that the problem was solved, only after an all-night session.

Notes

1. *Newsweek*, June 30, 1980.

2. Authors' interview with Ted Hoff, Santa Clara, CA, August 10, 1982.

3. Authors' interview with Robert Noyce, Santa Clara, CA, October 4, 1982.

4. Robert N. Noyce, "Creativity by the Numbers," *Harvard Business Review, 58*: (1980).

5. Certain parts of this section are based on the authors' interview with Robert N. Noyce.

6. Dirk Hanson, *The New Alchemists: Silicon Valley and the Microelectronics Revolution* (Boston: Little, Brown & Co., 1982), pp. 91-92.

7. Ibid., p. 100.

8. Ibid., p. 98.

9. Les Hogan (authors' interview, Mountain View, CA, November 15, 1982) provided insight into his celebrated move from Motorola to Fairchild Semiconductor, "I loved my work at Motorola, and was proud of our business success. Our 430 employees in Phoenix were shipping $20 million worth of semiconductors a month. And I had my arms around the whole operation; I knew every employee by first name. So I hated to leave. It wasn't because of the money, really. Certainly not the money alone. When Bob Noyce decided to leave Fairchild to start Intel, he flew down to see me in Phoenix and told me that I was his first choice to take his place. Sherman Fairchild took a liking to me, and he just kept upping the offer. It was a breathtaking offer. Fairchild was only about half the size of Motorola at that time. But Fairchild was the technology leader of the industry. So I decided to come to Silicon Valley."

10. Gene Bylinsky, "California's Great Breeding Ground for Industry," *Fortune*, June 1974.

11. Dave Lindorff, "The Venture 100: No Limits to Growth," *Venture*, May 1982. Co-founder Gordon Moore holds 9.8 percent of Intel's stock, worth $105.6 million.

12. Authors' interview with Robert N. Noyce.

13. William G. Oldham, "The Fabrication of Electronics Circuits," *The Microelectronics Revolution*, Ed. Tom Forester (Cambridge, MA: MIT Press, 1981).

Civil Society and Crisis 13

Culture, Discourse, and the Rodney King Beating*

Ronald N. Jacobs

editor's introduction:

Methodological Significance

Case study evidence also can include extensive if not exhaustive use of documents. For contemporary events, such documents may come from coverage by the local and mass media— whether in printed (e.g., newspaper) or electronic (e.g., television) form. This selection presents a "case within a case," its main concern being the differential newspaper coverage of a key community event—the beating of an adult, African-American male resident by three White members of the Los Angeles Police Department (LAPD).

The study tracks the event's coverage by the city's metropolitan-wide daily and the city's most important African-American newspaper, published weekly. The study

*Editor's Note: Abridged from "Civil Society and Crisis: Culture, Discourse, and the Rodney King Beating," in *American Journal of Sociology,* March 1996, *101,* pp. 1238–1272. Reprinted with permission. Many of the omitted portions, including a few footnotes, covered the original author's discussion between the case and sociological theory, with extensive citations to the literature, also omitted from the present selection. The bracketed words or phrases contained within quotations are those of the original author.

shows how the two newspapers differed in their rendering of "plot," "characters," and "genre," creating their own social construction of events. For instance, because the latter newspaper placed the events within the middle of a long and continuous "narrative" about historic brutality against African Americans, the newspaper also reported about a related trial that had begun a few days after the beating took place, but this trial was ignored by the metropolitan daily.

Case study investigators who rely on documentation as a source of evidence need to appreciate the differences in perspectives, if not ideologies, represented by the authors of the various types of documents. In this selection, the documents were published accounts of community events. Other case studies may rely on other types of documents. Whatever the source, you should be wary of the original authors' perspectives, as the authors produced the documents for reasons other than later serving as part of your case study.

Substantive Note

The Rodney King crisis was one of the most inflammatory community events in the 1990s. The nature of the beating had been serendipitously videotaped by an amateur cameraman. The police officers accused of the beating were acquitted a year later. Upon their acquittal ensued a civil disturbance in which 58 people were killed, 2,000 injured, and 11,000 arrested. Although only occurring in one U.S. city, the crisis demonstrated the continuing undertow of racial conflict in the United States. For instance, later in the 1990s, "racial profiling" by police officers became a widespread concern and is an issue that has not been resolved to this day.

The Case

...On March 3, 1991, an African-American motorist, Rodney King, was pursued for speeding. After a brief chase, King was met by 21 police officers, including members of the California Highway Patrol and the Los Angeles Police Department (LAPD). In full view of all present, King was severely beaten by three White LAPD officers as a sergeant and the remaining 17 officers looked on. Unknown to the police officers, the event was videotaped by an amateur cameraman, George Holliday, and sold to a local television station. The videotape, which was broadcast thousands of times, provoked a public crisis over police brutality and racism in Los Angeles. Interest in the crisis died down about a month after the release of the Christopher Commission report [described later in this chapter] on July 9, 1991, but exploded again in April 1992 with the return of not-guilty verdicts for the four police officers who had been indicted for the beating. By the end of the crisis, Police Chief Daryl Gates had resigned, Mayor Tom Bradley had decided not to run for reelection (for the first time in 23 years), and the city had experienced the most costly civil disturbance in the nation's history [see Figure 13.1 for a chronology]. Given that the city of Los Angeles had paid more than $20 million between 1986 and 1990 as a result of judgments, settlements, and jury verdicts against LAPD officers in over 300 lawsuits dealing with the excessive use of force, how is it that the Rodney King crisis came to define racial tensions in Los Angeles? How did the events surrounding the crisis affect political elites and other public actors in civil society? How did they affect social understandings about race relations? Answering these questions, I argue, requires an examination of the cultural dynamics of civil society.

. . . In the analysis that follows I focus on two newspapers with different (but overlapping) readerships. By examining the different narratives they constructed about the Rodney King beating—in terms of characters, character attributes, plots, event linkages, and genres—I show how the two newspapers constructed different but overlapping narrative understandings about the crisis. I also show how certain events became crucial turning points for the different narratives of both newspapers, whereas other events had significance only for the African-American press. Later I provide some historical information about the two newspapers and outline my methodological approach for analyzing texts.

Data and Methods

. . . To analyze the discourse surrounding the Rodney King crisis, I examined the entire universe of articles written in . . . [two newspapers, the *Los Angeles Times* and the *Los Angeles Sentinel*] between March and September 1991. In the *Los Angeles Times*, 357 articles were written during this period; in the *Los Angeles Sentinel*, there were 137 articles.[1] The *Sentinel*, which was founded in 1933, is the most significant newspaper for the African-American community in Los Angeles. In 1991 it had a circulation of 25,866, which was the largest among African-American newspapers in Los Angeles. In 1993 it received the John B. Russworm Award for the best

Date	Event
1991:	
March 3	Rodney King is beaten by members of the Los Angeles Police Department, an event recorded on videotape by amateur cameraman George Holliday.
March 6	Police Chief Daryl Gates calls the beating an "aberration."
March 11	A grand jury investigation is formed to look into the beating of Rodney King.
March 12	An FBI probe is formed to investigate the beating of Rodney King.
March 14	Four Los Angeles police officers are indicted for the beating of Rodney King.
March 30	Daryl Gates forms the Arguelles Commission to investigate the beating of Rodney King.
March 30	Tom Bradley forms the Christopher Commission to investigate the beating of Rodney King.
April 4	The Police Commission, on the urging of Mayor Tom Bradley, removes Daryl Gates from his position as police chief.
April 5	The Arguelles Commission and the Christopher Commission are merged into an expanded Christopher Commission.
April 6	The City Council, after criticizing the Police Commission's action, reinstates Daryl Gates to his position as police chief.
July 9	The Christopher Commission releases the results of its investigation, the "Report of the Independent Commission of the Los Angeles Police Department."
July 12	Daryl Gates announces that he will retire as police chief.
July 14	Daryl Gates announces that he might not retire until 1993.
July 17	City Councilmen John Ferraro and Joel Wachs make a public call for the resignation of Daryl Gates.
July 22	Daryl Gates announces that he will resign as police chief in April 1992.
1992:	
April 29	A Simi Valley jury acquits the officers charged with beating Rodney King. In the civil disturbances that ensue there are more than 11,000 arrests, 2,000 people are injured, and 58 people are killed.
June 6	Daryl Gates retires as chief of the Los Angeles Police Department and is replaced by Willie L. Williams.

Figure 13.1   Chronology of the Rodney King Case

Black-owned newspaper in the nation. The *Times,* which was founded in 1881, is the most significant newspaper for the "aggregated metropolitan community" (Janowitz & Suttles, 1977, 1991, p. 268) of Los Angeles. In 1991 it had a circulation of 1,177,253 and was the most widely read newspaper in Los Angeles, Orange, Riverside, and San Bernadino counties. It provides a reference discourse for many individuals and communities, including the African-American community. In fact, most of the people who read the *Sentinel* also read the *Times* (Lyle, 1967, pp. 169–70).

I analyze three different aspects of the news narratives about the crisis. The first is *plot,* which is concerned with the selection, evaluation, and attribution of differential status to events (Steinmetz, 1992, pp. 497–99). A narrative's plot is fluid and complex in its relationship to events; as Eco (1994) has shown, it can "linger" on a particular event, flashback to past events, or flash forward to future events. Plot is the best way to study what Abbott (1988) has called the "time-horizon problem," where events can differ in their speed and duration. A focus on which events are selected by a community for narration (and which events are not selected) provides important clues about how that community understands the past, present, and future.

In addition to plot, I also examine the *characters* portrayed in the narratives and their relationship to one another. The analysis of characters is particularly important for nonfictional narratives, because the narrators are often the same as the characters in the plot (Steinmetz, 1992, p. 500). I analyze the characters in terms of the opposition between heroes and antiheroes, using recent work on the analytic code of American civil discourse (e.g., Alexander, 1992; Alexander & Smith, 1993) to provide clues about how the characters are evaluated in various narrations. This research has demonstrated how public actors make use of the binary structure of civil discourse to "purify" themselves and their allies, and to "pollute" their enemies (Alexander & Smith, 1993, pp. 164–65). To narrate themselves and their allies as heroic, social actors try to cast themselves as rational and controlled in their motivations, open and trusting in their relationships, and regulated by impersonal rules in their organizational activities. Correspondingly, they try to narrate their enemies as irrational and uncontrolled in their motivations, secretive and deceitful in their relationships, and arbitrary and factionalized in their organizational activities.

The final component of my narrative analysis is *genre.* Because genre is infrequently utilized by most sociologists making the "narrative turn," I will describe in some detail how it can be incorporated into sociological analysis. Genre provides a temporal and spatial link between the characters and events of a narrative, and also influences the relationship between a story's characters, audience, and narrator. We can see how genre affects narrative by considering Frye's (1957, pp. 158–239) discussion of the four narrative "archetypes" of Western literature. In *comedy,* the protagonists, or heroes, are viewed from the perspective of their common humanity, and the general theme is the integration of society. The movement in comedy is usually from one kind of society, where the protagonist's wishes are blocked, to another society that crystallizes around the hero. Comic heroes have average or below-average power, and typically fall into three general types: the imposter, the buffoon, and the self-deprecator. In *romance*, the hero has great powers, the enemy is clearly articulated and often has great powers as well, and the movement takes the form of an adventure with the ultimate triumph of hero over enemy. Romantic genres are viewed by the audience from a perspective of wish fulfillment, where heroes represent ideals and villains represent threats. In *tragedy*, the hero typically possesses great power, but is isolated from society and ultimately falls to an omnipotent and external fate or to the violation of a moral law. Because the reader expects catastrophe as its inevitable end, tragedy "eludes the antithesis between moral responsibility and arbitrary fate" (Frye, 1957, p. 211). Finally, in *irony* the protagonist is viewed from an attitude of detachment and through the negative characterization of parody or satire.

The literary texts described by Frye differ in some important respects from the news texts of the present study. Most important, there are many competing narratives (and narrative creators) in news, all battling for interpretive authority over a particular event. For example, the Rodney King crisis was constructed in each newspaper through two competing genres: romance and tragedy. There was additional competition, in that the actual composition of the romantic and tragic narratives differed between the two newspapers. The point is that the analyst cannot assume any sort of narrative unity for newspaper texts. Instead, the sociologist employing narrative analysis must search for inconsistencies and determine how they are related to events and social setting (Wagner-Pacifici & Schwartz, 1991, p. 383).

Early Constructions of the Rodney King Crisis

An event does not become a public crisis automatically or instantaneously. Much like ritual, this process requires a period of "separation" (Turner, 1969) from ordinary, everyday life and a corresponding concentration of collective attention. Both of these, discursive separation and increased collective attention, were present in the early period of the Rodney King crisis. Although there was only one article about the beating in the *Los Angeles Times* the morning after it occurred, by the end of the first week there were 23. Similarly, although there were only two articles written about the beating in the *Los Angeles Sentinel* on March 7 (the first issue after the incident), there were 26 articles written over the next three issues. The event contained all the necessary symbolic elements to construct a narrative of crisis. First, the videotape of the beating—which was recorded by an "amateur cameraman," an ordinary citizen of civil society—showed visual and technical "proof" of the event: in a sense, a "video text," which itself placed the actors in relations of similarity and opposition to one another. The videotape served a naturalizing function for the subsequent interpretations that would be made. Second, the primary image of the videotape, the brutality of the White officers toward the African-American victim, Rodney King, was easily related to earlier historic images of White police violence against African Americans. Finally, there existed a history of conflict between Police Chief Daryl Gates and minority groups in Los Angeles (Sonenshein, 1993). For all of these reasons, the Rodney King beating threatened the idealized vision of American society, "a society composed of individuals equal in their human worth . . . [where] humanity composed of individuals found its fulfillment" (Greenfeld, 1992, p. 449). Rather than reinforcing such an idealized view, the images on the videotape related a story of particularistic and violent exclusion.

The earliest constructions of the event as a crisis occurred in the *Los Angeles Times*, as well as in the television media.[2] The *Times* represented the beating as a wild deviation and a "shocking" event. It represented the officers as being irrational and excitable in their work and as having used their powers illegitimately. Accounts from witnesses reported that the officers were "laughing and chuckling [after the beating], like they had just had a party" (*Times*, 6 March 1991, p. A22). These interpretations were not presented as evaluations, but were placed within the descriptive frame of the "news account," with each account attributed to a source. At the same time, the polluting, counterdemocratic discourse of civil society was operating within the text: through quotations, editorials, and descriptions. The following descriptions of the event appeared in the first days of the crisis:

> Accounts . . . suggested that what should have been a relatively simple arrest . . . escalated wildly out of control. . . . The violent images of White police officers pounding an apparently defenseless Black man have raised the ire of civil rights groups. (7 March 1991, pp. A21–A22)

> The beating of King, videotaped by an amateur photographer, has sparked an outcry over police misconduct in Los Angeles, as well as calls for the resignation of Chief Daryl F. Gates. The images of White police officers pummeling the Black motorist with their batons were aired by television stations across the country. (9 March 1991, p. B1)

The news was attributed to "accounts," "civil rights groups," and "images aired by television stations." This kept it within the constraint of news objectivity and the routine practices of using official sources. At the same time, the words "violent," "wildly," "pounding," and "pummeling" operated to place the actors in symbolic relation to each other and to the discourse of civil society. After two weeks, the *Los Angeles Times* had written 55 articles about the Rodney King beating.

Along with the construction of the event as a crisis came a specification of those violations depicted by the video images: violations of fairness, openness, and justice. News reports described the character attributes of the antiheroic police officers, adding to earlier descriptions of their "uncontrolled and irrational" motivations. The event of the beating, when linked to the videotape, was understood as a way to expose the evil that existed in the LAPD. An editorial in the *Los Angeles Times* proclaimed that "this time, the police witnesses, knowing about the videotape, will probably not compound their offense by lying about what really happened" (*Los Angeles Times*, 9 March 1991, p. B7). This narration, exposing the secrecy and brutality of the officers, was used by local leaders as well as "objective" news reporters:

> It exploded onto Los Angeles television screens last week. The scene: three Los Angeles police officers involved in a merciless, relentless, brutal beating of a Black man as he lay face down in the ground, while 12 officers observed in tacit approval. (*Los Angeles Sentinel*, 14 March 1991, p. A1)

> "This is not an isolated incident!" thundered Jose de Sosa, the rally's organizer and president of the San Fernando chapter of the NAACP. "This is the type of thing that occurs under the cover of darkness throughout our city." (*Los Angeles Times*, 10 March 1991, p. B1)

The police officers were condemned through visual images as well as linguistic discourse. On the one hand, the images of the videotape served to "naturalize" the relationships between the police officers, brutality, and "darkness." On the other, the news reports represented the videotape as a foil to the deceitfulness of the police department. In this double sense, the police officers were symbolically polluted by the videotape.

Still, if it was merely a problem of a few individuals in need of administrative control, crisis need not have ensued. True, the fact that such an event could have occurred was represented as evidence of a fundamental problem in officer selection and training, which by itself brought some criticism of the police organization. But the real threat to *institutional* legitimacy was constructed through representations of Police Chief Daryl Gates, who was described as unaccountable, racist, and ego driven. From March 7 to March 11, there were four editorials about the beating, but none focused on Gates or the institution of the police department. From March 12 to March 14, however, there were six editorials about the crisis, and all focused on Gates and the question of the institutional integrity of the LAPD. The following two excerpts are typical of editorial opinion during the second week of the crisis.

The people of Los Angeles have been unable to hold their chief of police accountable for anything—not his racial slurs or racial stereotyping; not his openly-expressed contempt for the public, juries and the Constitution he is sworn to uphold; not his spying on political enemies or cover-up of that espionage. (*Los Angeles Times,* 12 March 1991, p. B7)

Chief Gates is responsible for inflammatory comments, for the actions of his officers and for the $8 million in taxpayer money paid out last year to satisfy complaints against the department. But because of rigid civil service protections, the police chief is not accountable to the mayor, the City Council or to the city's voters. (*Los Angeles Times,* 13 March 1991, p. B6)

Attached to Daryl Gates in these two excerpts were many different signs, and all were damaging to his symbolic status. Gates was constructed in relations of opposition to the public, the Constitution, the mayor, and the City Council. He was constructed in relations of similarity to the LAPD officers, who themselves had already been polluted. Gates and the LAPD were also opposed to the mayor and the City Council, who in turn benefited symbolically by their semiotic contiguity to the public and the Constitution.

Narrative Tension and the Elaboration of the Crisis

With the event having been constructed as a crisis, it began to be represented through a tension between two competing narrative forms, which I have summarized in Figure 13.2. On one side was a romantic "drama of redemption" pitting the heroic actors of the local government (the mayor and the City Council) against the antiheroic ones (Gates and the LAPD). In this narrative, which was employed by both the *Los Angeles Times* and the *Los Angeles Sentinel,* the heroic actors were not constructed through any sort of positive discourse, but rather through a semiotic opposition to Gates and the LAPD. Because Gates refused to hold his police officers accountable for their actions, and because he was coded by the counter-democratic discourse of institutions, the remaining local governmental officials became the defenders of institutional legitimacy more or less by default. This occurred on several different levels. Semiotically, it operated through opposition, where every term implies and entails its opposite. In this case, symbolic opposition to Gates benefited the mayor and the City Council. Politically, it worked because of the need for an identifiably legitimate authority. This political dynamic was expressed quite well in a *Los Angeles Sentinel* editorial, which argued that "this community has had enough police brutality and if the chief of police won't stop it, then the commission must, and if not, the mayor and the City Council must take definitive action" (7 March 1991, p. A8).

Narrative Form	Heroes	Discursive Qualities of Heroes	Antiheroes	Discursive Qualities of Antiheroes
Los Angeles Times:				
Romance	Mayor, City Council	Semiotic opposition to antiheroes	Gates, LAPD	Out of control, irrational, deceitful, not accountable
Tragedy	"The world" "the people"	Isolated, factions	White, middle-class citizens	Passive, horrified
Los Angeles Sentinel:				
Romance	Local government	Semiotic opposition to antiheroes	Gates, LAPD	Brutal, merciless, secretive
Romance	African-American community	Unified, moral, active	Gates, LAPD	Brutal, merciless, secretive
Tragedy	African-American community	Ironic memory	White, mainstream society	Racist, insincere

Figure 13.2   Narrative Forms of Crisis Construction

In the *Los Angeles Sentinel*, however, the actual composition of the romantic narrative differed in important respects from that of the *Times*. An important reason for this was the construction of a second romantic narrative in which the African-American community itself was posited as the heroic actor. In this "romance of the community," the heroic actor was represented not through a mere semiotic opposition, but through actual and positive discourse. Employing a style common to the African-American press (cf. Wolseley, 1971), the newspaper invoked the ideals of American society while criticizing that society as it actually existed. In opposition to mainstream society, the *Sentinel* represented the African-American community as the true voice of unity and morality, and hence as the only agent able to truly resolve the crisis. We can see the construction of this second romantic narrative in the following excerpts:

Rarely, if ever, has an issue so united the Black community in the way the March 3 Rodney King incident has done. The savage beating of King has inspired Los Angeles's Black community to speak with one voice. (*Los Angeles Sentinel,* 14 March 1991, p. A1)

We must not allow ourselves to be set apart in this battle. Justice must be served and we must, at least in part, be the instruments of that justice. (*Los Angeles Sentinel,* 28 March 1991, p. A7)

The African American community itself has a distinct role in the account-ability equation. In fact, the community represents the proverbial bottom line: it is the ultimate determinant of values and enforcers of acceptable standards. (*Los Angeles Sentinel,* 11 April 1991, p. A6)

In this romantic narrative, the beating of Rodney King became a transfor-mative event, unleashing the potential power of the African-American community. While Daryl Gates and the LAPD were still the villains of this narrative, there were new heroes.

In tension with the romantic narratives, both newspapers also used a tragic frame to interpret some of the events surrounding the crisis. In a tragic narrative, as Frye (1957, pp. 36–37, 282–87) notes, the drama must make a *tragic point;* that is, although the protagonist must be of a properly heroic stature, the development of the plot is one of ultimate failure. Thus, in the *Los Angeles Times* the public—what Sherwood (1994) has called the heroic actor of the "drama of democracy"—became represented as a series of factions, and it became more difficult to imagine a plot development where a new actor could successfully step in and do battle with Gates and the police department. Within the tragic genre, reaction to the beating was interpreted through a narrative of class, racial, and ethnic segregation rather than public unity. As an editorial in the *Los Angeles Times* lamented, "It is profoundly revealing that while middle-class viewers recoiled in hor-ror at the brutal footage, the victim, like many others familiar with police behavior in poor and minority neighborhoods, considered himself lucky that the police did not kill him" (*Los Angeles Times,* 14 March 1991, p. B5).

These types of accounts in the *Los Angeles Times* represented a "tragedy of fate," in the aporetic sense of resigned acceptance, a tragedy pointing to an evil "already there and already evil" (Ricoeur, 1967, p. 313). However, as Figure 13.2 shows, the tragic frame of the *Los Angeles Sentinel* diverged in important respects from such a tragedy of fate. The *Sentinel* combined ele-ments of tragedy and irony, calling up other recent instances of brutality against African Americans. News reports in the *Sentinel* juxtaposed the outrage and collective attention about the Rodney King beating with the relative lack of attention concerning another beating case whose trial had begun on the same day. The trial stemmed from the "Don Jackson case," a 1989 event where two Long Beach police officers were captured on videotape pushing an off-duty, African-American police officer through a plateglass window, "followed by the sight of Jackson being slammed onto the hood of their patrol car, after a 'routine' traffic stop" (*Los Angeles Sentinel,* 7 March 1991, p. A1). Although the *Los Angeles Times* had given the Don Jackson story significant coverage in 1989 (12 articles), it failed to make the textual attachment to the Rodney King beating in 1991. For the *Los Angeles Sentinel,* however, the Don Jackson story served as an important interpretive filter through which to view the Rodney King beating. Other historical events also found their way into the *Los Angeles Sentinel's* coverage. In a feature interview, Brotherhood Crusade leader Danny Bakewell noted, "When I saw what happened to that brother on television, I thought I was watching a scene out of the distant past: a Ku Klux Klan lynch mob at work" (*Los Angeles Sentinel,* 14 March 1991, p. A5). By recalling other instances of brutality against African Americans, writers for the *Los Angeles Sentinel* placed the event of the beating in the middle of a long and continuous narrative, rather than at the beginning of a new one.

It was unclear at this point which narrative form would prevail as the dominant understanding of the crisis in either newspaper. For both, the final act of the social drama would depend on the responses of political actors and on the interpretation of these actors' attempts to resolve the crisis. Even at this early point in the crisis, however, important differences were developing in the reports of the two newspapers. Specifically, the *Los Angeles Sentinel* constructed two competing romantic narratives and a more ironic–tragic narrative, both of which would have important consequences for subsequent news coverage.

Genre Strategies and the Formation of Official Investigations

With the crisis developing rapidly, members of the political elite launched investigations to try to maintain the romantic narrative (where they were the heroic figures) and to deflate the tragic one. Yet, just like the construction of the crisis, the success of these attempts was neither automatic nor guaranteed. In fact, the initial attempts to resolve the crisis through "official investigation" failed miserably. The first attempt was a grand jury investigation, begun the week after the beating. This investigation ultimately led to the trial of LAPD officers Theodore Briseno, Laurence Powell, Stacey Koon, and Timothy Wind. Despite the fact that it produced these indictments, however, the grand jury investigation was not selected by either newspaper as a significant event in their developing plots about the Rodney King crisis. There are several possible reasons for this. The first is that the indictments lacked temporal immediacy, in the sense that they could only provide symbolic closure in the far distant future, after the conclusion of a lengthy criminal trial. The second reason, and perhaps the more significant one, is that the grand jury actions did not follow any of the plot lines of the various narrative constructions. They did not involve the local government or the African-American community as heroes, they did not address the problem of the police chief, and they left unresolved the questions of fragmentation and segregation. Although the sequence of events following from the grand jury investigation eventually led to the extremely meaningful "not guilty" verdict of 1992, the initial event was insignificant to the narration of the crisis.

The second investigation came in the form of an FBI probe, begun March 12. This action did get incorporated into some of the different plots, but it was evaluated negatively by all of them. In relation to the *Los Angeles Sentinel*'s romantic narratives, the FBI probe failed to include the African-American community. In relation to the other romantic frames, the national-level FBI probe could only purify the police department by polluting the political actors who had been constructed as the romantic heroes: the mayor and the City Council. Resolution of the crisis by the FBI would have placed the political leaders of Los Angeles in a symbolic position of dependence, and the crisis would have ended with a new genre and a new plot: a comedy about the city's political leadership. The city's leaders would have been symbolically transformed from active leaders to *imposters* who, unable to fulfill the requirements of their office, would have been viewed instead as "blocking characters." Although this comedy could still have been constructed as a narrative of inclusion through the reconciliation or conversion of the imposter characters, it would have necessarily decreased political legitimacy for local government. The FBI probe was quickly criticized for being divisive and coercive, particularly in the *Los Angeles Times,* where the "romance of local government" seemed to resonate more strongly. Although the police officers were usually represented together with Daryl Gates as the antiheroes, when reporting about the FBI probe, the *Los Angeles Times* linked Gates to the FBI and the police officers to the symbols of citizenship and rights (26 March 1991, pp. A1, A19, and 3 April 1991, p. A10). This homology with Gates undercut the symbolic strength of the FBI; the event of the FBI probe soon faded from the plotlines of the Rodney King crisis.

The third attempt at resolution failed most completely and with the greatest effect for the discursive environment surrounding the Rodney King crisis. This was the effort by Mayor Tom Bradley to remove Gates from his position as police chief. Initially, Bradley had refused to call for Gates's removal. But the failure of the FBI and the grand jury investigations, as well as growing public opinion against Gates, led Bradley to change his mind. Bradley called publicly for Gates to resign and represented a Gates resignation as a means of healing for the city and as a way for Gates to purify himself for the good of the public. He urged Gates to resign "for the good of the LAPD and the welfare of all of Los Angeles," and by doing so to show "uncommon courage" (*Los Angeles Times*, 3 April 1991, pp. Al, A10).

When Gates refused to step down from his position, the Police Commission, at Bradley's urging, temporarily removed Daryl Gates from his duties as police chief. This action, far from resolving the crisis, only inflamed it, reinforcing and respecifying the tragic narrative. The City Council criticized the Police Commission for being dependent on Bradley, attacked Bradley for being motivated by power instead of the public good, and described the action as "illegal" and "irresponsible" (*Los Angeles Times*, 6 April 1991, p. A1). One prominent City Council member, Joel Wachs, linked the action to the Watergate crisis, calling it "a shocking abuse of our time-honored system of government" (*Los Angeles Times*, 5 April 1991, p. A23). The Police Commission (which had been powerless until Bradley's mayoral victory in 1973) responded that "the action we have taken is on sound legal grounds and the court will back us" (attributed to Police Commission member Melanie Lomax and quoted in the *Los Angeles Times*, 5 April 1991, p. A1). Bradley tried to connect this emerging crisis with the larger Rodney King crisis, in which he was the hero, Gates was the villain, and any action against Gates was therefore a heroic act:

> It is my hope that today's Police Commission action will give us all time to bridge the differences that have grown between us since the Rodney King incident. . . . The Police Commission is using a well-established procedure. (*Los Angeles Times*, 5 April 1991, p. A23)

> "I acted in good faith in what I felt were legitimate concerns," Bradley said Saturday. "There was divisiveness in the city. The chief was at the center of the storm of protests and so long as he remained in the position it was not likely to change." (*Los Angeles Times*, 7 April 1991, p. A30)

It was certainly understandable for Bradley to link the Police Commission's action to the larger Rodney King crisis. However, the pollu- tion of power and ego proved to be more powerful than his metaphor of healing or his discourse of procedure. The *Los Angeles Times* increasingly described the mayor as "working behind the scenes" and "cranking up the political pressure," descriptive terms which resonated with the counterde- mocratic code of motives and relationships. On April 6, just one month after the beating, the *Los Angeles Times* reported the results of a poll show- ing that 60 percent of those surveyed believed that "the mayor was trying to further his political aspirations rather than . . . to mend a divided city" (*Los Angeles Times*, 6 April 1991, p. A1). Bradley had been successful in making the removal of Gates a turning point for the Rodney King crisis; however, the direction of the narrative development was not what he had wanted.

Narrative Updating Amidst
Failed Attempts at Resolution

As I have shown, none of the initial attempts to resolve the crisis were successful. The grand jury investigation was largely ignored by the press, the FBI probe was eventually deemphasized after being criticized, and the conflict between the City Council and the Police Commission did little except hurt the mayor's approval ratings. News reports in the *Los Angeles Times* responded to these failed actions of the political elites by updating the two narrative constructions and shifting the relative importance accorded to each genre. On the one hand, reports from "civic leaders" strengthened the tragic narrative of factionalism, claiming that "the intense fight over Gates's tenure has further polarized the city, politicized the issue and obscured the fundamental questions of brutality, racism, and police training raised by the King beating" (*Los Angeles Times,* 1 April 1991, p. A13). At the same time as the tragic genre was reinforced, other reports weakened the romance of local government, noting with irony the lack of heroism among city leaders. As an editorial in the *Los Angeles Times* noted, "The Rodney King beating has brought to the surface ugly problems in Los Angeles: not only the allegations of police brutality, but the now exposed factionalism among races and ethnic groups and the tensions between longtime city powers who fear too much change and new line city powers who fear too little" (*Los Angeles Times,* 29 March 1991, p. B6). In this new plot, the event of the beating was not only linked to the problems of police brutality, but also to the weakness of local leaders.

. . . For the *Los Angeles Times,* the romantic "drama of redemption"— positing local government as hero—had devolved into a *satire* of romance, where "a slight shift of perspective . . . and the solid earth becomes an intolerable horror . . . [showing us] man as a venomous rodent" (Frye 1957, p. 235). In this satirical form the romance threatened to turn into bitter tragedy, but without the usual sympathy for the tragic figure. Charged with the task of cleansing society from the evil of Police Chief Gates and the LAPD, local government leaders instead became represented as selfish, egotistical, and deceitful. As a result the tragic genre resonated more strongly in the *Los Angeles Times.*

In the *Los Angeles Sentinel,* too, the tragic form resonated strongly during this period. However, for the *Sentinel,* the romance of the African-American community continued to exert a powerful influence on the interpretation of the crisis. In this plot, the *Los Angeles Sentinel* continued to represent the African-American community as a unified group who needed to demand their right to economic and political empowerment (4 April 1991, p. A1; 11 April 1991, p. A6; 16 May 1991, p. A6). This depiction of heroic action on the part of the African-American community contrasted with that of the LAPD. Reports in the *Sentinel* editorialized about the commonality of unpunished police brutality and reported that African-American police officers had to deal with racist behavior from other police officers in their daily police routines (11 April 1991, p. A7; 18 April 1991, pp. A1, A7; 25 April 1991, pp. A1, A16; 2 May 1991, pp. A1, A14; 9 May 1991, p. A1; 16 May 1991, p. A1; 23 May 1991, p. A1; 13 June 1991, p. A1).

In this narrative context, where the negative characteristics of the police department continued to be described through the romantic genre, the conflict between the Police Commission and City Council had a different meaning. News reports in the *Los Angeles Sentinel* placed Bradley and the Police Commission in a heroic context and Gates and the City Council in an antiheroic one. There was no causal link here between the event and "factionalism." Rather, the *Sentinel* accepted the discourse of procedure and the metaphor of healing in its representation of the Police Commission's decision to remove Gates (*Los Angeles Sentinel*, 11 April 1991, p. A6). By contrast, when the City Council reinstated Gates, the *Sentinel* described the council members through the same attributes used for the police officers—deceit and unreasonableness:

> With regard to the council's decision to pay the police chief's legal fees . . . that probably will be millions of dollars out of the taxpayer's pocket. . . . I guess the City Council will have to answer to their voters about their decision to pay what could be millions in legal fees on the chief's behalf. (*Los Angeles Sentinel*, 2 May 1991, p. A14)

> This last proviso, regarding monetary damages, seems a hollow gesture to lend authenticity to the City Council action, because Gates out of his own mouth states that he seeks no money damages. (*Los Angeles Sentinel*, 11 April 1991, p. A6)

Thus, during this period the romantic narratives of the *Los Angeles Sentinel* remained relatively stable, with the only real change being a specification of which local government leaders were heroes (and which were antiheroes). In fact, whereas White support of Mayor Bradley decreased from 49 percent to 41 percent after the temporary removal of Police Chief Gates, African American support of Bradley actually increased during this period, from 54 percent to 64 percent (Sonenshein, 1993, p. 213). In a discursive environment where the conflict between the City Council and Mayor Bradley was represented in such unambiguous terms, the tragic–ironic narrative also remained stable. Within this frame, the *Sentinel*'s monitoring of the mainstream media meant that it began to interpret the reactions of the "mainstream" community, where support for Bradley had dropped, in an increasingly negative light. The *Los Angeles Sentinel* began to evaluate the mainstream public, and its reactions to the crisis, through the polluting discourse of factionalism and falsity. The following news excerpt is indicative of this shift: "While America pretended to be in shock, Black America was not shocked at all. . . . The attack on Rodney King is a part of the historical pattern of violent oppression of Africans in America which has been visited upon our people ever since we arrived here in a condition of involuntary servitude" (*Los Angeles Sentinel,* 11 April 1991, p. A7). In this type of interpretation, anyone who would be surprised by the beating in effect denied the history of racism and of slavery. This monitoring of the mainstream media led to the continuing resonance of the tragic–ironic narrative in the *Los Angeles Sentinel.*

The Christopher Commission and the Move Toward Resolution

Resolution of the crisis would, for the discursive community of the *Los Angeles Times,* require the creation of a new hero; for the *Los Angeles Sentinel,* it would require that this new hero, if not the African-American community itself, at least be attached to that community. The "hero" who was eventually to satisfy the conditions of both communities was the Christopher Commission and its "Report of the Independent Commission of the Los Angeles Police Department," released to the public on July 9, 1991. The Christopher Commission was composed of representatives from all institutional branches of "elite" civil society. It was co-chaired by John Arguelles, a retired California State Supreme Court judge, and by Warren Christopher, a former deputy attorney general and deputy secretary of state. Also included in the commission were two university professors, a college president, three accomplished lawyers, the president of the Los Angeles County Bar Association, and a corporate executive.

Despite these symbolic resources, the Christopher Commission was not automatically cast in its ultimate role as romantic hero. It had originally been formed as two separate investigations: the Arguelles Commission, formed by Daryl Gates, and the Christopher Commission, instituted by Tom Bradley. Like the preceding investigations, the *Los Angeles Times* initially represented both commissions in a negative light—considering them to be politically motivated and dependent. The Arguelles Commission was represented as being tied too closely to Gates, whereas the Christopher Commission was considered to be too close to Bradley. The decisive move toward symbolic resolution of the crisis came with the merging of the two commissions into an expanded Christopher Commission. As an event, the merging of the two commissions presented an opportunity for new narrations of the crisis to be made. Both Arguelles and Christopher made numerous public statements representing the merged commission as an independent, cooperative, and objective body whose orientation was directed toward the good of the public. They represented their merged commission as a movement away from the tragedy of factionalism and back toward the romance of local government. As the following excerpts demonstrate, their efforts were reflected in the *Los Angeles Times:*

> The heads of the panels . . . said they were seeking to distance themselves from the clash as the Police Commission forced Gates to take a leave. (*Los Angeles Times,* 5 April 1991, p. A23)

> "I think it would be good for everybody if we could come up with some kind of coordinated effort," said retired State Supreme Court Justice John Arguelles, the head of Gates's five-member civilian panel. "There are [now] two committees that might be perceived as having independent agendas that they might want to advance." (*Los Angeles Times,* 2 April 1991, p. Al)

> "In order to maximize the commission's contribution to the community," Christopher and Arguelles said in a joint statement, "we must concentrate on making an objective and thorough study of the long-term issues without being drawn into the controversy over the tenure of Chief Gates." (*Los Angeles Times,* 5 April 1991, p. A23)

In an environment dominated by satirical and tragic interpretations, even this merged commission was understood skeptically, and its report was forecast by some to be an "impressive study . . . that ends up just sitting on somebody's shelf" (*Los Angeles Times,* 11 April 1991, p. A10). Nevertheless, when the Christopher Commission's report was released on July 9— completed "within a restricted time frame because delay would not be in the public interest" (cover sheet of the "Report of the Independent Commission on the Los Angeles Police Department")—the density of media coverage about the crisis surged. In the *Los Angeles Times,* whereas there were three articles about the Rodney King crisis the week before the release of the report, there were 48 articles in the subsequent week; in the *Los Angeles Sentinel,* the density of articles increased from three articles to nine over the same period of time. But the report not only provoked a quantitative change in media discourse, but also engendered a qualitative shift. The event became a turning point for all of the narrative understandings of the Rodney King crisis. In the *Los Angeles Times,* it was interpreted through a religious metaphor of revelation strengthening the romantic narrative:

> Just as the Rodney G. King videotape gave the American public an unfiltered glimpse of police brutality, so did the Christopher Commission open a window Tuesday on the working lives of Los Angeles police, exposing strains of racism, violence, and callousness toward the public they are sworn to protect . . . Throughout the inquiry, both men said, they were acutely aware of the high expectations for their efforts. Arguelles talked of producing a report that would be seen as "visionary." (*Los Angeles Times,* 10 July 1991, pp. A10, A17).

The *Los Angeles Times* began to interpret the release of the Christopher Commission report as a symbolic completion of the crisis begun by the videotape. If the videotape provided the beginning of the narrative, the report enabled its closure. With this interpretive shift the satirical and tragic frames disappeared from the reports of the *Los Angeles Times*. At this point, the discursive environment of the *Los Angeles Times* began to resemble a cultural situation that Turner (1969) has called "reaggregation." Whereas authority figures had previously been represented as being divided and politically motivated, they were now represented as being open and cooperative, unified in their support of the Christopher Commission report, and motivated by the duty of office and concern for the public. Attention also shifted back to Police Chief Gates, who was represented as increasingly ego driven and out of touch with the public. As the following news reports demonstrate, the sharp opposition drawn between Gates and the remaining political leaders helped to increase the legitimacy of those leaders:

> "It appears as though a pattern is beginning to develop at Parker Center to punish or harass those who cooperated with the Christopher Commission and to intimidate others from cooperating in the future," [City Councilman] Yaroslovsky said. "This is an untenable situation, which the Police Commission should immediately move to restore." (*Los Angeles Times*, 16 July 1991, p. A7)

> The councilmen's good faith should not be trifled with by Gates. He can either cooperate with the council members and business leaders who would try to work with him on a transition or he can try to fight the many lined up against him. (*Los Angeles Times*, 17 July 1991, p. B10)

> Over a turbulent 10-day period, some of the most prominent political, business, and labor leaders wrestled with a difficult mission: how to persuade Police Chief Daryl Gates to commit to a retirement date. (*Los Angeles Times*, 24 July 1991, p. Al)

Former political adversaries, such as the Police Commission and the City Council, were now calling on one another to help in a common cause. Business and labor leaders, who had previously not been significant players in the social drama, were reported to be joining the unified effort. Articles in the *Los Angeles Times* reported that other area police departments, such as those in Pasadena, Long Beach, Santa Monica, Maywood, and the Los Angeles Sheriff's Office, were also conforming with the Christopher Commission reforms. Finally, when two of Gates's strongest supporters—councilmen John Ferraro and Joel Wachs—called for his resignation, the symbolization of political unity was virtually complete, at least for the *Los Angeles Times*.

. . . In the *Los Angeles Sentinel*, however, collective memory continued to play a significant role in the coverage of the crisis. We can see this from the earliest events leading up to the release of the Christopher Commission report. In its evaluations of the separate Christopher and Arguelles commissions, the *Sentinel* identified the latter with Gates and the former with Bradley and used the appropriate sides of the bifurcating discourse of civil society to interpret their actions. The *Sentinel* reported about the merging of the two commissions in a manner far different than the *Los Angeles Times*:

> Earlier Gates said that his Arguelles Commission would cooperate with Bradley's Christopher Commission. Subsequent reports indicate that the Arguelles Commission has had difficulty in attracting panel members and that the two commissions would merge—a prospect not too much to the liking of the Brotherhood Crusades' Danny Bakewell or acting Police Commission President Melanie Lomax. (*Los Angeles Sentinel*, 4 April 1991, p. A3)

The *Los Angeles Sentinel* interpreted the possibility of a merger between the two commissions as being necessitated by the weakness of the Arguelles Commission. In a direct metaphor of pollution, the Arguelles Commission was interpreted as something to be avoided, as a potential danger to the purity of the Christopher Commission.

Nevertheless, when the merged commission's report was released, the *Los Angeles Sentinel* described it as a "window of opportunity" and as an investigation of "extensiveness . . . forthrightness . . . and validity" (11 July 1991, p. A6). In this respect it mirrored the *Los Angeles Times*. At the same time, however, the *Sentinel* did not construct the commission report as a bridge toward the legitimation of local government leaders, but rather as a justification for the longstanding criticisms made by the African-American community. In this respect, the event of the Christopher Commission report was linked to the romance of the African-American community. John Mack, executive director of the Los Angeles Urban League, argued that the report "confirmed what we already know: that racism is rampant in the LAPD" (*Los Angeles Sentinel*, 11 July 1991, p. A15). By attaching the event to the romantic narrative of the African-American community, the *Sentinel* reinforced the heroic role of the Black community at the same time that it extended such a role to the commission and its report. If local leaders wanted to be narrated into a heroic role by the *Sentinel*, they would have to include the African-American community in the resolution of the crisis and would have to recognize that community's collective memory.

Notably, the focus in the *Sentinel* was on the reform recommendations, the findings of bias, and the issue of racism, rather than on the unity of the political leadership in its quest to remove Gates. Rather than relying on sources of support from the political and business leadership, the *Sentinel's* representation of support for the commission included City Councilman Michael Woo, Brotherhood Crusade leader Danny Bakewell, and the African-American Peace Officer Association, as well as "community leaders and various community coalitions long critical of Chief Gates and the practices and politics of the LAPD" (*Los Angeles Sentinel,* 18 July 1991, p. A1). The voices heard through the *Sentinel* did not readily forgive the political leaders, the police department, or "White society." They continued to represent the police department as exclusive and racist and to identify other area police departments (such as the Lynwood Sheriff's Office) as racist. The durable text of police oppression, always available for the *Sentinel,* was again brought forth as new incidents of brutality were revealed. As the following excerpts demonstrate, the *Los Angeles Sentinel* continued to represent the political system and mainstream society by using the antiheroic side of the discursive code:

> After the Rodney King beating, the barrage of nationwide media publicity and public disgust lulled citizens into a false sense of pride and complacency, encouraging them to believe that impending recommendations on LAPD practices and politics would serve to turn the department's mentality around. Then along came the Vernell Ramsey case—another Black Foothill victim alleging excessive force by the LAPD. (*Los Angeles Sentinel,* 19 September 1991, p. Al)

> Recent City Council debates—13 so far—over Christopher Commission recommendations have led to a barrage of complaints from community leaders and various coalitions. One of the main arguments has been the issue of power. Critics charge that the City Council has too much and has become lackadaisical about responsibly exercising its duties. (*Los Angeles Sentinel,* 22 August 1991, p. A1)

Thus ... there was no real narrative consolidation in the *Los Angeles Sentinel* after the release of the Christopher Commission report. The romance of the African-American community continued to be the dominant romantic genre for reporting about the crisis. It was supplemented by a "romance of the Christopher Commission," where the commission was constructed in relations of similarity to the African-American community instead of being attached to local government. Local government leaders, and the City Council in particular, were viewed largely as a threat to the resolution of the crisis. Similarly, the tragic–ironic narrative persisted. White citizens were interpreted as being not sufficiently concerned or vigilant enough to ensure that the reforms would be enacted. In other words, whereas the *Los Angeles Times* had narrated the event of the commission report as a link to political leadership and public unity, the *Los Angeles Sentinel* had narrated it as a link to African-American leadership and public complacency. In doing so, both newspapers were following the "narrative logic" that had developed during the course of events.

Conclusion

. . . The Rodney King crisis was socially constructed as several different problems in several different public spheres. In the *Los Angeles Times* it was constructed as a problem of police brutality, of factionalism, and of political divisiveness. In the *Los Angeles Sentinel* it was constructed as a problem of police brutality, of White insincerity, and of the need for African-American empowerment. The construction of these problems depended on the event, its narration by different social actors, and the ability of these actors to draw on codes and narratives that particular discursive communities found both plausible and dramatic. . . .

Clearly, the event of the Rodney King beating had important consequences for subsequent narrative understandings about race relations and civil society. But the event had neither a unitary nor a necessary meaning. Whereas it was constructed in the *Los Angeles Times* as the beginning of a narrative of crisis, in the *Los Angeles Sentinel* it was inserted into the middle of an ongoing narrative about civil rights and police brutality. Furthermore, the meaning of the beating changed as new events were added to the various narrative constructions. Some events, such as the grand jury investigation, were "meaningless," in the sense that they were not significant for the narrative constructions of the crisis. This is noticeable in that the sequence of events following the grand jury investigation ultimately became very meaningful following the not-guilty verdicts for the four officers indicted in the original investigation. Other events, such as the FBI probe, were initially meaningful but were soon removed from the ongoing narrative constructions and thus made inconsequential. Still other events, such as the conflict between the Police Commission and City Council, changed the earlier meaning of the crisis. The point is that both meanings and outcomes depend on the interaction between events and their narrative understandings, a finding supported by related studies of collective action (see, e.g., Ellingson, 1995; Kane, 1994) and violence (e.g., Wagner-Pacifici, 1986, 1994).

Finally . . . genre plays an important part in how events get narrated, linked to other events, and infused with social expectation. This is an important addition to narrative analysis and its focus on events, plots, and characters. Genre influences the expected outcome of a particular narrative construction by constructing a set of expectations for the hero and for the conclusion of the story. . . . The analysis of narrative and genre allows us to address more fully the relationship between the analytic properties of culture and their concrete articulation in real events. For this reason, a "narrative sociology" can help social scientists to better understand the dynamics of social process and social change.

References

Abbott, A. (1988). Transcending general linear reality. *Sociological Theory, 6,*169–86.

Alexander, J. C. (1992). Citizen and enemy as symbolic classification: On the polarizing discourse of civil society. In M. Fournier & M. Lamont (Eds.), *Where culture talks: Exclusion and the making of society* (pp. 289–308). Chicago, IL: University of Chicago Press.

Alexander, J. C., & Smith, P. (1993). The discourse of American civil society: A new proposal for cultural studies. *Theory and Society, 22,* 151–207.

Eco, U. (1994). *Six walks in the fictional woods.* Cambridge, MA: Harvard University Press.

Ellingson, S. (1995). Understanding the dialectic of discourse and collective action: Public debate and rioting in antebellum Cincinnati. *American Journal of Sociology, 101,* 100–144.

Frye, N. (1957). *Anatomy of criticism.* Princeton, NJ: Princeton University Press.

Greenfeld, L. (1992). *Nationalism: Five roads to modernity.* Cambridge, MA: Harvard University Press.

Iyengar, S. (1987). Television news and citizens' explanations of national affairs. *American Political Science Review, 81,* 815–31.

Janowitz, M., & Suttles, G. (1977, 1991). The social ecology of citizenship. In J. Burk (Ed.), *On social organization and social control* (pp. 251–71). Chicago, IL: University of Chicago Press.

Kane, A. (1994). Culture and social change: Symbolic construction, ideology, and political alliance during the Irish Land War, 1879–1881. Doctoral dissertation. University of California, Los Angeles, CA, Department of Sociology.

Lyle, J. (1967). *The news in megalopolis.* San Francisco: Chandler.

McCombs, M., & Shaw, D. (1972). The agenda-setting function of the press. *Public Opinion Quarterly, 36,*176–87.

Nelson, B. (1984). *Making an issue of child abuse: Political agenda setting for social problems.* Chicago, IL: University of Chicago Press.

Ricoeur, P. (1967). *The symbolism of evil.* Boston, MA: Beacon Press.

Sherwood, S. (1994). Narrating the social. *Journal of Narratives and Life Histories, 4,* 69–88.

Sonenshein, R. (1993). *Politics in black and white: Race and power in Los Angeles.* Princeton, NJ: Princeton University Press.

Steinmetz, G. (1992). Reflections on the role of social narratives in working class formation: Narrative theories in the social sciences. *Social Science History, 16,* 489–516.

Turner, V. 1969. *The ritual process.* Chicago, IL: Aldine.

Wagner-Pacifici, R. (1986). *The Moro morality play: Terrorism as social drama.* Chicago, IL: University of Chicago Press.

Wagner-Pacifici, R., & Schwartz, B. (1991). The Vietnam veterans memorial: Commemorating a difficult past. *American Journal of Sociology, 97,* 376–420.

Wagner-Pacifici, R. (1994). *Discourse and destruction: The city of Philadelphia versus MOVE.* Chicago, IL: University of Chicago Press.

Wolseley, R. (1971). *The black press, U.S.A.* Ames, IA: Iowa State University Press.

Notes

1. The *Sentinel*, like most other African-American newspapers, is distributed weekly. For a discussion of why the weekly format predominates for the African-American press, see Wolseley, 1971, especially pp. 87–90.

2. Being a weekly newspaper, the news reports of the *Los Angeles Sentinel* were constructed in an environment where the initial "agenda" of the crisis had already been set by the daily press. For a more detailed discussion of agenda setting, see McCombs & Shaw (1972), Nelson (1984), and Iyengar (1987).

Working

Growth of
High-Technology Culture*

Everett M. Rogers
and Judith K. Larsen

14

---

editor's introduction:

Methodological Significance

Data from open-ended interviews are another common form of case study evidence. Such interviews do not typically employ a structured questionnaire instrument but assume a more "conversational" mode—requiring the investigator to have a sound prior knowledge of the subject matter if not about the specific person being interviewed.

The present selection shows how the data from such interviews (as well as several interviews that appeared in the printed media) can be presented as part of a case study. Helpful in solidifying the evidentiary base is a series of footnotes, indicating the specific source and date of the interviews, including situations in which several interviewees are only identified by a pseudonym (see the names in quotation marks), to preserve their anonymity. Although the authors clearly make no claim that

---

they drew their sample of interviewees in any systematic fashion, the descriptive themes that emerge are plausible, and confidence in the findings is increased by both the large number of interviewees (about 20) and the in-depth presentations of some of the interviewees' experiences.

Substantive Note

The entirety of the book from which this selection comes is a case study of the high-tech culture of Silicon Valley. Each chapter of the book by Rogers and Larsen covers a different aspect of the culture. In addition to "working," the chapters include such topics as "networks," "lifestyles," "goodies," "losing—companies that don't make it," and other topics on the beginnings and future of Silicon Valley. The book also includes an embedded case about *Intel,* a successful high-tech firm. (See Chapter 12 of this anthology for part of this embedded case.)

The emergence and success of Silicon Valley symbolized a major evolution in the American economy and a significant shift of the entire American society to a high-technology culture, in the latter part of the 20th century. As such, the case study captures one of the most significant developments in American history. Although written 20 years ago, the book's main themes (e.g., the region's outrageous housing prices or the role of venture capitalists) still appear relevant to contemporary times. A possible exception is the book's discussion of the life of working women, who today have advanced with greater frequency into more technical and managerial positions. The origins of Silicon Valley, however, remain the same. These are captured not only as historical matters but also with (tape-recorded) personal interviews of key early leaders in the Valley's development, most of whom are now deceased. In this sense, the case study also was conducted at an important moment in history.

Talk to virtually anyone in Silicon Valley and you hear about the long hours. Why? Competition forces them, for one thing. Alan Shugart, originally of IBM, then Memorex, then president of Shugart Associates, and now president of Seagate Technology, stated, "You've got to pick out what the market is going to do and go for it. Seven years from now there will be a new technology doing what we do now. Someone will latch on to it. I hope I find it first." And a former Seagate employee now heading a spin-off said, "You get used to running 100 miles an hour while looking back over your shoulder."[1] Or as Karl Harrington, a semiconductor engineer, told us, "There is a real urgency here that is different from old-line industries. For us, the timing is tremendous. Beating a competitor to market by 60 days may be the difference between surviving and going under. Whoever gets to the marketplace first makes a splash."[2]

Some Silicon Valley people simply like to work. They put in long hours and cope with the job-related stress because they like microelectronics better than working in an established industry where they feel most people are bored clock-watchers. Many technical people are motivated by curiosity about how to make a device work, or how to make it work better. Such curiosity is also motivated by knowing that it will pay off in money, often lots of it. Adam Osborne of Osborne Computer said, "Here [in Silicon Valley] it is what you can get done and the faster the better."[3] Al Shugart confesses, "We all work hard because we all want to make a fortune in a hurry."[4]

Not only are the hours long and the pace fast, but also Silicon Valley workdays are intense. Rarely do people come to work and sit around chatting about news, weather, or sports. A production manager told us, "I've never had a cup of *coffee* in our cafeteria. I go to the cafeteria with my peers to discuss problems, but I have never taken a coffee break. I can get coffee and drink it in my office all I want. But there are so many things that have to get done each day that are waiting for you and you have to get going on them. There's a sense of urgency. These are requests from your colleagues and they need it right *now*."

Ray Brant, vice-president for human relations at National Semiconductor, contracted a rare blood disease that had to be treated with intravenous medication 24 hours a day. The disease required hospitalization, but Brant talked his way out of that because of his heavy workload. The semiconductor executive carried his intravenous bottle and pump with him to business meetings and arranged his car so the medication pumped as he drove. "If I backed off work for six weeks, I'd be too far off stream when I came back," he said.[5]

Some of the work intensity is self-induced; perhaps the ambitious people working in Silicon Valley prefer pressure. Nick Larsen commented, "We set the pace ourselves. If the wheel were running at 100 percent, we would spin it up to 120 every morning. Nothing's happening unless you're a little frantic. I've often seen design groups induce this frantic feeling themselves in order to get their juices flowing. There's nothing like a little fear and urgency to force creativity."[6]

It isn't enough just to be hard-working and dedicated. Meritocracy reigns supreme in Silicon Valley and that means knowing what you are doing. It's not who you know, who your parents were, where you went to school, or what clubs you belong to. It's *what* you know; intelligence is mandatory. Most who have made it in Silicon Valley have an extensive technical education. Budding entrepreneurs often started working on some technical problem while in college. Engineer Karl Harrington described the talent of employees in his small R&D company, "I report to a fellow who has four other managers reporting to him. Of the four of us, three have Ph.Ds. My boss has a Ph.D. and his boss has a Ph.D. I work with extremely bright and capable people who move quickly, both intellectually and conceptually. I have to use every wily trick I can think of just to survive."[7]

Lee Felsenstein, a Computer Kid and one of the main designers of the Osborne computer, thinks that engineering design work is so much fun that he never wants to leave it to become a manager. He had the title of "Research Fellow" at Osborne Computer Corporation, a similar job description to that of engineer Rod Holt's "Apple Fellow"—and to Ted Hoff's former title of "Intel Fellow." Felsenstein says, "It's fun to design a printed circuit board for a microcomputer. When we were designing the Osborne computer, I worked all three shifts on some days. The difference between tools and toys is not much."[8]

High-tech industry moves so fast that there is never time to relax and consolidate. People who work in Silicon Valley can't settle back and coast. If they do, they coast right out of the industry. Alice Ahlgren, director of communication at Cromemco, described this fast pace and its accompanying stress.[9] Cromemco, a computer manufacturer, had decided to enter the microcomputer market. Their new product, the C-10, was to be unveiled at the National Computer Conference. Just three days before this trade show, Cromemco engineers were still making final adjustments on the C-10. Ahlgren explained that if they weren't ready for this show, the opportunity would not come around again for another year. With three days to go, she balanced her anxiety against the fact that Cromemco had not yet missed a deadline; somehow the product would be ready—it was. Such an edge-of-the cliff existence doesn't make for nights of easy sleep. But on the other hand, life and work in Silicon Valley never gets dull either.

Frank Vella is a veteran engineer with 20 years in the valley. He has a paradoxical attraction and distaste for the work ethic, "A young engineer gets a macho thrill in working long days and all weekend. He has heard how everybody works long hours and now he has a chance to do it. He is earning his wings, the right to say 'I'm a bona fide member of Silicon Valley.' Wiser heads set the boundaries on what part of our lives we let work have. I've paid my dues and am interested in other things in my life. I worked my weekends and all those days in a row without a break. The longest stretch I worked was 59 days in a row, when the shortest day was 8 hours and the longest was 17. It simply doesn't turn me on anymore."[10]

How does the work ethic in Silicon Valley compare with other industries? Kleis Bahmann, who had worked in aerospace for 10 years and then switched to microelectronics, explains, "In aerospace the idea was not to get the work done, but to follow the freaking rules. Here we get on with the task; in aerospace you have to fill out the paperwork. People who think of themselves as doers rather than compliers are attracted to Silicon Valley. Hell, if my aerospace boss came over and said, 'You've written 100 engineering orders with no mistakes in the paperwork and that's good,' I would say, 'Any idiot can do that. You can tell me it's great, but both of us know it isn't.' But when you build a computer and get it working, it's obvious that you've done something neat."[11]

The Great Engineering Shortage

The Silicon Valley microelectronics industry sucks up university graduate engineers. The national shortage of engineers has roots in the public school system, where reductions in the number of qualified math and science teachers occurred as the result of budget cuts.[12] When students from the retrenched public schools reach college, there is a problem of not enough qualified professors. Salaries for assistant professors of engineering average $19,000, while salaries for engineers in industry begin at $25,000.

The United States graduates about 60,000 engineers annually. The Soviet Union, with a total population approximately equal to the United States, graduates 300,000 engineers. Japan, with half the population of the United States, graduates 75,000 engineers.[13] The United States awards about 6 percent of all undergraduate degrees in engineering. Comparable figures are 21 percent in Japan, 35 percent in the Soviet Union, and 37 percent in Western Germany. "Neither the strategic importance of education nor its close link to high technology is widely recognized and understood in America."[14]

In high-tech industry, a B.S. in engineering is a requisite for entry. Yet five years out of college, 50 percent of an engineer's knowledge is obsolete. Working engineers must be recycled.[15] There has been a call for universities to provide off-campus, part-time graduate programs for engineers, and for industry to encourage engineers to spend up to 10 percent of their time in graduate-level classes. The American Electronics Association and the Massachusetts High-Technology Council are collaborating in a campaign to convince 1,500 companies to give 2 percent of their R&D budgets to an engineering educational foundation, amounting to $40 million annually.

Women in Silicon Valley

The Silicon Valley microelectronics industry has been called "one of the last great bastions of male dominance" by the local *Peninsula Times Tribune*.[16] Women are mainly in positions as line operators, secretaries, and clerical workers. They are under-represented in management and administration. Few women have technical or engineering backgrounds, and they are thought to lack the necessary qualifications for these jobs. However, many men in administrative or managerial positions also lack technical backgrounds. Why there are few women in positions of responsibility in Silicon Valley is complex and puzzling. Until recently the overwhelming majority of engineering graduates were men. Women received only 175 degrees in engineering in the United States in 1950, but 6,100 in 1980.[17] Whereas in 1965 less than 1 percent of B.S. engineers were women, by 1980 the figure had increased to nearly 10 percent.[18] However, females have yet to enter the boardrooms or the executive suites of Silicon Valley.

Venture capitalists and entrepreneurs hold a firm grip over Silicon Valley. Most new firms are formed as startups with capital provided by venture funds. Scientific and engineering professionals in the finance community and in startups are likely to be men; these power-brokers rely exclusively on their personal networks, passing information about job openings, possibilities for expansion, and promising companies to their friends—other men. Women are virtually absent from the power centers of Silicon Valley corporations. Twenty of the largest publicly held Silicon Valley firms listed a total of 209 persons as corporate officers in 1980; only 4 were women. The boards of directors of these 20 firms include 150 directors. Only one was a woman: Shirley Hufstedler, serving on the board of Hewlett-Packard.

Although these limitations inhibit the participation of women in decision-making positions in the Valley, there are also opportunities. The need for trained employees exceeds the number of applicants; therefore, if you have the credentials, you stand a good chance of being hired. Ann Wells, president of Ann Wells Personnel Services, observed, "Anybody with a technical degree can be placed. A Martian with three heads could find a job in Silicon Valley. So for women with a technical background, it's terrific."[19]

Frances is in sales in a Silicon Valley semiconductor firm. Her story is typical of the experience of many Silicon Valley women. "I majored in French in college, taught for two years, and found I really didn't like it. So I got a job for a distributor in customer service where I learned about electronics. That was in 1972. I worked there for a year and then moved to my present job in semiconductor sales. At that time there were no women in product marketing or sales, so there was no place for me to go. An opening came up in product marketing dealing with the military group, where I could see there would be room for advancement. I got this job in 1979. I was the first woman in our company to get a marketing job. The people I worked for were leery about my ability since I'm a woman. The big problem was traveling. Now there are two women in product marketing. My next goal is to be a regional distributor sales manager. There are no women in this position now. The drawback is that I don't have field sales experience. How do I get it, if they won't let me travel?"[20]

An exception to masculine domination in engineering is Sandy Kurtzig, president of ASK Computer Systems. ASK is an OEM (original equipment manufacturer) that sells software computer programs for accounting, cost-control, and other financial uses to large companies. ASK's software is integrated into Hewlett-Packard minicomputer hardware, so that turnkey (ready to operate) systems are provided to customers. Sandy Kurtzig is a handsome woman but her competitors say there's nothing soft about Sandy Kurtzig when it comes to cutting a hard business deal.

When Sandy and her family moved to Silicon Valley, she enrolled in a master's program in aeronautical engineering at Stanford, while at the same time raising her two young children. At Stanford, she was one of only two women in her class of 250 graduate students.

Like many other women, Sandy Kurtzig wasn't satisfied with just doing domestic chores, so she launched her company in 1974. "I wanted to start in a garage like Hewlett-Packard, but I didn't have one. So I started in the second bedroom of my apartment. But most of the work was actually done on my kitchen table."[21] At first, Kurtzig did sales, bookkeeping, and management of her startup. As long as ASK had only five or six employees, they worked out of her apartment bedroom. Eventually ASK moved into nearby offices in Los Altos and went into a rapid growth phase. Annual sales reached $23 million in 1982.

Kurtzig believes that one reason for her success was hiring good people. They, in turn, hired other good people. "I told my top managers they had to hire people better than themselves. They wouldn't get promoted until they had their replacement ready." ASK's employees are treated well, even by Silicon Valley standards. All get stock options; there is also twice-a-year profitsharing, averaging about 10 percent of base salaries. In addition, ASK has beer busts every Friday, at which wine is also served ("I don't like beer," says Kurtzig). ASK also has a hot tub and Jacuzzi for its employees.

The key to effective competition in the software field is R&D, a fact that Kurtzig recognizes, "We spent less for R&D last year than H-P spent on coffee and donuts in a week. But then we signed a long-term contract with H-P's main competitor, DEC (Digital Equipment Corporation). So we capitalized on their R&D investment." When asked who her competition is, Kurtzig immediately responds, "IBM." Actually, ASK's sales don't quite rival those of International Business Machines. But when Sandy Kurtzig divorced in late 1982, ASK paid her husband $20 million for his share of ASK stock. That left Sandy Kurtzig with about $54 million worth of ASK Computer Systems.[22]

Third World Women

Although women are underrepresented in decision-making roles in Silicon Valley, over 75 percent of Silicon Valley's assemblers are women.[23] Most have only a high school education and approximately 40 percent of these skilled manual workers are members of ethnic minorities. Many are recent immigrants: "Minorities used to be black and women . . . now they are Vietnamese and Chinese."[24] The pay for these production workers is low, compared to other U.S. industries.

Clerical and technical support positions are also usually filled by women. According to a survey by Professional Secretaries International (PSI) in 1981, the pay of Silicon Valley executive secretaries is somewhat above the national average: An executive secretary in Silicon Valley earns $1,534 a month, or $18,408 a year. The national average is $1,364 a month, or $16,368 per year. Shirley Martin, president of the local chapter of PSI and secretary to the chairman of American Microsystems, Inc., figures that secretaries in Silicon Valley with at least five years' experience get salaries ranging from $20,000 to $35,000.[25]

Facilities

The egalitarian management philosophy of Silicon Valley is flexible, informal, entrepreneurial, and nontraditional. The goal of rapidly growing large companies is to retain the entrepreneurial spirit of the small company. A favored way is by decentralization, delegating greater responsibility to managers. When a division reaches 1,500 employees at Hewlett-Packard, it becomes a separate administrative unit, and employees are encouraged to identify with the division rather than with the H-P worldwide monolith.

Many observers feel that Silicon Valley firms display a distinctive management style. Compared to established firms in older industries, microelectronics companies believe in treating their workers like human beings, rather than like machines. Being nice to one's employees with financial rewards, exercise facilities, and calling them by their first names seems to make good business sense in Silicon Valley. Perhaps, as a result, employees will remain loyal to the company, rather than leaving for a competitor.

There are no factories in Silicon Valley, only "facilities:" modern, low-slung, clean, and quiet. Such buildings are located on a "campus," complete with beautiful lawns, immaculate landscaping, and lots of greenery. If criticism were to be leveled against the Valley's architecture, it might be about the routine sameness of the buildings. Most are one-level "tilt-ups," so-called because the concrete walls are cast on the ground and then tilted up into place. These tilt-ups house the thousands of small Silicon Valley firms that form the backbone of the microelectronics industry. Two-story buildings are the mark of larger companies; most of these are innovative in design and ultra-modernistic in appearance. Multi-story buildings in Silicon Valley can be counted on one hand.

If the buildings are like flat boxes, the landscaping is striking. The Valley's approximately 75 industrial parks are created, planted, and manicured by accomplished landscape architects.

Certain companies are famous for their settings. Rolm has hired tour guides to answer questions from the many visitors to their award-winning grounds. A brook meanders through the Rolm campus, rounding patios with umbrella-shaded tables, and gurgling past swimming pools and tennis courts to an outside eating area. Patios adjacent to the cafeteria furnish employees with a luncheon rendezvous. Vine-covered trellises, flowerpots, and lush landscaping provide a bit of serenity in an otherwise intense day.

The interiors of these buildings are an extension of the patios, alive with the vibrant green of plants. Hanging ferns and potted trees are everywhere, houseplants are common, radios play softly, and the walls of the bay seating dividers are covered with colorful, modernistic posters. Areas designed for the public—front offices and reception areas—sport plush, modern furniture; posters of fashionable art shows; macramé wall hangings; large plants and trees; and plate-glass windows looking out on green lawns. Coffee or tea is provided for visitors waiting for an appointment.

Stories about corporate recreational facilities are told throughout the Valley. Country club ambience is conveyed by pools, tennis and volleyball courts, parcourses, exercise equipment, and shower facilities. Silicon Valley workers want to stay in shape. The companies are not entirely selfless in providing these highly visible emoluments. They provide a counter-to-job mobility, and exercise improves health, cutting down on employee sick-days, as a Rolm spokesman pointed out. Rolm's million-dollar sportsplatz may thus be a shrewd investment.

Employees are encouraged to bring their families to use the swimming pools and tennis courts on weekends. Flextime, a policy of allowing employees to set their own hours of arrival and departure from work, is spreading. Rolm, Tandem, and Intel give their employees paid sabbaticals after several years of work. The official explanation is that this is a time of refreshment for the employee, but it also means that someone else is trained to perform the individual's job (and step in, should the employee leave).

In contrast, retirement plans are virtually unknown in Silicon Valley. Most companies have no retirement plans at all; youthful employees do not consider retirement benefits when making a job change. Nobody expects to be with the same company long enough to retire. Silicon Valley employees perceive their current job in terms of months or years, but certainly not in terms of lifetime employment. . . .

Casualties

Silicon Valley myth implies that success is almost inevitable for engineers and scientists. Although at first the pace will be fast and stress will be high, after a few years of struggling, rewards will accrue. Pay will increase, stock options will produce a substantial profit, and a promotion to management will come, the result of job performance and the overall explosion of the industry. Perhaps the company will be another superstar and one's co-workers will become millionaires too. Life will be pleasant—a comfortable home with a big pool, a new sports car, and money to do whatever one wants.

The Silicon Valley myth is a dream. The proportion of people who have the dream come true is, in fact, minuscule. Very few articles, books, or TV shows are about Silicon Valley casualties.

The standard successes are trotted out for display—attractive, young, bright, and rich. Those who didn't make it aren't mentioned. They are ignored, with hope to fade away, inconvenient reminders that Silicon Valley pressures demand a heavy toll from its workers.

These victims of the Silicon Valley work ethic probably outnumber the successes by a factor of ten to one. No one who lives in the Valley is unaware of its casualties, but no one wants to admit that it happened to him. They avoid remembering failures, being unable to handle pressure, being passed over for promotion, being laid off, or watching a company go under. But casualties exist, even if they are ignored. Most Silicon Valley workers encounter the caprice of the work ethic via layoffs. It is commonly understood that to be laid off is not necessarily a result of poor job performance, but rather a result of one's particular company or job. For example, a firm's sales department may actually be hiring at the same time production workers are being laid off. Few experienced engineers in Silicon Valley have not been laid off at least once.

Richard was an Intel engineer who experienced the 1975 layoffs. "I was a line supervisor. My boss came to me and said that I would have to lose all the people in my group. So I called them in and said, 'Guys, I know this is really tough, but you've all been laid off.' I walked them out to the parking lot and shook hands. Fifteen minutes later, I was back in my office thinking that was really unpleasant but thank goodness it didn't get me. My boss called me in and asked me if I'd taken care of the layoffs. I said yes, and he said 'I'm really sorry to tell you this, but you yourself are now laid off.' So fifteen minutes later I was out in the parking lot talking to the guys who were still leaning up against their cars, guys that I had just laid off. Fifteen minutes later, here came the plant guards with my boss. They had now walked three levels of personnel out to the parking lot. All of us really cared about the company and wanted to be working there. We were real people with real lives. But now we didn't have a job."[26]

The timing of a layoff is critical. If one is laid off during a Silicon Valley depression like 1971, 1975, or 1982, the prospects of finding another job soon are not good. Working conditions—competition, the importance of being first to market a new product, peer pressure—encourage marathon "pushes." Mammoth give-it-all efforts to develop a new product are ways a company demonstrates its aggressiveness and validates its claim as a real "comer." Employees can get wrapped up in this team spirit, allow nothing in their lives but work, turned on to being part of a team that makes a supreme effort. They can do it once, maybe twice, but not more than that. Especially if a marathon effort doesn't succeed. Then they burn out, like the circuits with which they work.

Several competing companies will each mount a supreme effort to reach the same goal; only one will be first. For the rest there is questioning of whether the tremendous outpouring of effort and energy was worth it. The cost is burnout of key employees, often at an early age. Charles Peddle, president of Victor Technologies, his fifth startup in a dozen years, said, "I put my three VPs in the hospital within the past two years, and three of the top four officers in Victor lost their families through divorce in the past year. Suddenly you wake up and realize your kids are two or three years older, and one of them is in trouble. If it costs 10 years of your life for every year you are president of the United States, each startup in Silicon Valley costs you five years."[27]

Three engineers in their mid-30s discussed "pushes" over salad and a sandwich at an industrial park deli. According to one, "That stuff is for young guys who don't know better. I did it, but I don't want to do it again. What would I get out of it? More money? Probably not. I can't spend time with my kids and go sailing on weekends if I get involved in a 'push.' It's for young guys who don't have anything else to do."[28]

Burnout can occur in any job in any industry, not just high-tech. But burnout is especially characteristic of work in the Valley. Here it happens fast, hitting people while they are still young. What happens to these people is something of a mystery. The industry is new and there has not been time for the full impact of burnout to be determined, but it is definitely a casualty factor in Silicon Valley.

The final step in many Silicon Valley careers is "dropping off the edge." No one really expects to leave the microelectronics industry, but it does happen: Sometimes a decisive event occurs—a layoff or a merger of companies which leaves some employees out in the cold. More commonly something happens which may not seem that important at the time—assignment to a different job, being moved to a different building out of the mainstream, or getting a new supervisor who is difficult to work for. The employee may attempt to cope with the new unsatisfactory work situation, but eventually there comes a parting of ways. The employee is out of work and must summon the energy to try once again to act enthusiastic about commitment to a company that will probably dump him, or her, when things go bad.

A drop-out pattern occurs that is fairly predictable. First the employee decides not to work full time. It may be possible to arrange a half-time position with a company, or to work on specific assignments on a part-time basis. But the unsettling gnawing feeling that things aren't working out continues; the job isn't as rewarding as it is supposed to be. A next step is for the employee to become an independent consultant (almost a Valley euphemism for someone who isn't working full time). Silicon Valley is full of consultants; many are engineers who worked for several companies and are well acquainted. Some have specialized expertise that is much in demand. Others were laid off some time ago and will consult on almost any issue. They keep active by lining up deals, maintaining old contacts, and postponing the time when, inevitably, they drop over the edge. And then one day you realize that they aren't around anymore.

The long hours and dedication to work required in Silicon Valley make sense in light of the rewards that are offered. But Valley successes share an invisible and powerful contribution from luck. The winners were "there" at the right time; they knew the right people; the economy was ready for their product. The more typical case is someone just as bright and just as dedicated, but one step out of phase with luck. Unlike Steve Jobs, the millions did not flow in for these entrepreneurs. Their dreams did not come true. Why does someone like Jobs or Sanders or Bushnell make it while others do not? To dream great dreams is to invite great disappointments. And Silicon Valley is the land of both.

The Silicon Valley work ethic may be the wave of the future. It is functional in an information society where high-technology plays an increasingly vital role. However, if the work ethic that dominates the high-tech industry is a model for the future, serious issues with far-reaching implications are raised.

Meritocracy is a positive side of the Silicon Valley work ethic: The single important criterion in determining success is work performance. But there is also a sinister side to the work ethic—one is left with few resources and little self-esteem when one's job is pulled away. The same forces that combined to produce the microelectronics industry, highlighted as the shining example of American innovation and entrepreneurial success, also can produce work-obsessed technocrats with a limited life experience and a stunted human understanding.

Notes

1. *San Jose News,* November 9, 1981.

2. Authors' interview with "Karl Harrington," Sunnyvale, CA, July 12, 1982.

3. *San Jose News,* January 18, 1982.

4. *San Jose News,* November 9, 1981.

5. *San Jose News,* October 28, 1981.

6. Authors' interview with Nick Larsen, Palo Alto, CA, December 9, 1981.

7. Authors' interview with "Karl Harrington."

8. Lee Felsenstein, "Why not stay an engineer?" speech delivered at meeting of IEEE, Sunnyvale, CA, February 16, 1983.

9. Authors' interview with Dr. Alice Ahlgren, Mountain View, CA, August 17, 1982.

10. Authors' interview with "Frank Vella," Palo Alto, CA, October 4, 1982.

11. Authors' interview with "Kleis Bahmann," Sunnyvale, CA, February 10, 1982.

12. Elizabeth Useem (1981), *Education and high technology industry: The case of Silicon Valley*, Boston: Northeastern University Institute for the Interdisciplinary Study of Education.

13. *The New York Times*, March 28, 1982.

14. *Christian Science Monitor*, October 6, 1982.

15. James W. Botkin et al. (1982), *Global stakes: The future of high technology in America*, Cambridge, MA: Ballinger.

16. *Peninsula Times Tribune*, July 24, 1980.

17. National Science Foundation (October 7, 1981), *Trends in science and engineering degrees, 1950 through 1980*, Washington, DC: Science Resources Studies Highlights.

18. Betty M. Vetter (December 18, 1981), "Women scientists and engineers: Trends in participation, *Science, 214*.

19. Authors' interview with Ann Wells, Sunnyvale, CA, December 30, 1981.

20. Authors' interview with "Frances," Mountain View, CA, March 1, 1982.

21. Sandy Kurtzig, speech delivered at the Innovation 2 Conference, Palo Alto, CA, November 3, 1982.

22. *Peninsula Times Tribune*, December 8, 1982.

23. Robert Howard (1981), "Second class in Silicon Valley," *Working Papers, 8*.

24. *San Jose News*, March 28, 1982.

25. *San Jose News*, April 19, 1982.

26. Authors' interview with "Richard," Santa Clara, CA, January 25, 1982.

27. Charles Peddle, from remarks at the Student Entrepreneur Conference, Stanford University, Stanford, CA, May 21, 1983.

28. Authors' interview with "Kleis Bahmann."

Head Start 15

The Inside Story of America's Most Successful Educational Experiment*

Edward Zigler and Susan Muenchow

editor's introduction:

Methodological Significance

Rather than highlighting any specific type of case study evidence, as in the three preceding selections, the present one illustrates the use of a broad mixture of traditional case study evidence. Strewn throughout the selection are direct quotations from interviews with key individuals or written documents. The selection also includes citations and discussions of data from existing research studies on pertinent topics (see especially the section on "A program that works"). Finally, the study benefits from the insights derived from direct participation in the case study events by the lead author—offering a more intimate portrait of other key participants (the lead author served as the director of the *Head Start* program during its formative early years).

*Editor's Note: Excerpted, with light edits, from Chapter 9, "Surviving the Reagan Years," in *Head Start: The Inside Story of America's Most Successful Educational Experiment* by Edward Zigler and Susan Muenchow, Basic Books, New York, NY, pp. 191–193 and 199–206. Copyright © 1992. Reprinted with permission of Basic Books, a division of Perseus Book Group via Copyright Clearance Center.

Because of the lead author's participant role, the credibility of the text is strongly reinforced by the work of the second author, who apparently conducted hundreds of interviews and also reviewed an extensive array of documents in completing the entire case study, represented again by a whole book. These sources are cited throughout the book (and many of them appear in the excerpt reproduced in the present selection). As a result, the entire case study combines the insights of an inside participant with research evidence amassed by an external observer and analyst.

Substantive Note

The book from which these excerpts are drawn is a case study of the country's most important preschool program, *Head Start*. The nation's school systems had traditionally begun at the kindergarten level, but young children can benefit greatly if their education starts a year earlier, at the "pre-K" level. The aim of pre-K programs is to get children ready to learn and also healthy for starting kindergarten.

When *Head Start* first began as a federal program in the 1960s, publicly funded pre-K programs were not widespread. *Head Start* was further innovative because it provided such educational opportunities for young children from low-income families. *Head Start* had to develop an appropriate array of services and collect sufficient evidence to show its effectiveness in benefiting the later education and development of the children. Over the decades, *Head Start* has continued to provide these services, now collaborating with many public school systems that in turn have extended their reach to support pre-K programs.

However, establishing and maintaining support for *Head Start* has been a continued challenge. Program continuation may be legitimately threatened by other federal priorities or a desire to reduce federal taxes, or both. The excerpt presented in this selection describes one such threat and how program officials garnered political support as well as research evidence to deal with the threat—processes that many other public programs have tried to emulate.

The election of President Reagan was widely regarded as the death knell for many federally funded programs for children. Federal human service officials adopted a bunker mentality. At the White House, the atmosphere of a prolonged wake prevailed among Carter's domestic policy staff in the last weeks before the Reagan inaugural.

As a symbol of their impending loss of power, the White House staff had no money left for travel. Peggy Pizzo, who had helped develop the administration's last proposal for a Head Start budget increase, was scheduled to attend the National Association for the Education of Young Children conference in San Francisco. A colleague in the Department of Health and Human Services [HHS] had to pass a hat to buy Pizzo a ticket.

To get free meals, Pizzo decided to hit every reception at the conference. The only problem was that there was nothing but wine to drink. Feeling a bit brave, she bumped into Larry Schweinhart of the High Scope Educational Research Foundation.

"I hear that High Scope has some new research data on the effectiveness of preschool," Pizzo said.[1]

"Yes, and I'm having the hardest time getting Carnegie to hold a press conference on the Perry Preschool data," he told her. The Carnegie Corporation of New York was convinced that no reporters would come to hear what had happened to a little over 100 children who had participated in a preschool program many years ago in Ypsilanti, Michigan. All of the children came from extremely poor minority families, and fewer than 20 percent of their parents had completed high school.

Pizzo offered to help. As a former Carnegie grant recipient who worked in the White House, she called key executives at Carnegie on High Scope's behalf. Then she recommended that High Scope tie the Perry Preschool findings, too. If the research had implications for Head Start funding, reporters would be interested.

By mid-December, there were editorials all over the country about the benefits of "Head Start-like" programs. The Perry Preschool findings were similar to those of the Cornell Consortium for Longitudinal Studies, which included some earlier High Scope data. But whereas most of the Consortium researchers had stopped following the preschool graduates after a few years of elementary school, High Scope continued to collect data on them as they became teenagers.[2] Thus, the Perry Preschool study was able to show that program participants were more likely to graduate from high school, get a job, and stay out of trouble with the law. Moreover, the High Scope researchers did the first cost-benefit analysis indicating the long-term taxpayer savings associated with investments in early childhood education for disadvantaged children. For every $1 spent on the Perry Preschool program, researchers estimated that taxpayers would ultimately save $4 to $7.

While these new data were being circulated, another Carter administration official who had just taken a job as NHSA's first lobbyist was laying some other groundwork to protect the program. On the day after President Reagan's inauguration, Harley Frankel, who had served as Carter's deputy director of personnel, placed a call to a telephone extension he knew in the Office of Management and Budget (OMB). Since no secretary had yet been hired in this particular office, one of the new Budget Director David Stockman's own deputies picked up the phone.

"I know you'll be cutting a lot of programs," Frankel said, describing himself as a former Nixon administration official, and neglecting to mention his more recent employers. "But to avoid bad press, you'll need to save a few, and let me tell you about Head Start: Everybody likes it, and it doesn't cost very much."[3]

A week later at the Cabinet meeting, Stockman suggested that Head Start be placed in the "safety net" of social programs that would not be cut. Before anyone spoke, Ted Bell, the new secretary of education, said he thought it was a good program and that it should be saved. Caspar Weinberger, Reagan's secretary of defense, who had protected Head Start when he served as secretary of health, education and welfare during the Nixon administration, also spoke on behalf of the program. No doubt there were additional factors that led to Head Start's inclusion among the so-called seven essential human services in the "social safety net," but sometimes Washington works very simply.

Although Head Start's budget, almost alone among social programs, remained intact during the Reagan years, its quality was eroded in numerous ways. The administration forced Head Start to serve more children while cutting back on the hours, services, and technical assistance. Stockman did try to turn over the program to the states, and Head Start's national leadership was almost destroyed.

Head Start's survival can be attributed to several factors: the dedicated federal agency staff who remained to administer the program; the increasingly sophisticated organization of Head Start directors, parents, and staff; the resulting bipartisan support in Congress; and the well-publicized research on the effectiveness of Head Start and "Head Start-like" programs. . . .

Loyal Protectors

Fortunately, some key experienced staff stayed on and managed, against all odds, to hold the program together during the Reagan years. Many of the strongest leaders among the remaining staff were Black, and had started out with the War on Poverty. These people had seen it all. Administrations would come and go, but they were determined that Head Start would survive.

Up to this point, Head Start had benefited from a series of strong national directors—Dr. Julius Richmond, the pediatrician who championed comprehensive services; Jule Sugarman, the administrative wizard; Richard Orton, who protected Head Start from an attempted transfer to the states; and Jim Robinson, who encouraged Head Start parents and staff to organize and help put the program in Caspar Weinberger's good graces.

The two Head Start directors during the Reagan years were no exception to this tradition. Henlay Foster, national Head Start director from 1980 to 1982, was very realistic about his task: It was, he said, to maintain the status quo. Foster had started out with the antipoverty program in 1965, then became Assistant Director of the St. Louis Head Start program in 1970, and then entered the federal civil service as a community representative in the Kansas City regional office responsible for monitoring local Head Starts in the state of Missouri. He joined the national Head Start staff in 1972.

Foster's biggest challenge was maintaining the Head Start Performance Standards, the basic framework we had worked so hard to establish to protect the program's quality. When the Reagan administration came in, newly appointed officials wanted to revise and relax these standards.

"I cooperated as a civil servant," said Foster, "but I expressed my opposition to what they were doing. Not only was the climate not conducive for changing the standards, but any reduction in the scope of the Performance Standards ran contrary, in my view, to the law and legislative intent."

The effort to revise the standards proceeded, but there were many complaints from the field. The revised standards finally reached HHS Secretary Richard Schweiker's desk. To our relief, he refused to approve them.

Foster said he viewed his two-and-a-half years as national Head Start director as a dual job. "It was to be the quintessential civil servant, and to do what I have always done—implement the policies and procedures of the administration, and try within those parameters to make sure the program did not deteriorate," he said.

Following Foster, Clennie Murphy, who had worked in the Head Start bureau since 1969, took on the federal direction of the program. Murphy served as acting Head Start bureau chief from August 1982 until March 1989. The Bush administration then appointed him as associate commissioner of ACYF, a position he held until his retirement in summer of 1991.

Murphy had worked in the Peace Corps, and his diplomatic experience showed. He acted as the administration's ambassador to the Head Start directors, parents, and staff. "My real struggle was to represent the administration," he said. "There was not one federal official I've known who wanted to hurt Head Start; even Dorcas [Hardy] was supportive. But I asked her to tell me if she was going to do something, so that I did not first learn about it in the newspaper." As a result, when administration policies conflicted with what he knew were the wishes of local Head Start leaders, Murphy was at least in a position to negotiate the differences.

At the same time, Murphy's many years as regional liaison had earned him the respect of Head Start directors, staff, and parents. "If I said, 'Don't take on that fight,' they wouldn't." Murphy said he worried sometimes, when an issue did not go the way the Head Start Association wanted, that he had injected himself too much in the process. But for his skill in negotiating and his ability to smooth things over, Murphy was dubbed, "Mr. Kissinger."

Perhaps the best measure of Murphy's talent is that while the Reagan administration proposed level budgets for the Head Start program throughout the 1980s, the president never opposed the much more substantial increases appropriated by Congress.

National Head Start Association

The staff trying to protect Head Start from within ACYF would have had far less success, however, were it not for the increasingly sophisticated organization of the National Head Start Association (NHSA).

"I had worked to build up the Head Start Association," said Jim Robinson, director of the Head Start bureau from May 1972 to May 1980. "I first raised the idea of establishing a national office in 1978, and discussed it again in 1980 just before I left. I said it was important for an association with several thousand members to have an office in Washington to be their eyes and ears, and to understand how legislation is put together."[4]

The NHSA went to work cultivating support in Congress. They drew up a contact list with NHSA representatives from each state who could testify on behalf of Head Start issues. Perhaps most surprising, NHSA members made friends with some of the most conservative members of Congress. Republican Senator Jeremiah Denton of Alabama was viewed as a Moral Majority leader. But when he became chairman of the Senate Committee on Labor and Human Resources, Subcommittee on Family and Human Relations, fellow Alabaman Nancy Spears went to see him. Spears, chair of NHSA's education and information committee, had no trouble securing Denton's support for Head Start. "Denton was a family man all the way," said Spears, "and he saw Head Start as a family program."[5]

Senator Orrin Hatch, Republican from Utah, another New Right leader, also quickly became a Head Start convert. Noting Head Start's success in attracting local volunteers and in highlighting "the role of parents as the prime educators of preschool children," Hatch pledged his support for an "expeditious enactment of reauthorization legislation continuing the goals and objectives of the Head Start program."[6]

The NHSA, working closely with Helen Blank, who has served as CDF's chief lobbyist for Head Start since 1981, managed to stave off a number of the Reagan administration's attempts to dilute the program's quality. The 1984 Head Start reauthorization bill was carefully drafted to ensure that a specific amount of funds would be continuously available for training, that the administration's plans to eliminate fording for the national Child Development Associate program would not succeed, and that Head Start's performance standards would be maintained. When it appeared that Congress might adjourn before completing the reauthorization, CDF placed an ad in *The Washington Post* which pictured young children over the caption: "400,000 Head Start children are looking for one good senator." Senator Hatch offered to be the senator, and with the help of Senator Stafford the bill was brought to the Senate floor just before Congress adjourned.

As a result of the continuing efforts of NHSA and CDF, in 1984 Congress appropriated an over $80 million increase for Head Start. In 1988 Congress approved a $50 million set-aside for Head Start salary improvements, another long-sought-after NHSA goal. "Then we sent thousands of thank-you letters," said Spears, "because most of the time Congress only hears from you when you want something."[7]

Throughout the Reagan years, NHSA officers also cultivated even the most intransigent of administration officials. By 1986, even President Reagan himself was willing to pay tribute to the program: "Head Start has demonstrated its worth and effectiveness over the past two decades," he wrote in a message to participants in a national conference.[8]

But the Reagan administration was trying to limit all children to one year of service. In this way, for the same amount of money, a larger number of children could participate in Head Start. But NHSA President Sarah Greene pointed out that many children, especially handicapped children, required a second year of Head Start to reap any significant benefits. In addition, she said, many parents only began to participate in the program after the first year.

Federal law explicitly stated that local programs had the right to provide more than one year of service to eligible children from age three to the age of compulsory school attendance. But despite assurances to the contrary, the administration continued to play the numbers game, covertly encouraging federal regional officials to limit services to one year in order to expand the total enrollment.

Finally, Nancy Spears, NHSA's education and information committee chair, got tired of hearing the administration deny that it was trying to stop the multiple years of service. She sent out a survey to Head Start grantees. In response, two-thirds of the grantees said they had received some pressure from regional HHS offices to restrict the enrollment to one year of service. Spears collected these regional directives and brought them to the attention of Congressman Dale Kildee, chair of the House Committee on Education and Labor. As a result, although the battle is ongoing, NHSA was able to stop, at least temporarily, the administration's effort to restrict Head Start to a one-year program.

A Program That Works

Head Start's survival during the Reagan years must also be attributed to the growing perception that the program works. Although Head Start is far from a panacea for poverty, there is ample evidence that it and other quality preschool programs make both immediate and lasting improvements in the lives of many disadvantaged children.

Head Start's immediate benefits are indisputable: Children's health is improved; they receive dental care; they have higher self-esteem and motivation; they score higher on academic tests; and many of their parents receive education and become involved both as volunteers and employees.[9]

As for the long-term effects of Head Start and other preschool programs, the Consortium for Longitudinal Studies offers probably the cleanest data. The 1978 follow-up research on 12 preschool programs (two of which were strictly Head Start and Head Start/Follow Through) showed that early intervention significantly reduces placements in special education and grade retentions. For example, a follow-up study on the Harlem Training Project found that the children were twice as likely to be in the right grade for the right age as were their peers who had not had the benefit of preschool.[10]

The High Scope Foundation's Perry Preschool study found that disadvantaged children who participated in the program fared much better than a control group who had no preschool experience. By age 19, the preschool graduates were almost twice as likely to be employed or in college or vocational training. Their arrest rates were 40 percent lower and they were also less apt to get pregnant as teenagers.[11]

Critics rightly point out that most of the aforementioned studies focused on early intervention efforts that were not Head Start programs, but that were in many cases more expensive projects operated under laboratory conditions. However, a 1987 study of more than 3,500 children who had been in Head Start programs in Philadelphia came up with similar, although somewhat less dramatic, findings as did the Cornell Consortium and High Scope.[12] Although, like earlier studies, the Philadelphia data showed no lasting effect of Head Start on achievement scores, children who had been enrolled in the program were more likely to participate in school. Even as late as eighth grade, Head Start children seemed more likely than their peers to be in the right grade for the right age. Most of these children were far from honor students, but the main point is that they were more apt to attend school regularly and to show up for the tests. Given this nation's concern with dropout prevention, that finding should not be minimized.

Similarly, a subset of longitudinal studies in a 1985 review of 210 studies—limited strictly to research on Head Start itself—documents that Head Start graduates fare better than their peers on such measures as being kept back in school and being placed in special education.[13]

There is even some indication that the management and quality improvements we made in Head Start during the 1970s, such as the introduction of the Head Start Performance Standards and the conversion of summer programs to full-year schedules, led to better outcomes for the children enrolled. When researchers compared long-range cognitive effects on Head Start children in studies before and after 1970, they found that the gains were greater among children who entered the program after 1970.[14]

Yet we must be careful not to oversell the effectiveness of Head Start. There is a classic design in most research on Head Start or other early intervention programs: A researcher looks at a group of children participating in a program, and at a control group of similar children who are not enrolled, and follows the two groups to determine if there are differences in outcome. Viewed from this perspective, Head Start and many other early intervention programs clearly "work."

If Head Start children are compared with their middle-class peers, however, we begin to see early intervention programs in a more realistic light. In a Montgomery County, Maryland, study, for example, there were three groups of children—Head Start children; non-Head Start children from similarly deprived circumstances; and middle- to upper-middle-class children. Compared to poor children not enrolled in Head Start, the Head Start children fared significantly better. But compared to their wealthier peers, the Head Start children still were disturbingly behind. Indeed, as a general finding in studies on the effects of quality preschool programs, a substantial portion of the participants still require remedial education, and/or get held back a grade or more in school. Head Start cannot by itself compensate for all the bad housing, substance abuse, violence, and lack of jobs in many communities. Head Start is merely one important tool for better preparing children and families to deal with a difficult environment; it does not inoculate them against all the social ills threatening America's children and families. . . .

A Bipartisan Consensus

Looking back over the Reagan years, it is clear that Head Start was not only salvaged, but, in many ways, strengthened. The program found protectors within the administration, and cultivated unexpected new friends in Congress. The National Head Start Association, with the help of CDF, became a force with which all politicians must contend. Cost-benefit studies convinced business leaders, including the top officers of Procter and Gamble and AT&T, that Head Start was a good investment. As a result, during a decade when most social programs suffered substantial cutbacks, Head Start's budget continued to grow.

By 1988 Republicans and Democrats were almost in the posture of competing to see who could provide the greatest boost for Head Start. Both party platforms that year called for extending services to all eligible children. A campaign document for one presidential hopeful clearly sang the praises of Head Start. "This program works: George Bush will sharply increase its funding."[15]

Notes

1. Peggy Pizzo, interview with Susan Muenchow, May 7, 1991.

2. Lawrence Schweinhart and David Weikart (1980), "Young children grow up: The effects of the Perry Preschool Program on youths through age 15," *Monographs of the High/Scope Educational Research Foundation, 7.*

3. Harley Frankel, interview with Susan Muenchow, September 12, 1990.

4. Jim Robinson, telephone interview with Susan Muenchow, March 13, 1991.

5. Nancy Spears, interview with Susan Muenchow, February 21, 1991.

6. Sen. Orrin Hatch, correspondence to Nancy Spears, National Head Start Association, December 3, 1984.

7. Spears, interview with Muenchow.

8. Ronald Reagan, message to 13th annual Head Start training conference on Child and Family Development Training, February 3, 1986.

9. Ruth McKey et al. (1985), *The impact of Head Start on children, families and communities: Head Start synthesis project,* Washington, DC: Government Printing Office, DHHS Publication No. (OHDS) 85-31193.

10. Irving Lazar and R.B. Darlington (1982), "Lasting effects of early education," *Monographs of the Society for Research in Child Development, 47* (195), 2–3.

11. John Berrueta-Clement et al. (1984), "Changed lives: The effects of the Perry preschool program on youths through age 19," *Monographs of the High/Scope Educational Research Foundation, 8.*

12. Carol D. Copple, Marvin G. Cline, and Allen N. Smith (September 1987), *Path to the future: Long-term effects of Head Start in the Philadelphia School District,* Washington, DC: U.S. Department of Health and Human Services, Office of Human Development Services, Head Start Bureau.

13. McKey et al., *The impact of Head Start.*

14. Judith Chafel (January 1992), "Funding Head Start: What are the issues?" *American Journal of Orthopsychiatry, 62,* 9–21.

15. George Bush (October 12, 1987), "Leadership on the issues," campaign document.

Section V

Analyses and Conclusions

The Organization of a Methadone Program* 16

Dorothy Nelkin

editor's introduction:

Methodological Significance

One of the most common ways of analyzing case study evidence is to array the evidence in chronological order, arguing that earlier events possibly led to later events. A case study is often the unfolding of events over time, and a detailed chronological rendition can represent a basic analytic strategy.

The strategy goes beyond simply "chronicling" the facts. As shown in the present selection, specific issues of program startup, implementation, initial client load, operational procedures, and the establishment of rules of behavior in a newly formed local methadone maintenance clinic all can be covered as part of the chronology. Important issues of dealing with community and staff relationships also can be included. (Other related topics omitted from the original work, due to the space limitations of this anthology, covered the establishment of the initial criteria for admitting and suspending clients.)

*Editor's Note: Excerpted, with light edits, from Chapter IV of *Methadone Maintenance: A Technological Fix* by Dorothy Nelkin. George Braziller, New York, NY, pp. 94–120. Copyright © 1973. Reprinted by permission of George Braziller.

This particular selection again comes from a larger book, whose case study is about the entire national strategy of treating drug addicts through methadone maintenance. The selection—from a single chapter in the book—represents a specific local experience within the broader national experience. Such a case within a case is yet another example of an "embedded unit of analysis." (See Chapters 9–12 of this anthology for other examples.)

Substantive Note

Despite its "advanced" economic and social structure, the United States has chronically suffered from high illicit drug use rates, among both youths and adults. For those persons addicted to heroin, methadone maintenance was developed as a biochemical treatment, and methadone maintenance programs were implemented throughout the country starting in the late 1960s. The programs have been a source of controversy, representing a "technological" fix that must be accepted by local communities and that consumes the precious time of medical workers in public health settings—but that appears only to serve as a palliative in dealing with the essence of the heroin addiction problem. Dorothy Nelkin's book captures the entirety of this controversy, and the selection shows how an actual clinic worked in Syracuse, New York.

The Onondaga County Department of Mental Health started the methadone maintenance program in a climate of urgency tempered by the ambivalence of other rehabilitation institutions, the police, and various community services. It was intended to broaden the type of treatment available to addicts and thus to help those not yet participating in existing programs. But a new program in a community represents a reallocation of scarce resources among new and existing interests. Careers and reputations are at stake.[1] Those who run other programs risk losing support if the new program succeeds; those sponsoring a new and controversial program risk loss of reputation if it fails. These attitudes affected all aspects of the Syracuse methadone maintenance program, from its initial funding and implementation to the eventual reception of its patients in the community.

Plans and Protocols

The Department of Mental Health initiated the methadone maintenance program with the stated purpose of allowing patients "to become free of the necessity of seeking money to purchase heroin on an undependable market, at an unpredictable dosage, at high personal risk, and with a great deal of total personal involvement which prevents them from participating in an ordinary way in the society of which they are a part."[2]

To set up such a program based on the controlled administration of an addictive drug required a four-level interaction among the County Department of Mental Health, a private hospital, and both state and federal bureaucracies. Dr. Donald Boudreau, head of the Department of Mental Health and coordinator of drug rehabilitation services, had to clear the proposal with the county legislature; negotiate with the hospital; apply for funds through the NACC; and acquire permits from the New York State Bureau of Narcotics Control, the New York State Department of Health, the Federal Food and Drug Administration, and the Internal Revenue Service. The process, required for all methadone programs, nearly smothered plans for the clinic in red tape. Problems of coordination were compounded by vague guidelines concerning application procedures and requirements, difficulty in mobilizing the hospital administration, and an uncertain funding situation.

The political use of the drug issue in the 1970 gubernatorial campaign had led to high expectations of state support. Responding to the encouragement of Rayburn Hesse in early 1970, Dr. Boudreau began to explore possible locations for a methadone maintenance program. St. Joseph's Hospital was finally selected because of its existing contacts with the Department of Mental Health and the interest of Dr. Robert E. Pittenger, head of Psychiatric Services. St. Joseph's is a Roman Catholic hospital founded in 1869 by the Franciscan Sisters of the Third Order. In 1969 it had a bed capacity of 388, a well-staffed social service department, and 200 attending physicians. Hospital policy has encouraged new social service programs, requests for which are reviewed by a medical staff executive committee, on the assumption that new programs will depend eventually on hospital back-tip services. Existing programs include the most extensive outpatient clinic in Syracuse, involving 41,779 patients. In 1964 the hospital added a 20-patient psychiatric day-care unit, which was proposed as the setting of the methadone program.

Although St. Joseph's was the logical location for the new methadone program, hospital psychiatric services were already overburdened and understaffed, and the hospital administration hesitated to use these scarce resources, especially for a program not fully accepted by the medical community. Furthermore, the staff viewed addicts as considerably different from psychiatric patients and were reluctant to take on the responsibility. In April 1970, however, the administration agreed to house the program.

Dr. Boudreau submitted application to the NACC for $162,000 for the remainder of the fiscal year ending March 31, 1971 (see Table 16.1).

In September 1970 the NACC provided funding prorated at $99,523 for the period between September 1, 1970 and March 31, 1971. The budget, intended to serve 100 patients, provided salaries for seven staff members—a social worker, two registered nurses, a rehabilitation counselor, two research assistants, and a receptionist—and one-fifth of the salaries of a psychiatrist, an internist, and an administrator. Equipment costs and laboratory fees were also included. Before the available funds could be used, however, both the Department of Mental Health and the hospital required permits, and the mass of complex paperwork created considerable confusion. It was March 1971 before accreditation was complete; the program could not begin to use its NACC funding until only five days before the termination of its contract. The program quickly spent $13,000 on equipment; the balance had to be returned to the state.

Meanwhile, on the expectation of contract renewal, Dr. Pittenger unofficially began to accept a few patients in April 1971. By this time the NACC had overcommitted its funds, and in August 1971, after several months of negotiation, the NACC decided to contract the program for only $50,000 through December 1971.[3]

. . . By October the NACC had still not signed the promised contract, a delay which gave rise to several rumors: that local political interests representing the pushers were interfering with funding,[4] that the legislature had gotten the political mileage it sought from the initial public announcement of the program and was no longer interested in exerting pressure to bring in funding, and that the NACC was favoring New York City programs at the expense of upstate New York. In the meantime the program was expanding, supported temporarily by the hospital and Medicaid rates, set at $6.32 per clinic visit. By November, when the contract was actually signed, the program was well underway, treating 45 patients.

The initial plan had been to provide new inpatient psychiatric services and a residential program for addicts without a job, family, or adequate living quarters. The reduced budget made these services out of the question; instead, the program was included, at first, in St. Joseph's psychiatric day-care clinic. Several patients who were admitted to the methadone program prior to its official opening came to this clinic. However, the association with the psychiatric clinic was quickly abandoned in response to objections from both the staff and the patients.

Months before the program was brought into the hospital, Dr. Pittenger had discussed the plans with the staff of psychiatric services. Yet at the last moment there remained serious objections. Nurses claimed the decision had been made without adequate consultation. In part, their objections were based on concerns common within hospitals over the distribution of authority and control. Hospital decisionmaking tends to be highly

Table 16.1   Syracuse Methadone Maintenance Program: Application and Accreditation Procedures

1970	
March	Boudreau discusses possibilities of methadone maintenance program with St. Joseph's Hospital and Dr. Pittenger.
April	Boudreau submits application for accreditation of the methadone program to the NACC for $162,000 for fiscal year ending March 31, 1971. Announces plans to *seek* local and state approval.
June	Negotiations between the county Department of Mental Health and St. Joseph's Hospital.
August 25	Health Committee of Onondaga County Legislature approves proposal and provides a $25,000 loan to initiate a program.
September 10	NACC approves county application and funded $99,523 from September 1, 1970 to March 31, 1971. Accreditation given through August 31, 1972.
September 10	County legislature unanimously approves program.
September 15	Request for FDA forms and approval procedures. Request for approval procedures from Internal Revenue Service. St. Joseph's Hospital is informed of application procedures and FDA forms are sent to the hospital.
September 22	Application for certification and registration is sent to New York State Bureau of Narcotics Control.
September	Negotiations concerning required laboratory support.
October 1	Intended opening date.
October 16	State Department of Health application is sent to St. Joseph's Hospital.
December 24	County Department of Mental Health fills out FDA form when it is realized that hospital had not yet done so.
1971	
January 5	St. Joseph's sends a note to the FDA requesting an Investigational New Drug (IND) permit in order to obtain methadone and to initiate clinical study.

(Continued)

Table 16.1 (Continued)

1971

January 8	New York State Department of Health certificate #2563 is signed approving the Syracuse methadone program as a class V program.
February	Internal Revenue Service tax stamp received.
February 18	Following a reminder letter from the Department of Mental Health, St. Joseph's submits State Department of Health application.
February 19	An IND number, 7567, is received from the FDA indicating approval.
March 16	Approval from State Department of Health for operation under provision of the New York State Hospital Code.
April	Request to NACC for budget renewal.
June 9	Program officially opens.
June 22	Revised budget submitted to NACC for $100,000. NACC asks for further budget revision.
July 17	Request to NACC for new contract of $50,000 for July 1–December 31, 1971.
August	Application to the Division of Health Economics of the state Department of Health for a Medicaid rate.
October	Medicaid rate of $6.32 per visit received.
November	Funds received from NACC through December 1971. January 1972 NACC approval for 1972, but funding delayed.

centralized, and nursing staffs, responsible for implementing programs on a day-to-day basis, often resent the authority of physicians and administrators. Nurses argued that the style of the psychiatric ward, based on trust, was inappropriate for addicts, who were accustomed to living by their wits and manipulating their environment; they would disrupt the daily routine.

The situation in this case was further complicated by stereotyped fears concerning addicts, who were believed to be "all psychopaths," violent, and likely to commit assault.[5] Husbands of several nurses forbade their wives to work in the clinic if it admitted addicts. Nurses denied that racial factors were involved in their reluctance to participate, but the situation was a new experience for most of them. Because of its Catholic affiliation and its location in a middle-income White neighborhood, St. Joseph's patients had been by and large middle-income people of Irish and Italian origin. Addicts themselves resented being placed with psychiatric patients; they differentiated between their own "voluntary addiction" and mental illness.

The combined attitudes of both patients and hospital staff resulted in a revised protocol which eliminated the inpatient phase except in the case of those who needed regular hospital care for medical reasons. Later, the methadone maintenance program moved to a separate facility across the street from the hospital. The program now has its own staff and no contact with psychiatric patients. Psychiatric services, if needed, were to be part of the methadone program, distinct from the regular hospital services.

When the plan to use a separate building was announced, the neighborhood was concerned about bringing addicts to the area. The hospital administration received several phone calls, one from a resident who requested that the hospital buy his house. But the hospital administration reassured the community, and the clinic quietly opened its doors on June 9, 1971.

The Patients

Requirements for admission to the methadone maintenance program assume, in the words of one of the program's administrators, that methadone is a "last resort."[6] Patients must be willing to involve themselves voluntarily in the program, which is open to both males and females of, in most instances, at least 21 years of age. Eighteen-year-olds are admitted if they meet the requirements of at least three years of heroin abuse and several prior attempts to abstain from drugs. Applicants who do not reside in the county are rejected, regardless of whether they meet the other requirements. In one case, an out-of-town addict asked if he could meet the residence requirement by leaving his clothes at a local church; he was refused. Finally, to be admitted, a patient must not have a serious mental illness, nor can he or she be a multiple-drug user.[7] The decision to accept or reject an applicant is made by the director following interviews by staff members. About 20 percent of those who applied were rejected because they had not been addicted long enough, or because they had never tried to "kick their habit" in other ways.

Who actually comes to the methadone maintenance program? In the first nine months of operation a total of 71 persons were actually admitted, though there were never more than 54 in the program at any one time. There are older patients who are tired of a life of hustling; there are those who are ill or whose habit is too large to maintain, and who are desperate for a period of relief and time to pull themselves together. Some come under family pressure, others under pressure from the police. Although the program is voluntary, its clients have limited alternatives: If not methadone, it is prison, perpetual stealing to buy heroin, and the continual dread of arrest. . . . Of the 71 persons admitted to the program, nine were awaiting trial and were offered conditional discharge if they entered a program, nine were on probation, and two were on parole when they applied. Thus some patients come to the program to avoid court action or to increase the possibility of a favorable judgment by a court or probation officer. In many cases, the addict simply walks off the street into the clinic.

The methadone clinic was not immediately deluged with applications. Six people were already involved when the program officially opened in June; enrollment increased as follows: June, 13; July, 25; August, 34; September, 51; October, 49; November, 52; and December, 54. Life is less difficult for addicts in Syracuse than in larger cities. According to one addict, "It's very easy to meet a connection. . . . You don't have to know where to go. You can get off a bus and within a matter of minutes be there if you have money in your hand." Many addicts feel they are their own masters and that they can control their habits. The opposition of DEN, the group with the most contact among addicts, may also have affected applications. DEN considered application to the program as an admission of an addict's failure to find any reasonable solution to his problem; only in a desperate case was the risk worthwhile.[8]

Because Syracuse is a relatively small city, most addicts know each other. This has significant influence on who decides to come to the program. Of the first group of 45 patients, 14 had heard of the program through a friend or a relative. In at least five of these cases, the friend was the former-addict research assistant working with the methadone program. Two others heard about the program on the street and just walked in. Two were referred by the Department of Mental Health; five came through referrals from hospitals or the neighborhood clinic; six came from DEN; and 13 from the NACC. (No information was available on three patients.)

The first 45 patients admitted to the program ranged in age from 18 years old to 49. . . . The average age of these first 45 applicants was 29.3 years. The average number of years of addiction was 8.9, ranging from as little as one year to as many as 25. Thirty-seven were Black and 15 were women. Fifteen of the patients were married, including four married couples who came to the program together. Of the others, 10 reported themselves as divorced or separated, the rest as single. Forty of the patients reported that they had been arrested: 18 from one to five times; 14 from six to 10 times; and eight more than 10 times. The average number of arrests for all patients was about seven. Though the demands of their habit had led most of the addicts to a similar life style, their backgrounds were diverse. Four of the patients had some college education, 12 others had finished high school, and another 12 had dropped out of the 11th grade. Only one person had not completed eighth grade. Over half had never worked at any time in their lives, others had had temporary menial jobs; five had permanent jobs: a musician, a teacher, and a nurse were included among these.

The heroin habit for these patients ranged from one bag a day to an alleged 23, a bag containing about 100 milligrams of material which is from 5 to 10 percent pure heroin. The average habit was about six or seven bags daily. Only nine patients reported no previous connection with other established drug abuse programs in town. Twenty-two had been associated with DEN, and 18 had been at one time connected with the NACC criminal or civil commitment program. In each case, they had failed to stay drug free. Needing a respite, they saw in the methadone maintenance program a means to buy time: "It will give me a chance to get my head straight." Patients enter the program with the hope of getting themselves off drugs entirely once they "get straightened out." Relieved at first to be freed of hustling, as soon as they are stabilized on methadone and feel healthy, they think about getting detoxified and leaving the program.[9]

Procedures

Despite the needs that bring addicts to the methadone program, they have significant problems in adapting to its procedures and demands. An addict must take methadone every 24 hours to avoid withdrawal symptoms. Because of the potential for abuse of the drug, the Syracuse program, like others, requires that the patient swallow the methadone in the presence of a nurse, at least during the early part of treatment. Indeed, the need for staff control has been a major factor in shaping the formal structure of the program.

Each day the patient comes to the clinic located on the first floor of a two-story frame house. He enters a small waiting room separated from a dispensing room by a locked Dutch door. To the right are small staff offices, and there is a single bathroom and a double-locked closet for the methadone. The clinic is open from 9:00 A.M. to 10:30 A.M. and from 2:30 P.M. to 4:30 P.M. every day, with some flexibility for those unable to meet these hours. On weekends it is open several hours in the morning.

At 8:30 A.M., before the clinic opens, a staff nurse goes to the hospital pharmacy, where the methadone is stored and prepared. She picks up the daily clinic supply as requested the day before. During the first five months of the program, methadone came in a powdered form already measured by the hospital pharmacist in correct doses for each patient and mixed with Tang in unbreakable plastic four-ounce baby bottles.[10] In October, to relieve the pharmacist of the burden of mixing the solution, the program began to order the methadone powder in sealed vials, each containing the appropriate dose for a particular patient. It is mixed with Tang at the clinic and the patients must drink it immediately in the presence of a nurse to assure that it is not sold or illegally distributed.

Most patients arrive early, when the clinic first opens. As in a bakery, each person takes a number when he arrives and waits his turn. Regardless of the number of staff members on duty, patients can only be given methadone one at a time, for, as a part of the procedure, each person must provide his urine sample in the presence of a nurse, and there is but one bathroom.

During the first stage of his participation in the program, an addict begins medication at a level compatible with his habit, and this is steadily increased to a regular dose of approximately 100 milligrams per day. He will reach his stable dose of methadone in about six weeks, after which he must continue to come to the clinic each day for personal and vocational counseling until he is socially stabilized to the point of "being gainfully employed and self-supporting, his living situation adequate and orderly, and family relationships in most instances positive and emotionally satisfying."[11] At first, attendance at therapy groups was also mandatory, but patients were reluctant to participate. It was soon made voluntary, and relatively few continued to come.

The frequency of required visits to the clinic is reduced at the discretion of the program director, on the basis of the following guidelines: After 13 weeks "clean," that is, with no urine positives that indicate that a patient has taken heroin or another narcotic, he may take methadone home on weekends. After 17 weeks clean, he must come to the clinic only three times weekly; after 22 weeks, only twice weekly.[12] Some patients must participate in therapy groups if they are to take methadone home.

The analysis of urine samples is clearly a crucial part of the program, for it serves as a check on the presence of heroin, amphetamines, or barbiturates. Until December 1971 the analysis procedure was not able to detect cocaine, a common street narcotic, but the quinine with which cocaine and other drugs are often cut is detectable. The analysis is a complex procedure requiring sensitive equipment that can distinguish morphine from other narcotics by a thin-layer chromatographic procedure. . . .

Rules and Their Implementation

The aforementioned procedures follow the general guidelines provided by the Beth-Israel Medical Center outpatient program. . . . The implementation of these procedures reflects the objectives and concerns of the clinic staff. Decisions ultimately rest with Dr. Pittenger, the medical director of the program, but with only one-fifth of his time allotted to the clinic, and with a major responsibility as head of psychiatric services for St. Joseph's Hospital, he depends heavily on the program administrator. Because she too is part time, the day-to-day functioning of the clinic as it most directly affects the clients is in the hands of the full-time members of the staff. They feel a stake in the success of the program, and "success" is inevitably interpreted in terms of the response of patients. Yet the definition of success is controversial, and various staff members have very different views. These differences are evident in their ideas about how strictly or leniently the clinic should be run. Some think that the program is not sufficiently firm in stating and implementing rules, while others take the position that procedures should be flexible enough to accommodate the needs of individual patients.

At first there were no rules and patients were simply told the procedures. The medical director felt that rules were necessary to guide the staff but that one must always ask, "What do the rules cost the individual?" Claiming that patients would follow rules only because they were afraid to jeopardize their position, he preferred to be lenient, allowing mistakes, adjusting to patients' life styles and expectations. However, one staff member called Dr. Pittenger "a marshmallow" and, along with several others, insisted that rules must be clearly drawn. In August 1971 the staff made an abortive effort to formalize the procedures by strictly defining the limits of appropriate behavior at the clinic in a set of rules:

> Do not engage in anti-social behavior. The following activities shall be considered anti-social behavior: abuse of drugs, excessive use of alcohol, threat to or assault upon any individual, conviction of crime, abusive language to staff.

The rules went on to specify that patients must submit to physical and laboratory tests, relay information regarding physical condition when asked to do so, take no other drugs without authorization, make sincere efforts to find employment, call the clinic if delayed, and respect the fact that clinic premises are restricted to participants in the program. Finally, the rules concluded with a warning in capital letters that "Violation of any one or a combination of the above regulations may be used as cause for being dropped from the program upon decision of the clinic staff."

It is hardly surprising that patients objected to these rules as insulting and paternalistic. Some staff members also were concerned, and the list was withdrawn. For the moment, no further rules were distributed; later revisions omitted the list of antisocial behaviors and added a note that "this is not a final or fixed document, and suggestions from patients and/or staff will be considered for additions or changes."

The pressure to enforce rules continued, however. "Of what use are rules if they are broken all the time?" asked one of the nurses. This attitude reflected two concerns of the staff: They hoped that rules would minimize manipulation by patients, and they felt it in the best interest of patients to have a clearly defined structure in the program. Most of the staff felt that addicts, like children, are better off within a well-defined situation in which they are forced to make choices and to take responsibility for their own behavior. But also the staff felt threatened by a loose interpretation of the rules. If rules could be bent, their authority could be undermined. The first head nurse left the program after three months because he felt he was forced to "mollycoddle joyriders." He claimed that with few rules and limited possibilities of staff control, patients take advantage; he felt manipulated. Finally, the staff was concerned with the public image of the program. For example, the program administrator, faced with practical problems of funding, saw the need for increased strictness and control in order to protect against what outsiders might consider failure. The tenuous status of the program and its limited resources fostered a demand for visible evidence of order and short-term success, although, as in the case of the unfortunate set of rules, this could undermine the broader goals of the program. . . .

Notes

1. The pattern of commitment to existing institutions is discussed in Lloyd E. Ohlin, 1960, "Conflicting interests in correctional objectives," in Social Science Research Council, *Theoretical studies in social organization of the prison*, New York, NY, pp. 111–129. See also Florence Heynman, June 1972, "Methadone maintenance as law and order," *Society*, 9, 16.

2. Methadone Maintenance Program, "Purposes," April 1971 (mimeographed).

3. This $50,000 plus the $13,000 from the previous allocation gave the program a budget of $63,000 plus Medicaid funds. During this period of negotiation, the local uncertainty was so intense that Dr. Boudreau requested Emil Drysdale, the director of NACC agency affairs, to send in writing an indication that there was no intention to terminate the Syracuse program.

4. The program could have had, in fact, a sizable impact on the illegal drug market. If one hundred hardcore addicts with a habit of $50 per day were no longer to buy heroin, this would remove almost $2 million of annual trade from pushers.

5. There is evidence that addicts fill the entire span of categories of psychiatric diagnosis proportionate to the nonaddict population. According to Marie Nyswander, M.D., "Addicts may be schizophrenic, obsessive-compulsive, hysteric, psychopathic, or have simple character disorders. Although once addicted, the behavior of all addicts may closely resemble each other (at least in the social sense of behavior), basically the individuals may be very different indeed." Quoted in Nat Hentoff, *A Doctor among the Addicts* (Grove Press, New York, NY, 1970, pp. 76–77). See also Alfred R. Lindesmith, *Addiction and Opiates* (Aldine, Chicago, IL, 1968, pp. 157–172).

6. *Syracuse Herald-Journal*, June 18, 1971.

7. Admission rules have been waived in several cases: One case involved a delicate employment situation that required stabilization; others involved addict families in which both husband and wife were addicted.

8. Daniel Glaser (personal communication) has pointed out a similar problem in New York City where a central referral service was set up to refer addicts on welfare to various treatment services. Former addicts from drug-free programs who serve as classifiers refuse to send anyone to methadone.

9. Any patient who wants to be detoxified is helped by the clinic, because participation is voluntary. Eight people were detoxified on request, but four were back on methadone within a month.

10. This form of bottling is required by the Bureau of Narcotics, for the reason that if a box of bottles is dropped, losing a large quantity of methadone, there would be considerable problems of accountability to federal auditors.

11. Mimeographed protocol, "Revised Narrative—Methadone Maintenance Treatment Program," n.d., pp. 4–5.

12. Rules require that any methadone allowed out of the clinic be transported in a locked box. Stolen or lost methadone cannot be replaced. Nevertheless there are continuing reports of accidental poisonings.

Transformation in the New York City Police Department* 17

*George L. Kelling
and Catherine M. Coles*

---

editor's introduction:

Methodological Significance

Whether using qualitative or quantitative evidence, the most desirable case study analyses should include explicit discussion and interpretation of the findings. Data do not speak for themselves. Case study investigators, after having presented the data, must develop the main arguments, including the examination of rival explanations.

In the case of the present selection, at issue is whether certain strategies implemented by the New York City Police Department (NYPD) contributed to major reductions in crime. The authors, Kelling and Coles, mainly make their arguments in qualitative terms. However, the logic of their arguments would be the same, even if the arguments were presented in quantitative

---

terms. First, they explain how the implemented strategies directly affected criminal behavior and disrupt crime operations. Second, they examine citywide crime trends, showing how the *timing* of the initial reductions appeared to follow in sequence the implementation of the strategies, as well as discussing rival explanations (though they do not pursue the rivals with analytic vigor). Last, they discuss and argue in favor of the possibility that the implemented strategies had been an important influence on the citywide crime trends.

Substantive Note

Widespread and sharp reductions in crime rates, in virtually all communities across the country, were one of the significant social changes that occurred in the 1990s. Major cities like New York City, reputed for decades earlier to be unsafe and dangerous, led the reductions. Even in retrospect, no one knows for sure why or how these reductions occurred. Each local area across the country has its own story (and they're not necessarily the same).

In New York City, and following a parallel campaign to make the city's subways safer, the NYPD adopted many strategies that appeared to have influenced crime rates. The excerpt in this selection explains these strategies—from enforcing minor violations ("order restoration and maintenance"), to installing computer based crime-control techniques, to reorganizing the department *and* holding police officers accountable for controlling crime—and then presents data and argument that the strategies did lead to reductions in crime. Other law-enforcement agencies also have adopted these strategies. The NYC leaders, including Mayor Rudolph Giuliani and Police Commissioner William Bratton (who also had led the subway campaign), gained national recognition for their successful work. [Bratton subsequently became head of the Philadelphia and then the Los Angeles departments, putting into place similar practices in each of those cities.]

Within the New York City Police Department [NYPD], a reorientation toward crime control with a strong order-maintenance component was several years behind the [New York City subway's] Transit Authority experience. In fact, police treatment of panhandlers and an anti-begging section of the state penal code were challenged in court before the NYPD had even turned its attention to order maintenance. It was only when Police Commissioner Raymond Kelly [appointed by Mayor David Dinkins in 1992] launched an effort to combat squeegeeing in 1993 that the breakthrough in the NYPD's approach to disorder and quality-of-life issues occurred. . . .

The First NYPD Success: Squeegeeing

. . . Squeegeeing, or unsolicited washing of car windows, was widespread in New York City during the early 1990s. Squeegeemen operated in groups of three to six, with a few locations having as many as 14 to 16, usually youths in their late teens or early twenties. The most popular locations for such activities were at entrances and exits to tunnels, bridges, and highways where cars were backed up, or at intersections. Some window-washers worked sites regularly, others only occasionally. Hard-working window-washers claimed to earn $40 to $60 a day; some made over $100 a day if they persisted. At many sites, window washing continued day and night, year-round, although activity was heaviest during warmer months.

The behavior of squeegeers toward occupants of cars varied. Many squeegeers worked hard, running back and forth between cars, even climbing on the bumpers of trucks to wash windows. Some appeared good natured, clowning around and verbally sparring with each other and with drivers, generally behaving in ways that they believed citizens would not find threatening. If drivers waved them off or turned windshield wipers on to dissuade them, many squeegeers would retreat. Nevertheless, others behaved in a manner clearly calculated to menace: If drivers said no to them, these squeegeers would drape themselves over the hoods of cars to prevent them from moving, even after trafficlights changed. Some squeegeers would spread soapy water or spit on car windows, leaving them dirty and streaked. Often two, three, or even four window-washers would swarm around a car, washing all the windows in spite of the driver's protests. A few squeegeers appeared to be mere pathetic hangers-on, burnt out and seriously under the influence of alcohol, drugs, or both, staggering bewilderedly between cars, gesticulating at drivers and passengers. Carrying only rags or newspapers, they rarely washed windows or received "tips."

Commissioner Kelly contacted [coauthor of this selection, George] Kelling during the summer of 1993 to aid the NYPD in getting control of squeegeeing. Kelly himself had recently been "serviced" by squeegeemen, one of whom had spit on his windshield, while driving into the city with his wife. Acknowledging his own rage and frustration, Kelly appreciated how threatened and powerless citizens felt after such assaults. Using a problem-solving approach akin to that followed by the subway's study group, Kelling and NYPD staff, then Assistant Chief Michael Julian and Sergeant Steve Miller, began their work by unobtrusively observing and videotaping squeegeemen. They had plainclothes officers drive an unmarked car through intersections to make it available for window washing. They also interviewed "squeegeemen" and neighborhood police officers, and examined police department criminal records. Background information on the squeegeemen arrested during the study period provided a picture similar to that gained by the Transit Authority. The popular conception of squeegeemen was a group of homeless individuals simply "down on their luck." Norman Siegel, head of the New York Civil Liberties Union, urged that political leaders "could better solve the problem by providing apartments and jobs to those who squeegee." [1] Yet the data collected on squeegeers portrayed a different scenario: Of those arrested during a 60-day experimental period, approximately three-quarters had legitimate addresses at which they resided; half had previous arrests for serious felonies such as robbery, assault, burglary, larceny, or carrying a gun; and almost half had previous arrests for drug-related offenses. Squeegeers were not merely a troubled population, but also were capable of considerable mayhem. Citizens had good reason to be fearful.

Dealing with squeegeemen had proven to be an extraordinarily frustrating job for the few police officers who took it seriously. Because officers in cars and special units ignored squeegeeing, neighborhood officers were left to deal with the problem. Yet when they did so, the officers received only scorn from other officers who viewed squeegeeing as unworthy of police efforts or attention. Even more chafing for conscientious officers was the response of squeegeers. Since squeegeeing was a minor infraction, it was punishable only by a fine or community service. Consequently, officers were limited to giving squeegeers Desk Appearance Tickets (DATs), known derisively by New York police as "Disappearance Tickets" because offenders generally failed to appear to pay their fines, and warrants for arrest that were issued subsequent to nonappearance were never served. As in most departments, warrants issued for nonappearance were sent to a central warrant-service unit, where they were relegated low priority compared to a flood of warrants outstanding on more "serious" matters. Squeegeers learned this quickly, and would all but tell officers to "Keep your DAT, I've got plenty of them."

A simple comment by a patrol lieutenant proved to be the key to solving the problem. His suggestion—"If only we [neighborhood officers] could get the warrants for nonappearance for the DATs"—made sense, for although squeegeeing was not a jailable offense, nonappearance was.

Although a DAT for a minor offense might not mean much to a central warrant bureau, it meant a great deal to officers trying to restore order to neighborhoods, despite scorn and derision from residents. Arrangements were made with Paul Schectman, then counsel to Manhattan District Attorney Robert Morganthau and now New York State's Commissioner of Criminal Justice, to have warrants for nonappearance for squeegeeing flagged and sent directly to the officer who had issued the DAT in the first place. Thus, when an officer served a DAT for squeegeeing and the offender did not appear, that officer could make an immediate arrest, and jail time would follow. With punishment swift and certain, squeegeeing died out in a matter of weeks.

A New Mission for the NYPD

The anti-squeegee campaign took place during the 1993 Dinkins-Giuliani mayoral campaign, when squeegeeing became a metaphor for all that was wrong with New York City. Rudolph Giuliani ran for office as a strong anticrime candidate. A former federal prosecutor, he laid claim to a special competence for dealing with New York City's crime problem; like many other local political leaders he was also "streetwise," and understood the consequences of disorder and fear in New York City. And, [when his term began in 1994,] he appointed [William] Bratton as Police Commissioner of New York.

Several factors made Giuliani's choice of Bratton to head the NYPD a key to dealing with disorder in New York City. First, the new commissioner would have to make major changes inside the NYPD itself. As an outsider, Bratton was fully prepared to do this. Most of the NYPD command staff had been in place since the mid-1980s. Moreover, in 1993 the department was being racked by a series of corruption scandals that, although not implicating command staff, nonetheless suggested that a "hunkering-down" mentality had developed in the upper levels of the department, discouraging sergeants and mid-managers from bringing forward charges of corruption or abuse. Many in policing believed that a "stay out of trouble," do-nothing mentality had developed in the ranks of the department as well. The department was described by many as a bloated, inefficient bureaucracy that was controlling neither crime nor its officers very well. And although the department had made a commitment to community policing on paper, it was still deeply mired in a narrow law-enforcement strategy. Aside from being an outsider, Bratton's success in implementing a preventive order-maintenance strategy in the [NYC subway's] Transit Police Department (TPD), as well as reorganizing and energizing the department itself, made him a logical candidate for the commissioner's job in a Giuliani administration.

On taking over the NYPD, Bratton adapted and then implemented many of the techniques conceived by aggressive chief executive officers (CEOs) in both the public and private sectors to strategically reposition their organizations. He also repeated many of the tactics he had used as TPD head. He devolved authority from the 55 top-level chiefs downward to precinct commanders, primarily captains. At the same time he made it clear that precinct commands would be given only to the best and brightest captains, and that future promotions would come from this pool of precinct captains. As this message was disseminated in the NYPD, many precinct commanders retired, giving Bratton the flexibility to assign young and aggressive captains to command precincts: The average age of precinct commanders dropped from the sixties to the forties.

Bratton initiated a number of other moves, including gaining control of a runaway budget, especially for its spending on overtime; improving training for officers; using task forces to study departmental problems; involving precinct commanders in corruption control; and surveying officers to determine their views about improving the department and the quality of their working conditions. He reduced the number of special units and developed a variety of internal communication channels (such as videos and internal newsletters) for sending information from himself and other key personnel directly to line officers. And finally, the new commissioner established clear, measurable goals for the department, which he communicated to the public by publishing seven strategic plans that covered everything from improving the quality of life in the city to managing domestic violence and controlling corruption.

Although all of these changes were important, and many comprise the standard approaches of leaders trying to reinvigorate moribund organizations, Bratton was also implementing nothing less than a new strategy of policing—community-policing. Embodied in the new strategy was a strong, simple, and straightforward message about the business of the organization and the function of policing. And fundamental to the new strategy was the development of greater accountability to the community and involvement in solving local problems.

Bratton's message about the business of the NYPD in a community policing strategy focuses on crime. The logic is this: First, even though policing involves broad and numerous functions, the core function of police is crime control—aimed at disorder, fear, and index crime. Second, police have the capability for preventing crime. Third, officers must be both aggressive and respectful in their activities: Being aggressive in crime control does not require being combative, nor does being respectful of citizens embody weakness. Finally, although comprehensive organizational change is likely to take years, gains in crime control will accrue rapidly if police are energized and carefully directed. For Bratton, community policing can be "hard on crime," and he is convincing police officers as well as the public that he may be right.

Community policing as Bratton conceives it is a far cry from community policing as seen by many other police leaders, who couch their descriptions in "soft," social science terms. In their view, community policing is antithetical to the "crime-fighting" function that defined the role of police for decades. Faced with this notion of community policing, many police officers find unpalatable what they believe is in store for them if they adopt it: a strategy that is soft on crime, has little impact on crime, emphasizes social work, cares more about the rights of offenders than the interests of the community, and is in the "grin and wave" tradition of community relations. Bratton had to convince officers otherwise, and so he did, in both the TPD and the NYPD.

Bratton's approach starts where officers stand in their own thinking, that is with crime, and then attempts to move them beyond their traditional, narrow law-enforcement view. By communicating to police what we know about the links between disorder, fear, and crime, and helping them to interpret [what we know] in relation to their own street experiences, Bratton has steered the NYPD into some initial successes similar to those achieved by the transit police. Squeegeeing was a quick win and immediately attracted the attention of the public as well as that of the officers themselves. And, just as searching farebeaters in the subway yielded weapons and sent a message through the TPD that fighting disorder was effective as a means of addressing crime generally, so similar accounts are making their way throughout the NYPD: A person arrested for urinating in a park, when questioned about other problems, gave police information that resulted in the confiscation of a small cache of weapons; a motorcyclist cited for not wearing a helmet, on closer inspection, was carrying a nine-millimeter handgun, had another in his sidebag, and had several high-powered weapons in his apartment; a vendor selling hot merchandise, after being questioned, led police to a fence specializing in stolen weapons. These stories made concrete the importance of dealing with minor problems in order to forestall major problems. Just as every farebeater was not a felon, not every petty criminal is a serious criminal; yet enough are, or have information about others who are. Thus, contact with petty offenders alerts all criminals to the vigilance of the police and gives police legitimate access to information about more serious problems.

To implement his community-policing strategy successfully, Bratton needed simultaneously to empower his new precinct heads and create a means for holding them fully accountable. The process developed to serve these two ends—Crime Control Strategy Meetings—rivets the attention of managers on what is happening in the neighborhoods for which they are responsible, thereby creating another sense of accountability to the local community. Each Wednesday and Friday, from 8:00 to 11:00 A.M., NYPD precinct commanders from one of the five boroughs convene in the command center at One Police Plaza, the NYPD's central headquarters, for these meetings. Also present are Deputy Commissioner for Crime

Control Jack Maple, the NYPD's chiefs of patrol (Louis Anemone) and detectives (Charles Reuther), all five borough commanders, and representatives from schools, district attorneys' offices, and the parole department.

The format for each meeting is the same: In turn, each precinct commander, accompanied by a detective lieutenant and other representatives of the precinct, takes the floor to report formally on current conditions in the precinct, including problems related to disorder, crime prevention and control, efforts being undertaken by the district police to address them, and results. Portrayed overhead on a large screen for all to see are precinct data on index crimes, numbers and geographical distribution of arrests, shooting victims and incidents, precinct residents on parole who have outstanding felony or parole warrants, and whatever other data are available that reflect on the quality of life in the district. Data are organized by week, month, and year-to-date and are compared with the previous year's statistics. The precinct commander is questioned by Deputy Commissioner Maple and others present about specific problems: rapes may be up; robberies staying at high levels; grand larcenies down—and precinct commanders have learned that they must not only be intimately familiar with the data looming over their heads, but also must be able to "unpack" them when queried. Officers from other precincts may offer suggestions to the solution of particularly troublesome problems arising from their own experiences or may share information about a common problem. The themes that continually shape the discussion are Bratton's four guiding methods of crime control: accurate and timely intelligence; rapid deployment; effective tactics; and relentless follow-up and assessment. Finally, each presentation generally closes with the introduction of a patrol officer or officers who have been particularly resourceful in dealing with some neighborhood problem—as likely a quality-of-life issue as any other crime problem.

The Crime Control Strategy Meetings have sparked the New York City Police Department. In an elegant and simple way they constitute a process that embodies the decentralization of authority to precinct commanders, establishes the terms of accountability, dramatizes the department's new procedures for providing services to communities, and reinforces Bratton's vision of policing. Most important, the seriousness of the meetings; the status of those required to attend and the presence of their peers; the incessant grilling and challenges; and the high visibility of the process force precinct commanders to focus attention constantly on their neighborhoods.

With these changes, the NYPD has undergone a major reorientation and reorganization, embracing fully a quality-of-life approach to crime prevention and control. Although all the elements of organizational change are not yet in place, the NYPD has gone through a substantial shift in its strategy—a shift that is no longer merely nominal, supported only by the highest levels of command and in a few isolated outposts in the department. Capitalizing on early wins and considerable reductions in serious crime, the new leadership is changing not only the structure of the NYPD, but also its entire culture. . . .

Assessing the Results of Restoring Order

For those who live and work in New York City today, the changes in the sub-way and on many streets and public places are palpable as order is restored to the city. Graffiti is gone from subway trains. The facilities of Grand Central Terminal, Penn Station, and the Port Authority Bus Terminal have changed dramatically: One has only to walk through one of these stations to feel the difference, see the cleanliness, and notice that a sense of mutual respect now characterizes citizen interaction. Bryant Park has been restored and is a joyous place. Central Park has been largely reclaimed. Squeegeemen are off the streets. People who left the city during the late 1980s and now return to visit are stunned by the differences in the subways, parks, and on the streets. News articles about New York regularly highlight the improvements. In sum, independent of statistics, the experiences of citizens in New York are changing. Where many used to find life in New York City an unrelenting hassle, they now feel a renewed sense of urban pleasure.

And although change is clearly evident in terms of quality of life and a reduction in low-level crimes and incidents of disorder, a new development is the dramatic reduction in "index [more serious] crime," as reflected not only by what citizens experience but also in the crime statistics. Declines in crime in the subway began immediately after the institution of an order-maintenance strategy by Bratton in 1990 and have continued to the present time. Figure 17.1 illustrates the increases both in all felonies (including robberies) and in robberies, perhaps the felony of greatest concern in the subway, prior to 1990; it also indicates the decreases that began the next year and have continued since. These are startling statistics, unparalleled in the crime-control literature: Since the institution of an aggressive order-maintenance strategy, *felonies have declined 75 percent and robberies 64 percent*. In effect serious crime has ceased to be a major problem in New York's subways.

Although the order-maintenance program in the subway was not introduced or studied experimentally, at least two factors suggest that order-maintenance activities caused a reduction in crime. First, the onset of declines in crime occurred almost immediately after Bratton introduced the police order-maintenance activities. Second, although administrative and organizational alterations were plentiful in the Transit Police Department, *tactical* changes were limited to targeting on farebeating and restoring order: No major antirobbery or felony tactics were introduced. Are the changes in crime rates solely the result of police efforts? No, not

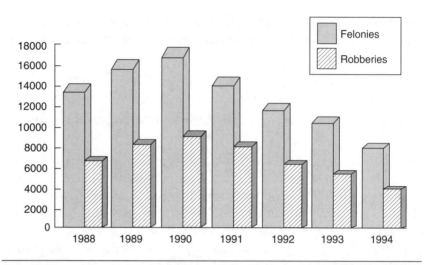

Figure 17.1   New York Subway Felonies and Robberies, 1988–1994

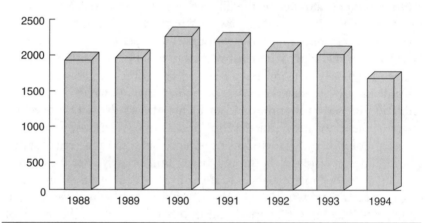

Figure 17.2   New York City Murder Rates, 1988–1994

likely. We believe that, most likely, they have come about as a result of the Transit Authority's total commitment to order restoration, which included eliminating graffiti, "target hardening" (that is, making targets less accessible), and assertion of civilian control over territory through the station managers program, as well as a result of police efforts.

This same pattern is now visible in New York City as a whole, where in 1995 citizens were less likely to be victimized than at any time since 1970. Figures 17.2 and 17.3 illustrate the significant declines that have occurred in violent crime, noticeable especially in 1994, during Bratton's first year as commissioner. Some of these declines are unprecedented. For example, the drop in the murder rate is without historic parallel in cities

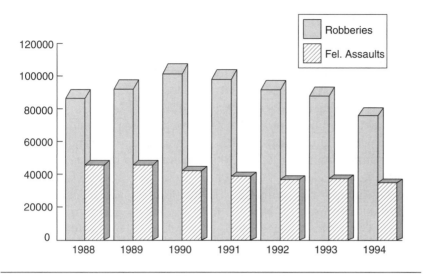

Figure 17.3 New York City Robberies and Assaults, 1988–1994

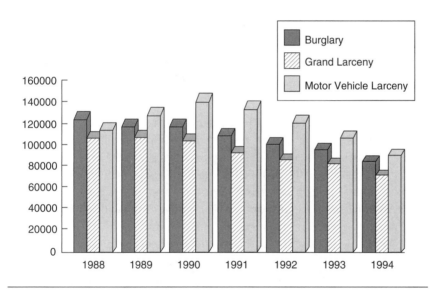

Figure 17.4 New York City Property Crimes, 1988–1994

throughout the United States. During 1994, homicide declined nationally by 5 percent, while the decline in New York City was 17 percent. Moreover, robberies declined in 1994 to their lowest rate since 1973. Assault declined as well. Preliminary statistics for 1995 suggest that the rate of decline in all categories of violent crime is even steeper than in 1994.[2]

As with declines in crimes against persons, property crimes have also decreased in New York, shown in Figure 17.4. In 1994 the burglary rate was down from 1993 levels by 10.9 percent; larceny 10.8 percent; and motor vehicle theft by 15.2 percent. Preliminary reports from 1995 again indicate that the rates of decline are accelerating.

Aside from looking at the data themselves, we can also test our conclusion that order-maintenance efforts have led to reductions in crime generally by returning to the perceptions of citizens in New York. Most believe that something quite profound is happening in their town. Although the citizens with whom we have spoken may not represent a random sample, there is little doubt that for them the quality of life in New York City is improving appreciably. One survey has a particularly suggestive finding. The widely reported Quinnipiac College poll regularly reports the most important concerns of New Yorkers. Its most recent findings were presented in a November 6, 1995, press release: "For the first time in a Quinnipiac College poll, New Yorkers list unemployment as the 'most important problem facing New York State today.' In April, New Yorkers listed taxes. In prior polls, New Yorkers always had listed crime as the biggest problem."[3] Adding up the changes in the subways and parks, as well as in the streets in many areas, over the last five years New York has become a much different place. We suggest that order-restoration efforts are a significant reason.

Because New York is a media center, and because the order-maintenance activities there are the cornerstone of police crime-control activities, considerable controversy has developed over whether Bratton's policies are responsible for New York City's widely reported reductions in crime. Within criminology circles, this debate has been rigorous indeed. The issue of whether crime is declining as a result of police actions raises some of the thorniest problems of causality in social science: How do we know that crime has actually dropped? Are the "books being cooked"? Are citizens changing their reporting habits, say out of concern for corruption? Are the changes a temporary blip that over time will return to previous "normal" levels? If crime has dropped, how can the effect be parsed out? What role does sentencing play? The increase in prisons? Are there structural changes in society—say changes in poverty levels—that could be responsible for the shifts? These and other legitimate questions abound.[4]

This debate has also been rancorous, because deep-seated ideologies are involved. One side argues that poverty, racism, and social injustice cause crime; because police can do little about these structural features of society they will never be able to do much about crime either.[5] An alternative and more optimistic view, to which we subscribe, asserts that addressing the "root causes" of crime, whatever they may be, need not be the only way of reducing crime itself: In fact, regardless of the causes of crime, police can, through the use of the proper strategy and a variety of tactics, affect crime rates. The key question for those who espouse this latter view is whether and how police can help to create the conditions in neighborhoods and communities that will allow other institutions—the family, neighborhood, church, community agencies and government, and commerce—to deal with these basic problems of society.

We believe the statistics reflecting current drops in index crime in New York City illustrate just these processes and effects. Specifically, our confidence that the crime reductions in New York City are real and have to do with police and community actions rests on a line of reasoning that goes something like this: prepare a city for 20 years; develop strong community movements; organize BIDS [business improvement districts] and private security; clean up the mess in the subway; restore parks (often privately, and keep them under private oversight); develop a community court and close linkages with prosecutors; and then have a new mayor and police commissioner walk in and say to the city, "Oh by the way, I have 38,000 police that I am going to assign to work with you and hold them closely accountable both for results and their behavior." In such circumstances, we would be surprised if crime did not drop.

Many of the initiatives for restoring order in New York City exist in cities throughout the country. A movement is gaining ground. This movement represents a basic shift away from the 1960s "criminal justice system" model, with its intolerance of citizen and private input into maintaining order and controlling crime, and its insistence that such matters are best left to professionals. To be sure, the move toward community collaboration and accountability is at this stage far from efficient and lacks refinement. But citizen initiatives are visible everywhere as grass-roots involvement—through neighborhood organizations, citizen advisory councils, and crimewatch groups. Private and corporate security organizations are reaching out to establish new relationships with citizens and with public sector agencies. Community- and problem-oriented prosecution, courts, and corrections efforts, widely dispersed and in their infancy, are affecting community efforts unevenly. Yet there is hardly a city in which the outlines of a community-based crime prevention paradigm are not apparent.

The shift to a community-based, problem-oriented approach to maintaining order and reducing crime, as promising as it is for cities, contains real dangers. The "system" model was reactive: As such, it used authority narrowly and frugally. The community model is active and interventionist, involving police intimately in neighborhoods as they attempt to solve problems before they worsen, and to some degree justifying intervention by citizens, directed at crime prevention, as well. Such actions by police and citizens must arise out of a broader base of authority and wider network of collaboration. How such use of authority is to be controlled so as to protect the fundamental rights of all citizens is a major issue in a democratic society.

Notes

1. Colum Lynch, "War on Windshield Washers," *The Boston Globe*, December 18, 1993, p. 3.

2. New York City Crime Control Indicators & Strategy Assessment, New York City Police Department, November 1995. Rape has not declined appreciably, and those data are hard to interpret. It could reflect that rapes really did not decline or it could reflect an increase in women willing to report being raped. Short of much more intensive study, no means of determining which is true is possible.

3. Quinnipiac College Poll, "Surveys of New York, New Jersey, and Connecticut," *Press Release*, Hamden, CT, Quinnipiac College Polling Institute, November 6, 1995, p. 2.

4. Harvard Professor Mark H. Moore of the John F. Kennedy School of Government has reflected on this issue in considerable depth and this enumeration of issues reflects his thinking.

5. See, for example, Richard Moran, "More Police, Less Crime, Right? Wrong." *The New York Times*, February 27, 1995, p. A15.

Communities Not Fazed 18

Why Military Base Closures May Not Be Catastrophic*

Ted K. Bradshaw

editor's introduction:

Methodological Significance

This selection provides another example of a case study analysis. Its main goal is to explain, through the assembling of appropriate documentary evidence and economic data, why the closing of a military base did not result in the predicted catastrophic effect. The analysis dominates the entire selection—which in turn, coming from a journal article rather than a book, represents the bulk of the entire case study. In this sense, the bulk of the entire case study is devoted to the analysis task and serves as another form of case study for you to consider in designing yours.

The analysis consists of amassing large amounts of evidence, quantitative and qualitative, to martial a strong argument. First, the evidence covers a broad variety of community economic conditions—ranging from retail and housing sales to health services to unemployment to the indirect effects of multipliers and local organizational capacity—whereby

*Editor's Note: Excerpted, with light editing, from "Communities Not Fazed: Why Military Base Closures May Not Be Catastrophic," in *Journal of American Planning Association*, Spring 1999, 65, pp. 193–206. Reprinted with permission.

catastrophic outcomes might have occurred. The breadth of the conditions covered—reflected by the case study's headings and subheadings—is extensive. Second, for each of the conditions, the case study presents data and an explanation to show why the actual outcomes were less severe than anticipated. Note that the data cover trends in the target community as well as comparisons to other communities and to statewide trends, during the same period of time.

The combination of these two features—a broad range of potentially relevant conditions and appropriate trend and comparative data—helps build confidence in the overall conclusions reached by this single-case study.

Substantive Note

The impact of federal policies and outlays on local economies has been a central concern of the entire American political system. The concern may reflect the presumed positive effects of new federal outlays in some local area (with legislators often accused of "pork barreling") or the presumed negative effects of the withdrawal of existing outlays. Among the latter, the closing and consolidating of military bases has sparked vigorous and highly visible, if not inflammatory, political debate. The present selection examines the effects of closing an important Strategic Air Command base that also happened to be the local county's largest employer.

When Castle Air Force Base near Merced California received notice that it was on the list of military bases to be closed, the public braced for a major catastrophe. Newspaper headlines announced the concerns of a community facing doom. Near the base, shopkeepers, bar owners, fast food restaurant managers, and local government officials tearfully anticipated that their community would become an economic backwater or ghost town. Local commissions were formed to try to save the base and the community. Leaders rushed to Congress to complain that closure would ruin their already fragile economy. Congressmen returned to assure citizens that closure would be fought. Task forces estimated the projected tragedy for the county—retail sales would fall $105 million, 3,700 jobs would be lost, county population would decline by 18,000 persons, the unemployment rate would increase by seven points, and decline would spiral (Castle AFB Task Force 2000, 1991). But . . . these well-meaning concerns were unfounded. Base closures are not necessarily catastrophes.

Announcements of military base closures stimulate an industry of cataclysmic prognostications. For example, the closure of Chanute Air Force Base in Rantoul, Illinois, was claimed by the mayor to pose the threat of a local economic loss of $340 million—over 2.6 times its payroll of $130 million (Hartwig, 1989). Another study reported that March Air Force Base's closure would result in a regional loss of $580 million, based on a 3.7 multiplier of the military budget of $157 million (Hannaford, 1989). A California government report on the closure of Fort Ord projected a private sector job loss of a quarter of Monterey County's nonagricultural workforce—over 25,000 workers—along with 17,200 base employees, and nearly a billion dollar indirect economic loss (Commission on State Finance, 1992). These projections of catastrophic impacts are not supported by good research, but seem to be political arguments aimed either to influence the military to keep a base open or to justify compensation to the local community.

. . . A growing body of research literature shows that base closures are not catastrophic in the short run, and that over time the base and its abandoned facilities can be an unprecedented opportunity for economic rejuvenation and public benefit. As to short-term impacts, evidence is mounting to show that closure can initially leave nearby communities unfazed (Hallissy, 1993). For example, a recent Rand Corporation study looked at the community impacts of three California bases—George, Castle, and Fort Ord—selected for closure in the 1988 and 1991 Base Realignment and Adjustment Commission (BRAC) cycles. Based on data collected through 1994, the Rand study concluded that "while some of the communities did indeed suffer, the effects were not catastrophic, [and] not nearly as severe as forecasted" (Dardia et al., 1996, p. xii). Comparing closed bases to matched pairs of communities with similar bases that did not close and to communities in the surrounding county, the researchers showed that the effects of base closure were "highly localized geographically" (pp. 44–45). . . .

Castle Air Force Base

Castle Air Force Base was located in Atwater, California, in the Central Valley about 125 miles southeast of San Francisco. Merced, the county seat, is a medium-sized city about 10 miles south of Atwater. Castle avoided the first round of military base closures, but learned in July 1991 that it was one of the bases scheduled for closure in the second round. The news was received with considerable local anger. Attempts were made to convince the military that the closure was a "Serious Military Mistake" (Castle AFB Task Force 2000, 1991). The local congressman spoke against the plan to close the base and intervened to suggest that Castle be retained instead of rebuilding Homestead Air Force Base in Florida after it was destroyed by Hurricane Andrew in the fall of 1992. All these efforts failed.

Castle Air Force Base was a well-established Strategic Air Command base and training facility for B-52 bomber and KC-135 tanker crews, with a 1991 contingent of 5,028 active duty military personnel and a payroll of $120.7 million. In addition, 1,208 civilian employees received a payroll of $17 million. The base had advanced equipment such as flight training simulators, facilities for large aircraft service and repair, a heavy-duty runway, and a campus-like setting. The military and civilian staff included a large number of skilled instructors, many of whom had been at the base for an extended period. Before final closure, the Air Force moved units out gradually, with the majority of departures in the first half of 1995; few personnel were left for the formal closure on September 30, 1995. The operations of Castle were transferred to Oklahoma and Louisiana. Most military personnel and their families were relocated. However, during the process of closing the base, military downsizing led to the discharge or retirement of 330 military personnel. A survey of these persons showed that only about 20 percent planned to stay in the area, and another 15 percent were unsure.[1]

Castle was the largest employer in Merced County, which is dominated by agriculture and related industries. The total civilian employment in the County was some 58,000 persons (California Employment Development Department, 1991–1997), which made the base employment of 6,000 persons about 10 percent of total civilian and military employment. The closure of the base resulted in the relocation of some 11,000 military personnel, spouses, and dependents.[2] The estimated county population was 184,000 on January 1, 1991, which means that the military exit involved 6 percent of the county population. Compared to other base closures, it is important to realize that Castle might be expected to experience more severe consequences because it is in a rural, agriculture-based county with very high unemployment, ranging from 12 to 20 percent. There are few other large employers near the base, and there are no federal government facilities into which civilians could be transferred. On the other hand, the county was spared worse consequences because the base employed few civilians in manufacturing or research, and the whole region was experiencing moderate population increase as part of the Central Valley's rapid growth.

The closure of Castle was anticipated to have catastrophic economic and employment consequences for Merced County.[3] In 1994, the California Military Base Reuse Task Force prepared a report that projected the base closure would lead to an increase in unemployment from 14.4 percent in October 1993 to 21.7 percent in October 1995. The county's analysis projected that closing the base would lead to the loss of 3,694 civilian jobs (5.8 percent of the employed laborforce), and to a population loss of 18,000 individuals. The impact on retail sales was estimated to be a loss of $105 million (Castle AFB Task Force 2000, 1991). As in other communities facing base closure, these projections reinforced local beliefs that, without the base, the community would spiral into a multifaceted decline.

The Case Study

This study is about the initial impact of base closure on its surrounding community. It was initiated before Castle closed, to help the community prepare for the anticipated problems. During the year prior to closure, data were collected and interviews were held with key economic developers, military staff, members of the base conversion Joint Powers Agency, government officials, and representatives of community organizations and private businesses. Increasingly, it became evident that the closure would not be a catastrophe because of many mitigating factors that might compensate for the loss of the military (Bradshaw, 1993). However, this optimistic finding was not popular with some government leaders because they wanted to demonstrate the severity of their losses in order to attempt to leverage additional compensation from the Department of Defense. After Castle officially closed, the research in the county continued with the objective of evaluating whether the preclosure predictions were correct. After closure, additional data were gathered to address the factors that had previously been identified as mitigating the impact of closure. . . .

Impact of Base Closure on Markets

One of the first impacts that communities worry about when a base closure is announced is declining sales by both consumer and military supplier firms. Local newspaper stories frequently quote small businesses near these bases as saying they serve mostly military personnel and their families. Their lost markets, generalized, mean that people will lose jobs, tax revenues will fall, and the community might decline with considerable loss of employment.

However, markets will not collapse as suggested by the catastrophic projections, because bases are relatively isolated economies—drawing little from the locality and generating little economic activity nearby. Bases import a high proportion of supplies and even personnel from national rather than local sources. The extent of their isolation has been demonstrated by earlier studies (Daicoff et al., 1970; MacKinnon, 1978), and by an interesting analysis of the impact of four new bases that located in small communities during the 1970s and 1980s. The more recent study (Muller, Hansen, & Hutchinson, 1991) found that the new bases did not create economic expansion in the local communities because the bases were weakly integrated into the communities, and because base employees spent money on the base rather than in local stores. Theoretically, this finding is consistent with Jacobs's (1984) observation that military expenditures are not used to advance local production. Rather than being an engine for local economic development, military bases are regional or national operations that have minimal or possibly even negative effects on local communities.

Local retail sales may stabilize. When a base closes, the public assumes that the large base payroll is the engine that has bolstered local retail sales and thus the local economy. However, a large proportion of that payroll never enters the local economy because bases have on-base retail commissary and exchange outlets for their personnel. In addition, military retirees in the area have privileges to shop on base. When the base closes, so do these internal markets. . . .

Data collected since the closure tend to confirm these anticipated effects of very limited retail sales loss. In spite of the base closure in the spring and summer of 1995, the reported quarterly sales in Merced County following closure increased $4.1 million in the third quarter and $3.7 million in the fourth quarter, compared to the year before. Sales growth in Merced County during 1995 increased 1.9 percent over the previous year, but Merced County lagged behind the overall state taxable sales growth of 5.6 percent. Neighboring counties such as Stanislaus and Madera, which also have high unemployment and an agricultural base, had growth rates of 3.1 percent (California State Board of Equalization, 1994 & 1995). Based on these comparisons, base closure resulted in growth that was slower by just over a percentage point than might have been expected.

The base closure did not lead to a quick decrease in the number of businesses in the county either. The data show that the county had a total of 3,900 sales tax permits in July 1995, up just slightly from 3,890 the previous year. During this same period, the number of tax permits increased 1.3 percent statewide (California State Board of Equalization, 1994 & 1995). Thus, base closure had the effect of slowing retail sales and tax permit growth in the county relative to other nearby counties and to the state as a whole. However, it is impossible based on this analysis to agree with catastrophic preclosure estimates that the total retail sales loss to the county would be $105 million (Castle AFB Task Force 2000, 1991).

Regardless of the overall trend, small shop owners nearest the base may suffer disproportionately, and business persons in town may not experience the stable retail environment that these data portray. The loss of military customers and sales perceived by small store owners and mall operators may be due only partly to base closure, because small community retail outlets are being hurt nationwide by transitions in the overall retail economy that hurt downtowns. Several of the major warehouse retailers have opened or are making plans to open in the Merced and Atwater area. Wal-Mart and Target have opened stores near Castle, and the Costco warehouse chain recently opened a store in Merced. An average Costco in northern California can be expected to generate about $75 million in sales per year,[4] nearly double the sales volume of the base outlets. These new retail chains obviously did not believe that the base closure would be a catastrophe for the Merced economy, and they are drawing a considerable amount of business from smaller local merchants, including those near the base. Thus, small merchants near the base may incorrectly blame the base closure for all of their sales loss, although the new big-box retailers may be as much to blame.

Military purchases from local equipment suppliers and service providers are little missed. As with retail, the isolated base economy purchases very few supplies and services from local businesses. Therefore, when a base closes, few of these businesses suffer greatly. Federal procurement policies take many purchasing decisions away from local bases, and most of the things that are needed to run a base are not manufactured in a small county such as Merced in any case. . . .

One of the most significant economic impacts of the closure of Castle was ending the construction program on base. Many facilities were upgraded and several hundred construction workers were employed at an annual spending level of $25 million. When closure was announced, these projects stopped, which undoubtedly reduced employment in the construction industry. It is not known how many construction workers resided in Merced County or where they went to work after construction on the base ended.

Surprisingly, expenditures for toxic cleanup replaced construction at the base, almost on a dollar-for-dollar basis, meaning that the construction budget suffered little loss. The annual toxic cleanup effort at Castle amounts to about $20 to 25 million for the first 3 to 5 years after closure, with lesser amounts after that. These expenditures had other similarities with the canceled construction budget as well, specifically that primary contracts went to firms outside the area. Some local workers were employed doing cleanup work along with significant numbers of workers from elsewhere, but it is not known if any workers employed in construction at the base found employment with the cleanup firms.

New housing sales increase, while resale housing prices fall. In all the previous case studies of base closures, declining housing values and increased vacancies in rental units followed. While the loss of retail sales in Merced County was small, with the effect mainly consisting of slower-than-expected growth, the picture for the housing market was very mixed. A large proportion of the military personnel lived on base or in the town of Atwater. Base dormitories and a housing complex provided housing for 1,874 military personnel and 2,600 dependents: The remaining 3,200 personnel and their dependents lived off base. Within the town of Atwater, military families constituted a large part of the town's 22,000 population, occupying about 30 percent of the town's residential units (Castle AFB Task Force 2000, 1991).

Housing prices started falling when closure was announced, and owners of rental units reported high vacancy rates as military personnel and their families left town. After closure was announced, housing prices initially declined about 10 percent (Dardia et al., 1996). Atwater city planners estimate that housing prices fell a maximum of 25 percent and vacancies increased by the same amount when military personnel left town. The county records report that 1995 home sales declined 23 percent from 1994, largely due to slow sales of existing properties such as those vacated by military families. Departing military families who owned housing were given price and sales assistance as part of their relocation, so individual military families did not suffer the loss of housing values. Clearly, the existing housing market was hurt by the base closure.

On the other hand, new housing sales increased by about 25 percent at the same time the base was closing. In spite of the base closure, seven new subdivisions in Atwater just outside the closed base are building houses, and sales are brisk, totaling several hundred houses a year, an increase of 37 percent over the preclosure sales level. Most of these houses are relatively inexpensive ($90,000), entry-level housing, but they compete strongly with the existing housing being sold by departing military families. In spite of the countywide drop in housing sales of 23 percent, Atwater's housing sales actually increased 3 percent because of the new housing development. The planning department reports that these new developments represent approximately $35 million in residential valuation, a significant sign of strength in the housing market just when the base was closing. . . .

Hospital and health care services are privatized. Base closure privatized the significant expenditures for health care that had been provided on base. Health care services including dentistry and most specialties were provided to active duty military personnel at on-base clinics and a hospital, which had been well equipped to handle most health care needs. The hospital had a 50-bed capacity, though only about 15 beds were in use during the last several years the base operated. More important in terms of local impact of the base closure, military retirees could use base medical facilities and services free of charge on an as-available basis. It is estimated that at least 25 percent of the medical workload at Castle was in- and out-patient services for retirees. The total 1991 health care budget for the base was $7 million, of which $1.5 million was allocated to retirees. As the base closed, retirees were offered insurance coverage that allowed them to get services from doctors and hospitals in the community.

Since the closure, retiree health care spending has added to the total economic base of the county. The value of retiree health care services to the local economy is about 25 to 30 percent higher than the $1.3 million allocated to them on base, giving a shift from military to private providers of about $2 million. This expenditure comes largely from insurance, which is paid by the military from national funds.

The base hospital has been turned over to the community and will be used as a clinic for people in the Atwater area, where health facilities are limited. The sense among local leaders is that this will improve local health care access.

Impact on Employment and Population

Prior to closure, it was expected that the predicted loss of retail sales, loss of base purchases of supplies and equipment, and falling housing markets would result in fewer jobs and higher unemployment. However, as has been shown, each of these factors either has been stable or declined minimally. Thus, it would be reasonable to assume that cumulatively the employment level and unemployment rate would follow the same pattern, avoiding the huge loses projected, but lagging behind the growth expected from California's post-recession economic recovery.

Civilian employment losses are balanced by job vacancies left by military spouses. About 1,000 civilian employees lost their jobs at the base, and many were concerned about whether and where they would find new jobs. Even without the base closure, the unemployment rate in Merced County hovered between 15 and 20 percent, so any new job-seekers would increase competition for relatively few available jobs. Increased unemployment was strongly anticipated because these civilian employees would remain in the area. Although displaced civilians can apply for jobs in other government facilities and may even qualify for transfer assistance, many are not able or willing to relocate.

The rise in unemployment was mitigated, however, because civilians who lost their jobs on the base were more successful than expected in relocating. Interviews with base personnel officers indicated that virtually any person wanting to relocate was accommodated. In addition, many of the civilian employees were spouses who were relocated with their families.

The overall civilian unemployment situation, however, was not aggravated by the base closure because of the jobs vacated by military spouses. About 2,050 spouses were employed in public and private jobs in the region near Castle, and most left their jobs to go with their spouses when base operations ended. No exact data are available on the number of spouse employees or their occupations, because a survey conducted to determine spouse employment had such a low response rate that the data are not useful.[5] However, it is believed that the spouses had a wide range of skills, including teaching and nursing. School and hospital administrators expressed concern to county staff working on the base closure that they might face a shortage of skilled workers, but no reports of worker shortages were uncovered after closure. The jobs made available by departing spouses might be available to displaced base employees or to others in the community who suffered a base-caused layoff. Future research will have to investigate whether jobs vacated by departing spouses were filled by those displaced by the base closure, or if the jobs went unfilled as firms readjusted their workforce or downsized. However, interviews with employers, training providers, and employment-development officials disclosed no major disequilibrium in employment after closure.

Unemployment rates do not escalate. Discussion of unemployment needs to be placed in context; Merced County consistently has had one of the highest unemployment rates in California due to its agricultural base. For example, in April 1995 just as the base was starting to close, the unemployment rate was 18.2 percent, ranking 56th out of 58 counties, and more than double the state unemployment rate of 7.8 percent. The neighboring county, Stanislaus, had an April 1995 unemployment rate of 17.4 percent. Employment and unemployment rates also swing wildly by season (due to agricultural employment), further masking the impact of the base closure. In pre-base closure years, total employment in the slowest periods was 8,000 to 10,000 less than the summer peak, and unemployment rates varied from a high of over 20 percent to about 12 percent.

Figure 18.1 shows employment and unemployment rates from 1992 to 1996. After the departure of the majority of the base personnel during the middle quarters of 1995, the seasonal pattern of employment and the unemployment rate fluctuated much as before. In October, just after the base closed, total employment in all industries[6] fell by several thousand compared to the years before. However, by January 1996 total employment actually increased by 100 compared to the year before the base closed. The average annual employment in Merced County in 1995 fell by 1,375 employees compared to 1994, but gained back 1,100 of these by 1996. Thus, after a brief decline, county employment regained almost all

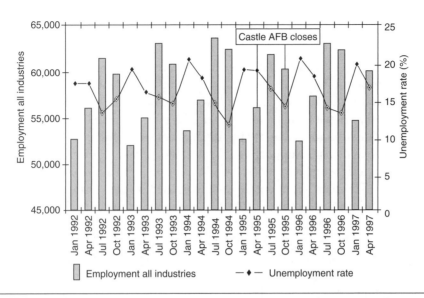

Figure 18.1   Employment and Unemployment Rate in Merced County Before and After
the Closure of Castle Air Force Base

SOURCE: Data from California Employment Development Department.

the preclosure jobs. Of course, county employment did not grow in this
period as it did in neighboring counties.

The annual average unemployment rate in Merced County during
the period of base closure followed seasonal patterns, but overall it rose
from 15.5 percent in 1994 to 17.1 percent in 1995, reflecting the impact
of the base closure. By 1996, unemployment had partially recovered by
dropping to 16.2 percent. The base closure period was associated with about
a 2.5 percentage point increase in unemployment, a significant but not overwhelming effect of base closure in a high-unemployment area. Perhaps
more serious, however, is the fact that Merced County did not share in the
improving employment prospects that favored the rest of the state. The state
unemployment rate fell from 8.6 percent in 1994 to 7.2 percent in 1996, a
decrease that was not reflected in Merced County. Interestingly, neighboring
Stanislaus County, which is too far away to have experienced much direct
impact from the base, did not fully benefit from the statewide improvement
either, and only reduced its unemployment from 15.7 percent in 1994 to
15.5 percent in 1995. Still, Stanislaus County improved slightly compared to
the 2.6 percentage point worsening in Merced County. Although it is unde-
niable that unemployment rose in Merced County due to the base closure,
the impact was much less than feared. The projection was that the October
1995 unemployment would jump to 21 percent, whereas it was only slightly
higher than the previous October at 14.1 percent. . . .

Impact on Population Stability

One would expect the net loss of economic vitality in a base closure community, combined with the disruption of many community services and functions, to lead to a loss of population. The movement of 11,000 military personnel and their families from Merced County is a significant reduction to the county population, which could be multiplied by the loss of civilians in supporting jobs. In theory, base closure should lead to significant population loss, even in a county with a history of rapid growth.

The data show population stability, however. Instead of base closure leading to a decline in the total population in Merced County, the estimated population increased by 600 persons (0.3 percent) to a total of 198,500 between January 1995 and January 1996 (California State Department of Finance, 1995–97). The high birth rate in the county must have been supplemented by a wave of new immigrants to replace the military personnel who left.

Merced's population did not grow as fast as if the base had remained open. The state as a whole grew 1.0 percent in 1995, while neighboring Fresno County grew 1.9 percent and Stanislaus County grew 1.0 percent. Merced County's population rebounded and began to grow again in 1996, reaching 201,000 by January 1997—an increase of 1.3 percent. People are moving to all the Central Valley counties because of low housing prices and a perceived high quality of life, as well as an expanding economy that creates jobs in fields for which the currently unemployed residents are not qualified. Merced County's 1996–1997 population increase exceeded the state population growth rate of 1.2 percent over the same year. During the three years prior to base closure, Merced County's population increased on average somewhat over 3,000 persons (about 1.5 percent) per year, similar to California's overall growth rate. The reality of a stable and slowly growing population contrasts with the projected catastrophic decline of 15,000 persons (Castle AFB Task Force 2000, 1991).

Multipliers and Community Response

A pervasive fear in base closure communities is that the loss of base employment and purchases will be multiplied many times in the county, and that the loss of revenues from base spending will cascade through the economy, causing employment and business to spiral downward out of control. The fear is based on high economic multipliers that amplify whatever loss there is. Another great fear is that the loss of the base will leave the community hopelessly disorganized and unable to respond adequately to these problems. However, in both cases the fears are overstated.

Job and income multipliers are not so high. Prior to base closure, the projections of catastrophe were based on the belief that the impact on local employment and income would be multiplied two or three times by the cumulative effects on one business after another. Multipliers are one of the most commonly misunderstood tools of economic analysis, and pundits who wish to show that a base closure will be a local catastrophe misuse and overestimate multipliers to make their point. In fact, however, economic multipliers in a small county like Merced with a specialized agricultural economy are quickly dissipated because so few things are actually purchased and supplied from within the county.

One typical misunderstanding about multipliers is how low they actually are when considered within a small region. Considering the sum of direct, indirect, and consumption-induced effects, multipliers are rarely 3.5 or more for a locality, state, or even region; the typical multiplier for an industry in a small county is within the range of 1.3 to 2.0, whereas in a large county multipliers of 1.5 to 2.5 are typical. Because of the isolated nature of military base supply systems, base multipliers (which are not usually available) are likely to be no more than 1.3 or 1.4, meaning that for every dollar the base spends, only 30 or 40 cents of additional economic activity is generated in the county (Bradshaw et al., 1994). At a state level these multipliers go up somewhat, as they do in large metropolitan areas, because more of the things purchased by the base and its employees are produced within a larger area. . . .

Building Local Organizational Capacity

In most base communities, the military is a significant organizational power, sometimes as a resource and partner with the community in many programs, and other times contributing only volunteers through a few organized efforts, When a base closes, this organizational capacity will be lost just when it is most needed. Realizing the military's responsibility to the communities where bases are closing, the Office of Economic Adjustment (OEA) has become a sophisticated resource for economic revitalization of closed bases. With the ability to fund significant planning activities at the closed bases, the OEA has also contributed a methodology for reuse that has continually improved. The U.S. Department of Defense *Base Reuse Implementation Manual* (1995) outlines a three-phase process based on intensive local planning by a designated local reuse authority (LRA). The LRA conducts a number of required studies, including the environmental impact report, and obtains local input on reuse options. In the second stage, the military makes a wide range of decisions about conveyance and disposition of the property. In the third stage, parcel-by-parcel decisions are implemented and reuse begins.

Successful base reuse planning begins before closure. Bases with strong leadership and organizational capacity minimize the panic of closure and position the community for a stronger response. In contrast, bases where the reuse planning process resulted in lawsuits, conflict, lack of leadership, and the inability to reach consensus wasted considerable energy throughout the closure. George Air Force Base in southern California, for example, shows the problems caused by failing to reach a consensus, with one town separating from the Joint Powers Agency and suing the other participants. Their reuse efforts have been delayed because of these problems. Yet, because of the persistence of the OEA reuse process, the communities near the base got another chance and progress is being made (see Hartwig, 1989; Murphy, 1993). . . .

Conclusion

Closure of a military base is not catastrophic to its local community because even fully operating bases have weak links to the community and the economy in which they are located, and because several compensating factors work to mitigate some of the losses that do occur. The people who lose their jobs and the communities that lose a major employer must make painful adjustments that cannot be minimized—in some areas the losses will be greater than in Merced. However, in this study, the catastrophic losses that were projected prior to closure failed to materialize. The impact of a base closure may be greater under other circumstances, and the findings do not suggest that all communities experiencing a base closure will have such mild consequences. Some of the most important limitations of the findings of this study include:

- Most significantly, communities whose bases employ large numbers and/or proportions of civilians, especially in industrial or repair facilities, will suffer more serious consequences than those whose bases use mostly military personnel, because civilian workers are not routinely relocated and they are not easily re-employed by private industry.

- Previous findings show that base closures in rural areas and small towns have more serious effects than base closures in urban areas. Also, areas that are growing will adapt more easily to a base closure than areas that are declining.

- Minority groups may be overrepresented among dislocated workers.

- Even base reuse will not necessarily re-employ the civilians initially laid off when a base closes.

- Workers dislocated from a base often must take new jobs at lower wages.

- Base closure does slow community and economic growth somewhat compared to what would have happened if the base did not close. The size and balance of these effects will be specific to the particular base and community, depending on how much growth is occurring nearby and the extent to which losses are compensated for by changing markets and populations.

At the same time, this study suggests some of the reasons why a base closure may not be as catastrophic to the local area as most of the preclosure estimates suggest.... When the military leaves, the impact is mitigated through processes that are more complex than usually realized: Military retiree spending shifts from the commissary to private stores and replaces lost retail sales by military personnel who are transferred; expenditures for toxic cleanup replace those for base construction; military spouses who are relocated leave jobs which can be filled by others; health insurance covers payments for medical services that had been provided by military doctors; affordable housing becomes available; and base reuse commissions stimulate regional cooperation among communities.

Studying how the closure of Castle Air Force Base affected communities around it can help other communities estimate the types of impact to expect if a nearby base closes, even if they have different base and community characteristics. In areas where there is no large military retiree population whose commissary shopping will be eliminated, or where retirees have easy access to other commissaries, one would expect to see a larger loss of retail sales, regardless of whether it is a rural or urban base. If the base employs a large number of civilians in manufacturing or research and development who have no other job opportunities in the community, then there will be a significantly larger pool of unemployed workers remaining in the area, creating many negative effects on the local economy. If the region is losing population anyway, the vacant housing stock is less likely to be repurchased and reused. If the overall region is stagnant or declining economically, public or private employers will be unable to hire as many displaced employees. If the local region supplies a large proportion of the base's goods and services, then the multiplier will be higher and the community impact will be greater. In short, by knowing how to evaluate the claim that a base closure will be catastrophic and identify which losses will be significant, the community can better prepare for the economic development challenge that it must undertake to convert a closure to an opportunity....

References

Bradshaw, T. K. (1993). *Which impact? The local impact of base closure needs closer examination* (Working Paper No. 602). Berkeley: University of California, Institute of Urban and Regional Development.

Bradshaw, T. K., et al. (1994). *Defense industry conversion, base closure, and the California economy* (Working Paper No. 631). Berkeley: University of California, Institute of Urban and Regional Development.

California Employment Development Department. (1991–1997). *Monthly labor force data for counties.* Sacramento Employment Development Department, Labor Market Division.

California State Board of Equalization. (1994 & 1995). *Taxable sales in California: Sales and use tax.* Sacramento: State Board of Equalization.

California State Department of Finance, Demographic Research Unit. (1995–1997). Estimates of the population of the state of California and counties, July 1. (Report E-2). Sacramento: State Department of Finance.

Castle Air Force Base, 93rd Wing/FMC. (1991 & 1992). *Economic resource impact statement.* Atwater, CA: Castle Air Force Base.

Castle AFB Task Force 2000. (May 1991). *May 1991 report on Castle AFB proposed closure: A serious military mistake.* Merced, CA: Merced County.

Commission on State Finance. (1992). *Impact of defense cuts on California.* Sacramento: State of California.

Daicoff, D., et al. (April 1970). Economic impact of military base closings. *ACDA/E-90, I and II.* Washington, DC: U.S. Arms Control and Disarmament Agency.

Dardia, M., et al. (1996). *The effects of military base closures on local communities: A short term perspective.* Santa Monica: Rand Corporation.

Hallissy, E. (November 13, 1993). Navy towns not fazed by closing of bases. *San Francisco Chronicle,* p. 1.

Hannaford, W. (July 1989). Military base closings: For better or worse? *State Government News,* 10–13.

Hartwig, R. P. (June 1989). Life after death of a military base: The case of Chanute Air Force Base. *Illinois Business Review, 46*(3), 8.

Jacobs, J. (1984). *Cities and the wealth of nations.* New York: Random House.

MacKinnon, D. A. (July 1978). Military base closures: Long range economic effects and implications for industrial development. *AIDC Journal, 13*(3), 7–41.

Muller, T., Hansen, R., & Hutchinson, R. (1991). *The local economic and fiscal impact of new DOD facilities: A retrospective analysis.* Bethesda, MD: Logistics Management Institute.

Murphy, K. D. (September 1993). Making the most out of base closing. *Governing,* 22–24.

U.S. Department of Defense. (July 1995). *Base reuse implementation manual.* Washington, DC: Office of the Assistant Secretary of Defense for Economic Security.

Notes

1. Data from interviews with Castle Air Force Base personnel, 1993.

2. Estimates in 1991 were for 16,000 military and dependents, but this was probably an error corrected in 1992 (Castle Air Force Base, *Economic resource impact statement,* 1991 & 1992).

3. The county is a reasonable level of analysis given the large size of California counties. The two nearest towns outside the county, Modesto and Fresno, are 38 and 56 miles away from Merced.

4. Based on phone interview with Costco executive, 1995.

5. Estimates calculated in consultation with base personnel officials using the following ranges: Officers comprised about 25 percent of all base military personnel; the best available data indicate that about 75 percent of these were married and of these, about 45 percent of spouses were employed. This means that about 450 employed spouses of officers worked in Merced County. The remaining 75 percent enlisted military personnel were younger and, although only about 60 percent were married, more of their spouses were employed—about 70 percent. This means that about 1,600 spouses of enlisted military personnel were employed, for a total of 2,050 spouses employed. Data provided by base personnel office interviews, 1995.

6. The data series on employment in all industries is used because it is based on place of work, whereas total laborforce is based on employment by place of residence. However, employment in all industries excludes self-employed persons, unpaid family workers, household workers, and workers on strike.

Lessons From Houston 19

Fighting to Save Our Urban Schools*

Donald R. McAdams

editor's introduction:

Methodological Significance

A final analytic challenge is to bring a case study to conclusion. Nothing may be more difficult than when this is to be done with a single-case study, especially if the real "case" is still ongoing. How to define an appropriate endpoint, and also identify broader lessons learned beyond the single case, remains a constant challenge.

One workable strategy leaves the reader at the end of a logical cycle in the sequence of events. In the present selection, such a cycle was defined by a new round of school board elections, to occur in late 1997. Because such an election would inevitably create a new dynamic for overseeing the school system that was the subject of the case study, the author chose this juncture to conclude his case study.

*Editor's Note: Excerpted, with light edits, from "A New Beginning for HISD" and "Lessons From Houston," the last two chapters in *Fighting To Save Our Urban Schools—And Winning!: Lessons From Houston* by McAdams, Donald R., Teachers College Press, New York, pp. 229–247 and 248–266. Copyright © 2000 by Teachers College Press. Reproduced with permission of Teachers College Press in the format Other Book via Copyright Clearance Center. A few footnotes have been omitted or integrated into the text.

However, case study authors usually also want to impart some broader message in drawing their conclusions. For the present selection, the broader context was defined by the reasons for doing the case study in the first place: to provide insight into the challenges and strategies in reforming school systems in large American cities. The author claims that his single case represents a successful example of such reform. As a result, the broader message is directed to audiences who must deal with other similar urban school systems, and the concluding passages include references to five other urban systems in the same state.

Within this context, and still as part of the conclusion, the author briefly reviews the educational processes and accomplishments in his single case. The goal is to leave the reader with the understanding that the lessons from this single case may be especially pertinent because the case covers the specific steps taken to produce an exemplary experience.

Substantive Note

The case, the workings of the Houston Independent School District (HISD) from 1990 to late 1997, probably *was* an exemplary case. HISD excelled among school districts in Texas and also within the nation at large. Whereas many other urban school districts had struggled during the same period of time, HISD had implemented a series of educational and administrative reforms, in turn producing disproportionately positive outcomes in student achievement scores. Along the way, HISD adopted many educational policies (e.g., accountability, private-sector contracts, decentralization, and expanded school choice) that became popular during the first decade of the 21st century.

As with other selections in this anthology, the present selection has been extracted from the complete case study, which covers an entire book. As with one of the other selections, the author was an intimate participant in the case. (He was a school board member during the entire period of time covered by the case.) He uses this knowledge as an insider (information not usually shared in published form by school board members)— complemented by citations to local news articles (found throughout the book but not illustrated in the material extracted for the present selection), other external documents, and interviews with key participants—to provide a degree of comfort regarding the accuracy and validity of the case study's findings.

Equally important, the author brings a flair for writing that makes this case study eminently readable, and it is, in fact, exciting to read. The selection, as with his entire book, combines a "close-up" style of writing with the citation to external evidence about the accomplishments of a school district in the real-life world. You could do worse in conducting your own case study.

A New Beginning for HISD

The defeat of the $390 million bond issue in May 1996 and John Sharp's audit report to the taxpayers in October were defining moments for HISD. The failed bonds proved to HISD watchers that the public had no confidence in Houston's public schools. The Sharp audit confirmed for most Houstonians that the bond vote was justified.

In the year that followed, however, attitudes changed. The public began to notice that most HISD performance indicators were improving significantly. Also, almost every month the board of education approved another bold reform initiative. HISD was getting better after all.

The prevailing opinion was that these improvements and actions were a response to the failed bonds and the Sharp audit. The public had at last gotten HISD's attention. There was truth in this view, but the reality was far more complex.

The reform of HISD began with *Beliefs and Visions* [HISD's strategic plan] in 1990 and the selection of Frank Petruzielo as superintendent in 1991. Frank's achievements were not insignificant: shared decisionmaking in every HISD school, school improvement plans, school-based budgeting, the establishment of a professional district police force, massive changes in school attendance boundaries, several significant management audits, and a start toward more effective employee performance evaluations.

But the real improvement of HISD began with Rod Paige [later appointed the first Secretary of Education under President George W. Bush]. His election as superintendent in February 1994 was the single most important event in the reform of HISD. Without Paige, shared decisionmaking would never have taken root, accountability would not have become firmly established, and decentralization would never have happened. Also, without Paige, there would have been no *PEER* task forces, no performance contracts for administrators, no modified vouchers, no business outsourcing, and no incentive pay for teachers.

The reform of HISD started well before the failed bond election and the Sharp audit. But these two events accelerated the pace of reform. They focused attention on the politically driven behavior of board members. They pushed Paige into hiring an effective press secretary.[1] They gave Paige the opportunity to come forth with a fresh, bold reform agenda for HISD. And, perhaps most significantly, they put into the hands of Paige and the board reformers a powerful argument to obtain board support for Paige's agenda.

Paige's New Beginning for HISD. . . . On October 16, [Paige] unveiled his *New Beginning for HISD* in a whirlwind of staged media events.[2] Rod's message was clear and strong. The district had been under enormous pressure. It had not been an easy time. The bond election and the Sharp audit had been wake-up calls. HISD did many things remarkably well, but there were a multitude of things HISD either did not do well or should not even have been trying to do. Almost everything could be done better.

Since 1990, board members and superintendents had changed. *Beliefs and Visions* had been largely overwhelmed by events and changing circumstances. The time had come to revitalize these beliefs and visions from 1990; Rod said, "I view the bond election in May and the Sharp Audit this month as providing us with precisely the right opportunity to outline some very basic, but bold, new principles which can guide this district well into the next century." "Today," continued Rod, is "a new beginning for HISD."

Rod's four basic reform principles were Accountability, Best Efforts, Choice, and Decentralization. HISD would establish objective, believable measures of accountability so that the community could track progress. Teacher salaries would be based on direct measures of teacher skills, knowledge, and student performance. Where HISD could not perform a business function as cheaply as the private sector, the function would be outsourced. All HISD students would be allowed to attend the public school of their choice, as long as space was available. Students would have "academic free-agency" and schools would have to compete for students. Innovative proposals to manage schools from nontraditional providers would be welcome. Over the next three years, HISD would transition to a budget system that allocated money to schools on a weighted-per-pupil basis.

News coverage of Paige's media blitz on October 16 was disappointing. The media were far more interested in Paige's comments about HISD's response to the Sharp audit than they were in his new initiatives. Most employees and parents acted as if the new beginnings principles had never been announced. Paige's press conference of October 16 was largely forgotten.

It would have taken formal endorsement of these principles by the board of education, extensive promotion by the district, and widespread media coverage over *many* weeks to capture the attention of the public. That was not possible. Powerful interest groups—employee groups, organized labor, the NAACP, and others—opposed one or more of Paige's four principles. At best the board would have supported them five to four after a bitter vote.

The reforms of 1996–97. But in the year that followed, month by month, agenda item by agenda item, through clever scheduling, a great deal of arm-twisting, enormous staff work behind the scenes, and very close votes—sometimes fights—at the board table, HISD began to embrace the principles of competition.

The policy changes and contracts approved by the board from October 1996 to August 1997 could almost be called a revolution. They were changes that could not have been imagined just a few years before. The board relinquished its authority to approve personnel appointments, promotions, and transfers. Within the constraints of HISD's overcrowded schools, an effective public school choice program was established. Nineteen charter schools were approved. A contract was signed with a private company for the education of at-risk adolescents. Several significant student achievement initiatives were launched. Employees became more accountable for their performance. And except for student transportation, the management of almost every major business activity of the district was contracted out to private companies. . . . [Ed.'s Note: The original text, omitted here, then gives a lengthy discussion of these reforms, summarizing the initiatives.]

. . . The last battle of 1997 was over the budget. By making hard choices, and with some good news from the Harris County Appraisal District, Paige was able to recommend a 1997-1998 budget that provided a 5 percent across-the-board increase in teacher pay plus another 1 percent for performance pay without a tax increase. There was a furious battle with the HFT [Houston Federation of Teachers] over the 5 percent increase (HFT wanted 10 percent) and performance pay. But the board was unmoved and the city did not seem to notice. The budget was approved on August 29.

In the days that followed, talk among HISD watchers shifted from school improvement and taxes to the upcoming board elections.[3] Indeed, some community leaders and parent activists had been talking about the 1997 elections for over a year. For at least two years everyone had known that [board members Paula, Ron, and myself were not planning] to seek a third term. Clyde and Laurie's terms also ended in 1997, and though both were seeking re-election, re-election was not certain. Paige was managing with a narrow, unstable majority on the board of education. Changing even one trustee changed the dynamics of the board. In 1998, the board reformers who had started and sustained the reform of HISD would be gone. Everyone knew an era in the history of HISD was coming to an end.

As Ron, Paula, Cathy, Rod, and I reflected on our work together since the battle for *Beliefs and Visions* in 1990, we had reason to be proud. We had not achieved what we had hoped. We had not turned the pyramid upside down. Too many of Houston's children were still not receiving the quality education they deserved. But we had made a start.

We had not always worked together. Paula had opposed the negative appraisal of Joan Raymond [superintendent of HISD prior to 1991] and the initial decision to hire Rod as superintendent. She also had voted against several of Rod's most important recommendations. Rod, Paula, and Cathy saw Frank's limitations before Ron and I. Early on Ron and I were the only enthusiasts for outsourcing. Over the years we had disagreed on a host of minor issues. We were all quite different.

Yet we shared core principles, trusted and believed in each other, and happily deferred leadership to one another. We started as strangers with a common goal, developed into an effective power bloc on the board, and became friends. We had set out to transform Houston's public schools. We had not. But we had at least started HISD down a new path.

Of course, we had not done it by ourselves. Most of our policy initiatives were supported by other board members. We could never have deposed Joan Raymond without Felix Fraga and Wiley Henry. We could never have hired Rod Paige without Arthur Gaines. Clyde Lemon, following his election in 1995, was the key fifth (though sometimes it appeared reluctant) vote that enabled Rod to move forward with his reform agenda. And Laurie Bricker was as strong for the principles of *Beliefs and Visions* as Rod himself.

There were also scores of business and community leaders, parent activists, and district personnel who made critical contributions to the improvements in HISD: the members of the Coalition for Educational Excellence, the Hook committee, the decentralization commission, more than a dozen PEER committees, business leaders and business partners, Parents for Public Schools, thousands of parent and community volunteers, Paige's senior staff, thousands of HISD principals and teachers, John Sharp, and even John Whitmire. HISD was improving because the leadership of Houston and a great many parents and voters demanded that it improve and because district employees were able and willing to make it happen.

Finally, without the permission (and sometimes prodding) of the Texas legislature, many of our reform policies would not have been possible. We were fortunate to serve Houston at the same time that educational reformers such as Senator Bill Ratliff (R-Mt. Pleasant) and a host of others were serving all of Texas.

Nevertheless, the leadership of the reformers on the board had been decisive. And this leadership was about to change. The upcoming board elections would fundamentally change the board. If Paige lost his slim majority, the further reform of HISD would probably come to an end and much of what we had accomplished would be at risk. Even if the voters elected strong, reform-minded trustees, the old *Beliefs and Visions* board would be history. Nineteen ninety-eight would be a new beginning for HISD.

In July, I decided to seek a third term on the board. The decision surprised me almost as much as it surprised others. For four years I had known I would not run again. Board service was not good for my family life or my business. I did not want to go through another election. And the endless controversies had left me tired and much too cynical. Eight years was enough. But in the end, the entreaties of Rod and others convinced me that I was needed. Perhaps as a link to the board of *Beliefs and Visions*, I could help the new board find its voice and continue the journey Cathy, Rod, Ron, Paula, and I had begun in 1990.

But even if I were re-elected, my life in 1998 would be part of another story. The board elections of 1997 and the other events of autumn belonged to the future. The voters of Houston would decide what that future would be. . . .

Houston's Achievements

What have I learned in eight years as a Houston school board member? What can elected officials, educators, business and community leaders, interested parents, and school reformers everywhere learn from the Houston experience? Obviously, the Houston story is unique. Time, place, circumstances, and individual actions shaped events.

But the issues and dynamics of school reform in Houston cannot be that dissimilar from the issues and dynamics in other American cities. Urban school reformers everywhere must deal with public opinion, the media, state education agencies, business interests, teacher unions, organized labor, political parties, taxpayer groups, neighborhood interests, discrimination and ethnic conflict, and the core educational issues of curriculum, teaching, learning, assessment, accountability, and management effectiveness. I believe urban school reformers everywhere can learn from the Houston experience. . . .

What has been achieved in Houston since 1990? A lot. Active shared decision-making committees at each school are now the rule, not the exception. At most schools they are meaningfully involved in developing school improvement plans and major campus decisions—budgets, schedules, uniforms, student discipline, and so on.

In 1990, [then Houston superintendent] Joan Raymond selected principals with input from her trusted advisers. As a courtesy, she informed trustees just days, sometimes hours, before presenting her recommendations to the board for approval. Sometimes upward of 25 principals were moved by one board action. School communities waited nervously to see who the superintendent had chosen as their leader. Political deals between the superintendent and board members were not uncommon.

Today most school communities, guided by a district superintendent, select, de facto, their own principals. The process is participative, open, and thorough. Board members are completely out of the loop. Selection decisions are better, for the most part. And school communities are now stakeholders in the success of new principals.

The HISD accountability system has had a huge impact on student achievement. In the years that followed its approval in 1993, behaviors changed. Principals, on whom the rewards and consequences fell most heavily, began demanding more control over their schools and better support from central office. All over the district, principals began adding more phonics to their instruction in reading, working on better curriculum alignment, examining student performance data student by student, and pushing to improve classroom instruction.

The impact of private-sector contracts for administrators has also been significant. Paige has exercised his option on a number of occasions to terminate principals and other administrators, including district superintendents. The word from administrators is that the loss of job security has significantly sharpened their focus on student performance. New teacher contracts, teacher evaluations, and termination and grievance processes have also improved teacher accountability. Many of these changes have been made possible by changes in the Texas Education Code.

District decentralization has significantly shifted power away from central office, but real decentralization is still a dream. Some of the district offices have become little central offices instead of service centers for schools. And schools are still budgeted with staff positions, not dollars. The principal of a typical elementary school, with a total operating budget of nearly $2 million, usually controls less than $100,000. Also, because middle-class schools tend to attract and keep experienced teachers at or near the top of the salary schedule, and schools full of at-risk students are more likely to be staffed by young teachers at or near the bottom of the salary schedule, resource inequity still exists. Until schools are budgeted with dollars, based on weighted student enrollment, and given the freedom to configure their workforces as they wish, central office will rule.

Peer Examination, Evaluation, and Redesign task forces have made an enormous contribution to the improvement of HISD operations. PEER has also become the methodology of choice for addressing complex student services and instructional issues. PEER recommendations, the recommendations of Texas comptroller John Sharp, and the aggressive contracting out of most of HISD's major business functions have improved significantly the management of business operations and support services.

The bottom line for HISD is productivity: output divided by input. Productivity is difficult to measure, but consider HISD's key outputs (student performance, the drop-out rate, and school safety) and most easily measured input (money).

Table 19.1   Changes in HISD and State TAAS Percent Passing for Non-Special Education Students for All Tests Taken From Spring 1994 to Spring 1998

	1994			1998			
	HISD	State	HISD–State Gap	HISD	State	HISD–State Gap	Decrease In Gap
Grade 3	51	58	7	73	76	3	4
Grade 4	47	54	7	77	78	1	6
Grade 5	51	58	7	83	83	0	7
Grade 6	40	56	16	66	79	13	3
Grade 7	37	55	18	64	78	14	4
Grade 8	31	52	21	59	72	13	8
Grade 10	38	52	14	62	72	10	4

SOURCE: Houston Independent School District (HISD) Research Office.

In Texas, the best measure of student performance is the Texas Assessment of Academic Skills [TAAS]. Since 1994, the best baseline year for TAAS, state TAAS scores have improved, as one might expect. But HISD scores have improved even more (see Table 19.1). During this same period, the percentage of Texas students eligible for free and reduced-price lunch increased from 45.1 to 48.4. The percentage of HISD students eligible for free and reduced-price lunch increased from 57.3 to 77.

These improvements in student performance have dramatically improved school accountability ratings. On the HISD accountability matrix, which measures schools against a fairly constant baseline, the number of exemplary schools has increased in five years from 10 to 84. The number of recognized schools has increased from 19 to 117. At the bottom of the matrix, the number of low-acceptable schools had decreased from 81 to 0. The number of low-performing schools has dropped from 68 to 2.

HISD schools have also improved their ranking on the Texas Education Agency accountability rating system, which has increased performance standards since 1993 and measures subgroup performance as well as overall school performance. Since 1993, the number of exemplary schools has increased from 0 to 36. The number of low-performing schools has decreased from 55 to 8. In 1998, HISD had a higher percentage of exemplary schools than any of the other six largest urban school districts in the state (Houston, 12.2 percent; Dallas, 2.8 percent; Ft. Worth, 5.1 percent; Austin, 8.5 percent; San Antonio, 12.1 percent; El Paso, 5 percent).

Accurately determining the number of dropouts is difficult, and various ways are available to calculate drop-out rates. By any measure, however, HISD has fewer dropouts. According to the Texas Education Agency, which calculates the drop-out rate by dividing the total number of annual dropouts by the cumulative enrollment for the year for students in the 7th through 12th grades, the HISD drop-out rate has declined from 10.4 percent in 1990 to 2.8 percent in 1997.

HISD schools are also safer than they were in 1990. School safety is difficult to measure. HISD did not begin keeping uniform crime report data on police-related incidents until 1993–1994. And for the first three years, as principals—under a new Code of Student Conduct that required reports to local law enforcement—kept better data, the number of police-related incidents increased. But in 1996, Sharp's auditors, basing their opinion on focus groups, concluded that school safety and security had improved. And from 1995–1996 to 1997–1998, the number of incidents leading to arrest fell from 2,664 to 2,155; the number of violent crimes—defined by the Federal Bureau of Investigation as rape, robbery, murder, or aggravated assault—fell 38 percent.

School finance is complex in Texas, as it is in most other states. But it is not misleading to note that HISD's tax rate, at $1.384 per hundred valuation, is the lowest among the 21 school districts in Harris County and 28 cents below the county average. HISD also has the lowest effective tax rate among the large urban school districts in Texas (these numbers are for 1997–1998; in July 1998, the Board of Education approved a $.075 property tax increase per hundred valuation for 1998–1999, bringing the tax rate to $1.459). And weighted general fund spending per pupil per year in 1995–1996—$4,206—was third from the bottom among Harris County school districts and, when adjusted for inflation, less than in 1992–1993. . . .

Notes

1. In December, Paige hired a media consultant, Terry Abbott. In March, Abbott was appointed press secretary with a salary of over $110,000 per year. Board members had been pushing for years for a professional to handle media relations. Most of us recognized that HISD was, in effect, in a continuous political campaign and that only a media professional with political experience had the expertise we needed. We also recognized that to hire a press secretary with political experience, HISD would have to pay $100,000 per year or more. Both Petruzielo and Paige had been unwilling to endure the criticism that would inevitably follow a decision to pay $100,000 per year to a press secretary, who HISD's critics would immediately dub a spinmeister. The defeat of the bonds and the Sharp audit convinced Paige that it had to be done. As expected, there was widespread criticism of Abbott's salary. But Abbott, who had been press secretary

for former Alabama Governor Guy Hunt, was perfect for the job, and within months we could see that he was worth every dollar the district paid him. His work contributed in no small measure to the improvement of the district's image in the months that followed.

2. At 10:00 a.m. he held a major press conference at Mark Twain Elementary. At noon he addressed the Galleria Chamber of Commerce at the Hilton Hotel, Southwest. At 7:00 p.m. he met with parents at Will Rogers Elementary. To support his media blitz, Rod scheduled three additional evening meetings with parents at schools in different parts of the city and outlined his proposals in letters to community and parent leaders (Paige, "Letter to Community Leaders," October 18, 1996; Paige, "Letter to PTA and PTO presidents," October 21, 1996).

3. Other important issues demanded the board's attention during 1997. In April, the district's guidelines for admission of students into magnet and gifted and talented programs—65 percent African American and Hispanic and 35 percent White and other—were challenged in federal court. But this issue and others really belonged to the future.

Index

About the Editor

Robert K. Yin, Ph.D., serves as Chairman of the Board and CEO of COSMOS Corporation, an applied research and social science firm that has been in operation since 1980. Over the years, COSMOS has successfully completed hundreds of projects for government agencies, private foundations, and other entrepreneurial and non-profit organizations. At COSMOS, Yin actively leads various research projects, including those in which the case study method is used. He has authored numerous books and peer-reviewed articles, including *Case Study Research* and *Applications of Case Study Research.* In 1998 he founded the "Robert K. Yin Fund" at M.I.T., which supports seminars on brain sciences, as well as other activities related to the advancement of predoctoral students in the Department of Brain and Cognitive Sciences.